revolution. The result is an unusual interpretation of Marx as a rationalist and the last great philosopher of universal enlightenment. Because he assumed that men calculated shrewdly in pursuing their material affairs, Marx could construct a science of political economy; because proletarians could perceive their common interest in a social revolution that could extend the scope of freedom, a practical sense of progress and the meaning of history seemed possible as well.

Since neither Sartre nor Merleau-Ponty wrote a detailed study of Marx, *History and Human Existence* is unique. It offers a critical reappraisal of Marx and the existential Marxists; and it supplies a lucid introduction to an important area of modern thought.

JAMES MILLER is in the Department of Government, University of Texas, Austin.

HISTORY AND HUMAN EXISTENCE

HISTORY
AND
HUMAN EXISTENCE

FROM MARX TO MERLEAU-PONTY

James Miller

UNIVERSITY OF CALIFORNIA PRESS
Berkeley   Los Angeles   London

Parts of Chapter 10 appeared as "Merleau-Ponty's Marxism: Between Phenomenology and the Hegelian Absolute," in *History and Theory,* Vol. XV, no. 2, © 1976 Wesleyan University, Connecticut, reprinted by permission of Wesleyan University Press.

University of California Press
Berkeley and Los Angeles, California
University of California Press, Ltd.
London, England

ISBN 0-520-03667-0
Library of Congress Catalog Card Number: 78-51747

Printed in the United States of America

For Barbara and Jim

Contents

Acknowledgments

To my professors in the History of Ideas Department at Brandeis University—Gerald Izenberg, George Armstrong Kelly, Alasdair MacIntyre, Heinz Lubasz, Kurt Wolff, and Mark Hulliung—thanks are due for providing the interdisciplinary framework and intellectual stimulation that allowed an earlier version of this essay to be written as a dissertation. That this department no longer exists is symptomatic of the mean spirit and narrow professionalism of the modern academy in America.

To my friends Jay Eisenberg, Peter Levin, Anne McCammon, Andrew McCammon, Phil Harris, Darrell Hawthorne, and particularly to my special friend Sarah Minden, thanks are due for tolerating my immersion in philosophy, and for discussing ideas, even when their intelligibility seemed questionable.

To my farflung colleagues William Galston, Cyril Levitt, Stan Spyros Draenos, Brian Milton, Bruce Miroff, Paul Breines, James Schmidt, Russell Jacoby, and especially Langdon Winner, thanks are due for giving generously of their time, sympathy, and critical acumen.

To Gary Kline, thanks are due for helping prepare the index.

And, finally, to Lee C. McDonald of Pomona College, a true mentor and a fine person, special thanks are due—for introducing me to politics and philosophy, and for enabling me to exercise the freedom to think.

J. M.

Austin, Texas
February, 1978

Introduction: Marxism and the Sense of Subjectivity

The present essay provides an introduction to the treatment of human existence and individuality in Marxist thought. The work will be primarily concerned with two related topics: the evaluation by Marxists of individual emancipation and their assessment of subjective factors in social theory.

By taking up these topics within a systematic and historical framework, I hope to generate some fresh light on several familiar issues. First, I pursue a reading of Marx focused on his treatment of subjectivity, individuation, and related methodological and practical matters; second, I apply this interpretation to analyzing the dispute between Marxist orthodoxy and heterodoxy over such matters as class consciousness and the philosophy of materialism; finally, I employ this historical context to clarify the significance of "existential Marxism," Maurice Merleau-Ponty's and Jean-Paul Sartre's contribution to Marxist thought.

Since the mid-sixties, questions of subjectivity and individuation have assumed a certain currency in radical circles, and not only from the standpoint of existential Marxism. In fact, the new left of the period presented demands not only for civil rights and a redistribution of wealth but also for a transformation of individual existence and a metamorphosis in everyday life. "People who talk," admonished one wall poster during the French student uprising in May of 1968, "about revolution and class struggle without any explicit reference to everyday life, without understanding what is subversive about love or what is positive about refusing coercion, have corpses in their mouth."[1] The temper of this radicalism marked a departure: where once Communists had discussed electrification, five-year plans and the collectivization of Soviet agriculture, young students, in search of authenticity and a new openness in human relations, now dwelled on eros emancipated, desire unleashed, existence transfigured.

Such departures had been anticipated by several leading neo-Marxian theorists of the postwar period: by Herbert Marcuse, with his discussion of surplus repression and one-dimensional man; by Henri Lefebvre, with his critique of everyday life; and by Jean-Paul Sartre, with his existential reconstruction of Marxism. What these theorists held in common was an heretical insistence on the human —the "subjective"—dimension of socialism. For Marcuse, this spelled an interest in Freud; for Lefebvre, an inventory of quotidian existence; for Sartre, a phenomenology of social institutions. Other Marxists, however, criticized these theorists for violating the aims of a scientific socialism. Thus Louis Althusser proclaimed in the late sixties that "the category of the subject is constitutive of all ideology."[2] Marxism, for the orthodox, was to be a purely *objective* discipline.

Since the turn of the century, Marxism has indeed been predominantly interpreted as an objective theoretical system, given to dissecting social facts and making empirical predictions. According to such orthodoxy, capitalism fosters, "with the inexorability of a law of nature," its own collapse. The capitalist mode of production gives rise to social relations rife with class antagonisms; this material infrastructure determines in turn the legal and political superstructure of any capitalist society. On all these levels, social conflict and economic contradictions lead inevitably to the demise of capitalism as a form of life. In the march toward communism, there may be detours, even temporary defeats; but the proletariat and its party may always claim this: History is on their side.

Given such putatively scientific claims on the part of orthodox Marxism, it might seem odd that a philosophical concept like subjectivity could find any adherents at all, especially within such a deterministic outlook. The very term "subjective" has often functioned as an insult in Marxist polemics. Not only does it suggest something less than the lucidly objective understanding all science covets; even worse, it smacks of an anachronistic world of philosophical disputation, where idealists discourse on the unreality of the material world.

Despite such prevailing prejudices, twentieth-century Marxism has spawned a number of heterodox schools, interested both in philosophy and in the problem of human existence as it informs social theory. Moreover, these heretics, from Georg Lukács to Maurice Merleau-Ponty, have often claimed the patronage of Karl Marx himself, and not without justice. Thanks to this subterranean stream of neo-Marxist thought, as well as to the new left that has made it fashionable, such philosophical issues as subjectivity and individuation have become alive again for radical theorists. Yet while a considerable literature has flourished around the question of Marx's relation to Hegel and philosophy, little attention has been devoted to the problem of the varying approaches to subjectivity within Marxism.

This problem would merit attention if only for the central role subjectivity assumes in the works of the existential Marxists. But the issue transcends intellectual history, as the purview of the new left suggests. Under the reign of advanced technology and its attendant imperatives for organization and control, such issues as autonomy, self-expression and individuation have assumed a renewed relevance for the critique of contemporary society. In a world that threatens to become literally inhuman, a philosophy of the human subject promises insight into the possibilities for a better form of life.

Similarly, the very currency of individualized variants on Marxism suggests a need to reevaluate Marxist views on individuation. For too long, Marx has been read as an apostle of the communitarian ethos pure and simple, a reading parodied by the contemporary advocates of a left-wing politics based in rural communes, as well as the cold-war critics of a communism cast as intrinsically totalitarian. Yet Marx himself highly valued the elaboration of human individuality as a progressive aspect of historical development.

This dispute, over whether or not Marx favored individuation as a paramount goal of social revolution, has clear ramifications for a radical politics. The treatment accorded subjectivity likewise affects the shape of radical strategy: if the human subject looms as a central element in understanding and shaping social reality, then the new left was not mistaken in addressing such issues as the quality of everyday life and the personal dimensions of any struggle against coercion, issues largely ignored in traditional left-wing organizing. The relation of the individual to social institutions becomes a focus of strategy and a source for a new vision of politics.

Unfortunately, the notions of individuation and subjectivity remain far from self-evident in their bearing on the main body of Marxian theory. What, for example, is the relation of individuation to that inherently "social being" Marx in his early writings identified with the human essence? What is the role of purposive action in an economic and historical development characterized by Marx himself as "necessary"? What kind of subjects did Marx presume would institute communism? How does the category of subjectivity square with the requirements of a rigorous inquiry into society?

This study attempts to unravel some of these dilemmas. By tracing the continuities and contradictions of Marxian philosophy from Marx to Merleau-Ponty, I will try to examine critically the rise of a social theory premised on the interaction of active subjects and aiming at the socioeconomic emancipation of the individual. My point is primarily philosophical and exegetical: to establish the cogency of "existential Marxism" within the Marxist tradition, to analyze and evaluate its key categories, and, as a consequence, to elaborate, in a preliminary fashion, a number of interrelated issues, such as the importance of individuation as a critical concept, the place of reason and freedom in human existence, the role of human agency in history, and the methodologies appropriate to social inquiry. Similar questions have increasingly preoccupied contemporary social philosophers of varying persuasions; so it may be timely to amplify such concerns within the radical tradition itself.

What exactly is up for grabs in the Marxist debate over individuation and subjectivity? Although the Cartesian sense of subjectivity coincided with individual consciousness and the *cogito,* in German philosophy after Kant the term came to connote a universal faculty (in Kant, the transcendental ego as the condition of the unity of empirical perception). The Marxian concept of subjectivity, then, invokes the Kantian rather than Cartesian tradition. Following Kant, the Marxian notion stresses the universal as much as the particular, while following Hegel, it accentuates the objective elements of human agency and the development of self-consciousness through intersubjective communication.

As used in the present work, "subjectivity" will refer to those distinctively human and largely internal or conscious aspects of any process, be it perceiving, thinking, willing, or the happenings of history; while objectivity, to oversimplify, will correlatively imply the primarily natural and largely external aspects of such processes. Subjectivity and objectivity appear here not as absolute opposites, but rather as inherently related aspects of reality. For the Marxist, as Karel Kosík put it, "the essence of men is the unity of objectivity and subjectivity."[3] Through the practical transformation of the world, the human subject objectifies itself, and the objective world becomes comprehensible to the mind. Thus, as Max Horkheimer has cautioned, "the subject-object relation is not accurately described by the picture of two fixed realities which are conceptually fully transparent and move towards each other. Rather, in what we call objective, subjective factors are at work; and in what we call subjective, objective factors are at work."[4]

There is also a danger in treating the analytic distinction between subject and object as a kind of ontological chasm; for it may prove reasonable to assume that social institutions and conventional norms exhibit a distinctive ontological character, neither wholly subjective nor wholly objective. But given the Marxist usage, the notion of subjectivity, far from delimiting a monadic rationalism, in principle accommodates intersubjectivity, cooperation, and social existence; nor does adopting such an understanding of subjectivity at the foundation of social theory necessarily entail "methodological individualism" — the reduction of all social phenomena to the beliefs and behavior of individuals. The concept of subjectivity must therefore be distinguished from the concept of the individual, which is established precisely in distinction to the general and collective, even though the individual may embody social interests and elaborate capabilities that are universal.

By "individuation," on the other hand, I refer to the process whereby human beings become distinctive, autonomous, and self-conscious agents, each capable of purposefully reshaping the natural world and of independently evaluating moral claims. Individuation thus delimits a broader range of possibilities than "individualism," the term used by Tocqueville to describe "a mature and calm feeling, which disposes each member of the community to sever himself from the mass of his fellows and to draw apart . . . so that . . . he willingly leaves society at large to itself." Unlike individuation, of which it represents but one form, individualism connotes selfishness and egoism; it first arises in modern society, which "throws" the individual, in Tocqueville's words, "back forever upon himself alone and threatens in the end to confine him entirely within the solitude of his own heart."[5]

In opposition to this pejorative notion of individualism, which he once equated with a "soulless materialism," Marx developed his own outlook on individuation from a variety of contemporary sources.[6] From the Enlightenment, Marx took over the conviction that men freed from institutional and cultural fetters could be shown to share equally in universal human faculties and capabilities. But Marx critically modified this doctrine of the essential sameness of abstract individuals, by elaborating what Georg Simmel once called a "qualitative" notion of individuality. Within this qualitative understanding, developed by Goethe and Hegel as well as the romantics and existentialists, the individual is valued not for his universally human qualities but for his unique and incomparable personality; to borrow Simmel's description, this form of individuation "means that the single human being distinguishes himself from others; that his being and conduct — in form, content, or both — suit him alone; and that being different has a positive meaning and value for his life."[7] Marx's concept of individuation distinctively combines aspects of the Enlightenment and qualitative notions, emphasizing the social and historical context of individuality, while criticizing the abstract and purely private forms of individuation characteristic of bourgeois society.

It should be stressed that the concepts of subjectivity and individuation are logically independent. Adhering to a social theory that emphasizes the role of subjectivity does not entail subscribing to individuation as a value of social development; nor does an esteem for individuation require a methodology that eschews a causal explanation of social facts. Nevertheless, a kind of conceptual affinity does link the notions of subjectivity and individuality held by many thinkers: the understanding of subjectivity may well help define those capacities to be unfettered and refined in the process of individuation, just as an interest in individuation may focus attention on questions of freedom and the methodological significance of subjective factors in historical explanation.

Ironically, little attention has been devoted to Marx's own views on either individuation or subjectivity, despite a wealth of references throughout his work to individual emancipation and to real individuals as the foundation of social theory. When Sartre and Merleau-Ponty came to restore the subjective dimension in Marxism, it was in large part these oversights they had in mind. Still, the goal of individuation and the notion of subjectivity have meant a lot of different things to different Marxists. The present essay seeks to elaborate some of the issues at stake.

Since Marxist theory represents a coherent whole, the sense attributed to individuation and subjectivity affects the bearing of the entire theory. Marx's own outlook on man as a practical as well as rational animal engendered a certain optimism in regard to his hopes for communism: the development of man's practical need to transform the natural world, as evidenced in modern industry, could also become an enlightened impulse to reshape the social world of human relations. In both cases, individuals (through social classes) had creative roles to fulfill. By contrast, if subjectivity were merely the reflexive response to prior stimuli, its voluntary role in social action could be but minimal; dispassionate science might instead point out the path history inevitably would follow, dragging individuals, classes, and nations in tow.

The significance attributed to subjectivity thus influenced Marxism at several levels. For example, it helped determine the epistemology at the basis of the theory: did the mind passively reflect external sense-data, as the orthodox supposed; or did consciousness contribute to, as well as result from, the practical transformation of the world through purposive action, as Marx believed? The sense accorded subjectivity also affected the meaning of materialism: did it signify the reducibility of reality to the motions of physical matter, as Engels argued; or did materialism instead mark out the preeminent role of active human beings in shaping a real world, as Marx thought? Finally, the meaning attached to subjectivity affected the strategy appropriate to a Marxist politics: was communism to be imposed by the actions of a vanguard party, as Lenin counseled; or was communism to be the outcome of a pedagogical process of self-emancipation by enlightened proletarians, as Marx hoped? Similar issues were at stake in the value different Marxists attributed to individuality. Would communism emancipate a class, an advanced technology, or individual men and women? Would it merely mollify material want or also facilitate self-expression and individual autonomy? What, in short, were the aims of socialism?

Almost fifty years ago, Georg Lukács vindicated the Hegelian philosophical foundations of Marxism in *History and Class Consciousness*. In a sense, the current work critically reexamines those foundations, describes their erosion, and explores one of the philosophical alternatives. For while Sartre and Merleau-Ponty loyally defend Marx and his commitment to individual emancipation, their existential version of Marxism implicitly challenges Marx's (and Hegel's) understanding of human existence, and the reason native to subjectivity in the faculties of labor and interest. In the process, both Sartre and Merleau-Ponty have undermined, often unintentionally, the central subjective premises supporting Marx's optimistic outlook on individuation. Their elucidation of human existence calls into question the primacy of reason, the desirability of freedom, and the possibility of revolution—especially a true communist revolution, which enables oppressed individuals to emancipate themselves, rather than letting a new elite mythologize a proletariat whose members in fact remain dominated.

The work is divided into three parts: the first covers Marx, while the third treats Sartre and Merleau-Ponty; the second discusses in brief a number of relevant Marxian theorists, including Engels, Plekhanov, Kautsky, Lenin, Luxemburg, Lukács, and Gramsci. In the later sections, I have largely limited my discussion to the "existential Marxists," both out of considerations of space and in an attempt to sharpen the argument. Many of the problems raised in these later sections, for example, naturally have their analogue in the psychoanalytic strain in Marxian thought (Reich, Fromm, Marcuse) and certainly in the critical theory of the Frankfurt School (Adorno, Horkheimer, Benjamin), which speaks powerfully to the possibility of individuation in the modern world. I nevertheless believe that Sartre and Merleau-Ponty have framed the key philosophical issues. With the critique of their contributions we can at least make a start.

Throughout, the reader should bear in mind certain additional limitations. In the first place, the present study is necessarily onesided, since it is largely confined to exploring the way each thinker has articulated the issues surrounding subjectivity and individuation. My analysis is also rather narrowly conceptual; much of the social and political context has been omitted, in part because a number of historical studies in these areas are already available.[8] Finally, I have decided to restrict citation to the works under discussion, with a few exceptions. In a field crowded with secondary sources, it is a constant temptation to articulate an interpretation by demolishing rival readings; at the risk of belaboring the obvious, I have preferred to stake out my own position without fighting a war of footnotes. On the other hand, this essay would have been unthinkable without the large and growing volume of first-rate studies in Marxist philosophy: I have tried to document my debt to this secondary literature in the bibliography, which lists all books consulted.

The present work was written during a time of widespread social unrest within the United States. An era of decline for the American empire, it has also been a time marked by diminishing prospects for an independent left, as well as renewed fears of an epidemic barbarism. At a time when established socialist and communist regimes offer scant hope for a libertarian and radical reordering of society, politics, and everyday life, it has seemed appropriate to reconsider the issues of subjectivity and individuation within Marxism itself. While few explicitly practical perceptions are given expression in this essay, it would be dishonest to pretend they did not play a critical role in its conception and execution. My real reason for taking up the question of subjectivity with regard to *Marxism* (rather than some other social theory) lies in the irrevocable commitment of revolutionary Marxism to abolish all social orders in which human beings are oppressed and degraded. That commitment seems to me the proper place for contemporary social thought to begin—even if it ends by discarding the Marxian theory.

PART ONE

Marx

1

Marx's Hopes for Individuation

He insisted on the social medium of existence, the public dimension of self-expression, the objective elements of human agency; he analyzed the conventional weight of institutions, the laws of economic exchange, and the cumulative momentum of history. And yet Karl Marx, in striving for a science of society, remained equally preoccupied throughout his life with the individual—not, it is true, as a self-seeking egoist, nor as spiritual avatar, but instead the individual as a sociable and objective being, rich in vocations and values, multifaceted in wants and talents, gifted with free time and a sense of wholeness.

A utopian prospect? Perhaps. But also an index of human possibilities: the "social individual" as the *telos* of a history rendered rational, not only via the political emancipation of the individual, but also, and more importantly, through the conscious appropriation, by associated individuals, of their collective powers and institutions. This, at least, was Marx's vision.

It is a vision that incorporates individuation as one of its central elements. Indeed, Marx maintained an interest in individuation throughout his life, an interest evinced in *Capital* as well as his earliest essays. To be sure, Marx's understanding of individuation as an historical accomplishment evolved as he developed his broader theory; yet while he abandoned the philosophical anthropology of his youth, he never ceased to value individuation as one of the most progressive and desirable tendencies of history. Rather than merely repudiating the modern ideal of individuality, Marx radicalized it: communism would complete the process of individual emancipation pressed forward by capitalism and liberalism.

During the first half of the nineteenth century, European liberals sought, and in some areas helped accomplish, the emancipation of the individual from the authority of monarchial and ecclesiastical institutions. In so doing, the liberal movement in politics furthered a process initiated by the rise of Protestantism, the growth of trade and industry, and the subsequent mass migration of people from the countryside to the burgeoning cities of Europe. During the Middle Ages, man had been conceived primarily in relation to a larger religious and communal order: this social and spiritual realm supplied the individual with a raison d'être and assigned him his station in life. The view of the individual which emerged during the modern period by contrast upheld as its ideal the autonomous personality, independent of the ties of religious and political hierarchy. Many of the leading philosophers and social theorists of the seventeenth and eighteenth centuries had anticipated the main themes of the new view: Descartes's theory of the self, like the economic man portrayed in classical political economy, could be used to support a novel vision of the individual as an essentially free agent.

The French Declaration of the Rights of Man and Citizen provided the classic political statement of European liberalism and its central tenets. Men were born and remained free and equal in rights; these rights included liberty, property, security, and resistance to oppression. Liberty, defined as the freedom to do anything that did not infringe on another person's freedom, was established by public law, before which all individuals were treated as equals, without regard to social position. Sovereignty resided in a people and nation, not a monarch or privileged estate.

A broadly defined image of the individual emerged from liberal thought. Autonomous and self-reliant, the individual also appeared acquisitive and self-interested. On the positive side, individuals were valued for developing their special capacities and perfecting their particular personality. But in any case, the individual was portrayed in contrast to the community; the liberal state was primarily to assume a negative role, mediating the interaction of individuals, since, without a minimum of public regulation, the utopia of monadic individualism threatened to degenerate into a nightmare of selfish egos competing for scarce resources.

Liberal ideas and institutions did not undergo a uniform development throughout Europe, however. In some countries, such as Germany, a more traditional view of the state persisted well into the nineteenth century; there, individual freedoms were often secured through concessions from the established authorities, a situation which reinforced the customary connection between duty and liberty. In this context, individual rights could be regarded as an attribute of a properly constituted sovereign, rather than a critical protection against the sovereign. Moreover, during the seventeenth and eighteenth centuries, a number of German theorists advocated enlightened despotism, an approach which continued to influence political thought in the nineteenth century.

After the July Days of 1830, demands for liberal reforms grew throughout Germany. But the chief response was increased repression and censorship; as a result the liberal movement was forced to operate without adequate public representation and under a suffocating set of restrictions on meetings and publications. The popular basis for a liberal politics seemed questionable, too. Throughout the first half of the nineteenth century, Germany remained a backward and predominantly agricultural country, even though peasants and artisans were being uprooted by the slow decline of older sectors of the economy. While these conditions forced the social question to the fore, political circumstances made articulating what popular discontent did exist difficult; liberalism consequently remained the creed of relatively isolated groups of intellectuals.

In the 1830s, the German liberal movement united around issues of anticlericalism and a cosmopolitan hostility to Prussian domination. At least in principle, most liberals claimed to represent "the people": in addition to constitutional reforms and freedom of the press, the liberals sought an end to economic privilege and restrictions on trade. But the movement was divided over how to attain these goals. One group appealed to established authorities for reform, while another hesitated between such appeals and autonomous claims in terms of popular rights. A radical group, finally, advocated uncompromising popular sovereignty, and a total break with the existing regimes.

For philosophical as well as strategic reasons, various factions split before 1848. The philosophy of Hegel, in particular, became a source of contention. Hegel himself had asserted the necessity of an hierarchical sovereign state which could impose common aims and ideals on the competing particular interests within civil society; as a result, his philosophy was commonly regarded as a justification of the Prussian monarchy, even though Hegel himself had proposed critical changes in the Prussian constitution. But some young Hegelians declared their mentor's apparent reconciliation of particular and universal interests premature. In their eyes, the arbitrary authoritarianism of Prussian politics thwarted human freedom, the avowed object of the Hegelian philosophy. A radical faction grouped around a militant reading of Hegel and demanded that political policies actually conform to the dictates of Reason as deciphered by a dialectical philosophy committed to a free state. More cautious liberals, by contrast, argued that contemporary institutions carried at least the promise of rationality within them already. For such liberals, reform could be accomplished within the bounds of established law.

THE INDIVIDUAL IN THE BOURGEOIS STATE

Although Marx came to criticize liberalism and its understanding of individual emancipation, his earliest writings take their bearings from this context of political theory. In his dissertation, completed in 1841, Marx had defended the liberal party as the only German movement that adhered to the "concept" of Hegelian philosophy, with its demands for a rational state. While positive philosophy exalted the existing state as rational, an authentically Hegelian and negative philosophy would demand, in the name of its unactualized concept, that the state be transformed so as to accord with rational norms. By remaining true to the concept of rational politics, and by seeing political rationality as a task yet to be accomplished, the liberal party could make progress: it could be "conscious in general of principle and aim."[1]

In his first journalistic writings for the *Deutsche Jahrbücher* and the *Rheinische Zeitung,* Marx brought such theoretical preoccupations to bear on the current issues of the day, among them the introduction of representative government, freedom of the press, and the social question posed by the unincorporated poor, who belonged to no guild or estate and yet constituted as much as half the population in some areas of Germany.[2] An article in 1842 attacking press censorship used the Hegelian premise of an ethical state to argue against Hegel's own conclusions. Marx agreed with Hegel that the state should embody an ethical community, publicly incarnating that "universal human nature" and rationality inherent in each individual; he also insisted that an *"ethical state* presupposes that its members" already have in mind *"the view of the state."*[3] While laws without objective norms would be "laws of terrorism," a free state would avoid setting itself against its subjects; instead, it educated men to become "part of the state, by transforming the aims of the individual into universal aims."[4] Only then might the individual find his satisfaction in the life of the state. Marx here sustained a democratic version of Hegel's political philosophy: in a truly representative state, each man, by obeying the laws of his own reason, would also obey the laws of the state, that "great organism."

The problems impeding the realization of such a truly representative state, however, were by no means negligible. In several articles on the plight of the impoverished, Marx protested the exclusion of the propertyless—in the new parlance of the day, sometimes called the "proletariat"—from full citizenship. Such an exclusion contravened the universality of a truly rational state. Moreover, the recent increases in the unincorporated poor suggested to Marx that the problem lay not with the poor but rather with the constitution, which refused even to recognize the problem. Marx thus placed the question of poverty at the center of his thinking about politics.

It was not until 1843, however, that he found the time to clarify the theoretical implications of his observations as a journalist. After reading books on the American and French revolutions, as well as Machiavelli, Montesquieu, and Rousseau, Marx turned his attention again to Hegel, to criticize *The Philosophy of Right,* a central text in the political polemics of the day. By mid-1843, he had drafted a section-by-section commentary on the book's later paragraphs. Although he published an introduction to this material, the main manuscript only appeared posthumously, as the *Critique of Hegel's "Philosophy of Right."*

This *Critique* bore the imprint of Ludwig Feuerbach's "transformative" method. As Feuerbach himself had explained it, "We only have to make [Hegel's] predicate the subject, and likewise the subject the object and principle—therefore we only have to invert speculative philosophy—in order to have the undisguised, pure and clear truth."[5] Feuerbach's example was instrumental in turning Marx's attention to the individual, both as the particular *this,* the tangible and perceptible "something" that founded all abstract thought, and as the conscious human being who conceived all philosophy, religion, and politics in the first place, according to Feuerbach's self-styled materialism.

In the *Critique of Hegel's "Philosophy of Right,"* Marx juxtaposed methodological and substantive criticisms: Hegel's proclivity to hypostatized abstractions abetted an antidemocratic politics. Hegel consistently divorced such human "predicates" as the state from their "real independence, their subject."[6] Because of his consistent inversion of real relationships, Hegel severed the state from its actual basis, interacting individuals, while transforming the family and civil society into predicates of the state through its "self-positing" activity. In Hegel's topsy-turvy world, the state itself becomes the creating subject, while the human subjects "become unreal, and take on the different meaning of objective moments of the Idea."[7] Thanks to his starting point, Hegel ended by making the monarch the embodied subjectivity of the state, and the true animating impulse of society.

Marx, like Feuerbach, proposed a new, more concrete foundation for political philosophy: "One has to start from the real subject and examine its objectification."[8] The subject was man; his real activity, his "objectification," was his outward creativity, in the form of ideas (like religion) as well as institutions (like those of politics). The methodological entreaty to return to the actual subject implied a political corollary: "The state is an abstraction; the people alone is the concrete."[9] With his transformative critique of Hegel, Marx thus definitively abandoned neo-Hegelian liberalism in favor of what he called "true democracy," a populist halfway house between liberalism and communism.

Yet Marx in 1843 was still willing to grant Hegel's social analysis a relative validity, since the ethical form of the Hegelian state at least responded to the fragmented form of life within civil society. Hegel had been appalled by the atomism of that society; left to their own devices, he felt that the people were only "the Many, as units . . . a formless mass whose commotion and activity could therefore only be elementary, irrational, barbarous and frightful."[10] Hegel hoped the modern state could provide civil society with a binding ethical order to combat this social disorder.

But Marx, while sympathetic with the Hegelian critique of civil society, by 1843 had also come to feel that any purely political accommodation missed the point. Even republicanism was denied Marx's blessing, since the political republic, as a mere constitutional form, provided democracy only within "the abstract form of the state." A political solution left the social bases of an atomized civil society intact and failed to solve the problem of poverty; as a result, the state, divorced from and set opposite the concrete forms of interaction within civil society, assumed the abstract form of rights and laws governing man qua citizen. Man qua man, on the other hand, pursued life in civil society as before.

As a consequence, the extent of individual emancipation within the modern state proved problematical. While bourgeois civil society represented the "accomplished principle of individualism," for most men that individualism remained partial and one-sided, rooted in the isolated struggle for survival. Where survival became the end, the individual's objective power of shaping the world, his labor, became a mere means. The bourgeois state ratified this inversion by vesting the individual's acknowledged universality in legal rights, where "man's content"—his practical pursuit of everyday life within civil society—"is not taken to be his true actuality."[11]

True democracy, by contrast, would reconcile the social and political realms, rather than merely counterpose them. As Marx portrayed it, democracy abolished the separation of the state from a civil society by transforming the latter, and making everyday life itself the basis of ethics. The preconditions for such a metamorphosis in social existence included the restructuring of property relations, the amelioration of poverty, and the establishment of universal suffrage. With the realization of popular sovereignty and the abolition of primogeniture, the state could disappear, while the legislature, by truly representing the will of the people, could shed its opposition to civil society. Institutions could then be treated as vessels of individual activity, rather than as mysteriously self-positing Ideas, à la Hegel. True democracy thus marked the "first true unity of the universal and particular."[12] The subjects of such a democracy might be acknowledged for what they were, rather than valued only as legal citizens.[13] To the extent that civic and political life at last transparently stood forth as the "free product of men," the individual became the active subject rather than passive object of communal life.

By repudiating liberalism in favor of his own radical populism,

Marx posed the question of individual emancipation on a new and universal level: freedom and a decent existence were now claimed as rights for all men, regardless of their estate. Marx also began elaborating his own philosophical anthropology, which treated man as a practical and sociable being, rather than the acquisitive and insular entity classical liberalism had found in civil society. Moreover, by 1843 Marx had come to view the practical project of individual emancipation as a social as well as political issue: any purely political program such as liberalism proposed would leave man's everyday existence intact, and thus sustain the contradiction between the privatized, self-seeking individual and the public-minded citizen of the ideal political community—an ideal that liberalism continued to profess without extending it to civil society.

THE ALIENATION OF LABOR

In 1844, Marx published two articles in the *Deutsch-Französische Jahrbücher*. One, "On the Jewish Question," restated many of the points raised in the longer Hegel manuscript; the other, intended as an introduction to that manuscript, signaled an important departure. Reflecting Marx's growing interest in socialism and communism, "Toward the Critique of Hegel's Philosophy of Right: Introduction" attempted to identify a collective agent that might historically embody philosophical ideals and seek to realize them: "It is not enough that thought should seek its actualization: actuality must itself strive toward thought." Although an agent that could realize universal freedom at first appeared to be lacking in Germany, Marx asserted that a deeper examination of the social question revealed the proletariat as the incarnation of philosophy. "As philosophy finds its *material* weapons in the proletariat, the proletariat finds its *intellectual* weapons in philosophy."[14]

Moreover, as Marx made clear in a third article published in 1844, the protest of the proletariat against oppressive conditions, passing beyond inherently limited plans to seize political power, embodied a plea that social relations be transformed, that everyday existence become humane. "A social revolution, even though it be limited to a single industrial district, affects the totality, because it is a human protest against a dehumanized life, because it starts from the standpoint of the single, real individual, because the collectivity against whose separation from himself the individual reacts is the true collectivity of man, the human essence." A merely political revolution, by contrast, aimed only at winning institutional influence and power, and thus took as its standpoint neither the real individual nor the transformed collectivity, but instead the institutions of state, "an abstract whole that only exists through a separation from real life."[15]

Given this analysis of the social question and its feasible resolution, Marx logically turned his critical energies from political philosophy to political economy—that young science which claimed to show the anatomy of civil society. Where the 1843 manuscripts had examined the *political* disunity of modern society, Marx's posthumously published 1844 manuscripts concentrated on the *economic* factors underlying that disunity. This time, he developed his argument primarily through a critical reading of Adam Smith's *Wealth of Nations*.

Following such classical economists as Smith and David Ricardo, Marx described modern society (and organized his notes) in terms of a tripartite division into capital, landed property, and labor, a separation which he saw as reducing to a confrontation between capital (incorporating landed property) and labor. For the most part, he confined himself to pointing out the contradictory consequences and evasions of political economy, that dismal science which recognized labor as the chief source of human wealth, yet justified denying the laborer a full share in his own product. But he also charged the economists with failing to analyze scientifically the *"subjective essence of private property, labor."*[16]

Marx sought to rectify this omission through an analysis of the alienation of labor, one that enriched his understanding of individuation under modern economic conditions. He started from the central economic relationship discussed by classical political economy, that of the worker to the process of production. The failure of the laborer to acquire a full share of his own product represented the estrangement of labor from its product. More fundamentally, the initial separation of labor and capital necessitated the alienation of the laborer from the act of production; the modern worker lacked the tools and machines essential to his very life activity. As the object of labor was alienated from the laborer, both in the act of labor and its product, so also was the complete activity of labor disrupted, by the disjunction of its essential elements.

This economic alienation had wide implications. Just as labor appeared a salable commodity external to the worker himself, the ultimate material of labor, nature, likewise seemed hostile and indifferent to the modern laborer. Yet the individual not only needed to labor to survive: his self-assertion also required objectifying activity, of which labor for Marx constituted the paradigmatic instance. The alienation of labor from the laborer thus entailed the alienation of the individual from himself. Instead of seeing his own objective activity publicly recognized as enriching the community, the worker competed with other individuals to sell his power of labor, and with it, his power of self-assertion. Estranged from himself and any public affirmation, the laborer became an abstract monad, depending on work merely to sustain an isolated existence. For the laborer, individuation necessarily occurred as alienation from social existence. Man was alienated from man.

The capitalist, by purchasing labor, had expropriated the individual's objective essence. Yet once lodged within the capital-labor relationship, the worker could only reproduce this relationship, in the very act of reproducing himself through labor. The only escape lay in an overthrow of the economic conditions which fractured social life. The liberation of the individual (bourgeois as well as proletarian), which Marx had previously shown to depend on a social transformation, now was seen to require specifically the emancipation of the working class. This emancipation proceeded through the struggle between capitalist and laborer which unavoidably developed within the capitalist mode of production.[17]

INDIVIDUAL AND SPECIES: MAN AS SOCIAL BEING

Although Marx devoted most of his attention in the 1844 manuscripts to political economy, his argument often hinged on an implicit vision of man. As the manuscripts amply attest, he had borrowed more from Feuerbach than a methodology; he had also acquired a philosophical anthropology which depicted man as inherently a "species being."

Feuerbach, in his introduction to *The Essence of Christianity*, had equated knowledge of the human species with science; he had also attributed genuine consciousness only to those beings capable of making their species an object of thought. That man could consciously reason signified for Feuerbach that the human "I" transcended its individuality in the very process of thinking; the highest expression of this transcendence was the infinity of God posited by religious thought, an infinity in truth representing the idea of the perfected species-essence of mankind.[18]

When Marx applied Feuerbach's anthropology to social life, he emphasized his own neo-Hegelian conception of man as a practical and objective being. For Marx, the highest expression of man's "species-being" came not in the consciousness of the infinite, as for Feuerbach, but in objective human activity. Man was the "subjectivity of *objective* essential powers, whose action, therefore, must also be something *objective*."[19]

Labor comprised the principal medium of man's objective being. Through labor, man's restless power of objective action transformed the world and appropriated it as *his* reality: humanity as a whole proved itself in work, if only by facilitating the survival of the species. The object of labor therefore represented the "objectification of man's species-life."[20] Although Hegel had grasped the genesis of humanity as the progressive real objectification of the human spirit, Marx criticized Hegel for equating objectification with alienation, thus insuring that the transcendence of alienation appeared either as an impossibility or an absurdity.[21]

The manuscripts insisted on man as a social being as well as a species-being. Human production had historically always proceeded in cooperation with others, either in the family, the guild or the factory; once exchange of goods had been instituted, the individual also depended on the others for material sustenance. But even on a philosophical level, man as an objective being implied man as a social being: for Marx, as for Hegel and Feuerbach, only another human being, by encountering the individual subject as an active object, could confirm this subject qua objective being, through the public recognition of is objectifications.[22] In 1844, Marx thus praised Feuerbach for making the relationship of man to man the guiding principle of his materialism.

In truth, man could not humanly exist outside society. "Men, through the activation of their *nature create* and produce a human *common life,* a social essence which is no abstractly universal power opposed to the single individual, but is the essence or nature of every single individual, his own activity, his own life, his own spirit, his own wealth."[23] The most cultivated and human projects of the individual were both universal and social; even the isolated scientist, in formulating observable laws and acquiring verifiable results, was active as a man and engaged in an indirectly communal enterprise, as part of the community of scientific reason.[24]

Communal social life did not arise initially through any conscious agreement or reflection among contracting men, but rather sprang directly from individual "need and egoism," neither of which could be confirmed or satisfied apart from society. Yet the individual's activity, even as inherently social activity, rarely occurred within the form of some *directly* communal activity, as the case of the scientist illustrated. Despite the implications of the phrase, the social being of the individual did not mean that his human being was to be identified with society, or even a particular social role; Marx's anthropology instead evoked an objectifying agent, open to a variety of social relations, but only mediately related to the larger community.

The individual indeed remained irrevocably particular for Marx: "It is precisely his particularity which makes him an individual, and a real *individual* social being." To be sure, the individual, precisely as an objective being, was characterized not by some ineffable, interiorized particularity, but by a "totalizing" particularity, that, in activity and thought, engaged in objective projects pointing beyond the individual, toward the universal and social community of man. In this sense, while the individual could never be subsumed under the universal for Marx, the individual could and did participate in the whole of social life, as the "subjective existence of society thought and experienced for itself."[25]

In the 1844 manuscripts, as in the 1843 Hegel critique, a philosophical anthropology anchored Marx's approach by specifying what essence modern man was alienated from. The notion of the *social* individual also allowed Marx to erect a universalistic social theory without relying on Hegelian abstractions, or a cult of renascent community; it let Marx reconcile the individual, as a concrete, particular person, with the individual as the vessel of human universality and species-being—a reconciliation expressed in the admonition that "above all, we must avoid postulating 'Society' again as an abstraction vis-à-vis the individual."[26]

Yet Marx's defense of the social individual remained ambiguous. It also in a sense begged the question of how the individual was integrated within a social community by simply asserting that the individual was, by essence, sociable. Marx later modulated his position to claim as a matter of observable fact (rather than philosophic essence) that the individual had become an intrinsically social being in the course of history. But he continued to emphasize the objective and social dimensions of human existence by focusing on the durable works created for humanity through the labor of individuals. As empirical science as well as prospective utopia, Marxist thought thus relied on the ability of the concrete individual to unite, in his own person, a concern for the universal as well as the particular.

A VISION OF FREE INDIVIDUALITY

The ultimate reconciliation of the individual with the social world awaited the conscious reappropriation, by individuals in society, of the objective world they had collectively created. Within bourgeois society, the individual's "nature, objectification and realization" were alienated precisely to the extent that "*my* means of life belongs to *someone else*, that *my* desire is the inaccessible possession of *another*," that my objectification in labor was simultaneously my loss of the object. The more the worker produced, the less belonged "to him as his own"; the activity of the individual consequently appeared "independent of him and not belonging to him."[27] Individual appropriation came to seem a matter of mere possession, rather than a process of sensing, feeling, thinking, acting, and loving, as well as possessing. Things themselves had lost the significance of being human property: "We ourselves are excluded from *true* property because our property excludes the other human being."[28]

If the abstract equality imposed by money expressed the "general overturning of individualities" within bourgeois society, then that society could be opposed by the demand that "everyone of your relations to man and nature must be a *specific expression,* corresponding to the object of your will, of your *real individual* life."[29] In communism, Marx saw the radical incarnation of this demand. He carefully distinguished his own concept of communism from earlier and more primitive notions, which involved a crude leveling of individual capabilities to a dull equality; Marx by contrast described communism as the fulfillment of individual capabilities, and the cultivation of a rich, "subjective *human* sensibility."[30]

Through a revolutionary transformation of the social world, communism would transcend the contradictions between subject and object, spirit and matter, activity and passivity; it would resolve the antagonisms between "existence and essence, objectification and self-confirmation, freedom and necessity, the individual and the species."[31] In the end, the human individual might stand forth in his essential nature.

Suppose we had produced things as human beings: in his production each of us would have *twice affirmed* himself and the other. (1) In my *production* I would have objectified my *individuality* and its *particularity,* and in the course of the activity I would have enjoyed an individual *life;* in viewing the object, I would have experienced the individual joy of knowing my personality as an *objective, sensuously perceptible,* and *indubitable* power. (2) In your satisfaction and use of the product I would have had *direct* and conscious satisfaction that my work satisfied a *human* need, that it objectified *human* nature, and that it created an object appropriate to the need of another *human* being. (3) I would have been the *mediator* between you and the species, and you would have experienced me as a reintegration of your own nature and a necessary part of your self; I would have been affirmed in your thought as well as your love. (4) In my individual life I would have directly created your life; in my individual activity I would have immediately *confirmed* and *realized* my true *human* and *social* nature. Our production would be so many mirrors reflecting our nature.[32]

While communism represented the "necessary form and dynamic principle of the immediate future," it was "not itself the goal of human development."[33] Instead, the individual's emancipation, *from* alienating social conditions, *to* unalienated social life, formed the ultimate aim. "Labor would then be *true, active property,*" affirming one's *"individual* life."[34] It was a vision that would animate Marx's thought long after he had discarded the philosophical anthropology behind its initial formulations.

REALITY DEPICTED

In 1845, Marx and Engels published their first joint work, *The Holy*

Family, a polemic aimed at the German philosophical radicals. Although they allied themselves with materialism, Marx and Engels, like Feuerbach, persisted in deploying notions such as the "true nature" of man. Throughout *The Holy Family,* Marx retained the essentialistic language of Feuerbach-cum-Hegel most fully elaborated in the 1844 manuscripts. Retrospective nature as well as prospective norm, the concept of a human essence enabled the "Idea" of man to appear within the "real itself," as Marx had once specified in his adolescence; idealism could hence be accommodated to materialism.[35] Yet the essence or nature disclosed by philosophical anthropology, no matter how materialistic its claims, remained a static substance outside of time, discernible primarily through its absence within empirical reality. Such essentialism, by juxtaposing essential human nature with its empirical alienation, covertly sustained the dualism of "is" and "ought"' which Marx had hoped to overcome.

The manuscripts comprising *The German Ideology,* dating from 1845-1846, represented a crucial break with this philosophical anthropology and its essentialism. After an abortive attempt to have the book published, Marx and Engels consigned it to "the stinging criticism of the mice." Yet in this work, as Marx acknowledged fifteen years later, he and Engels settled their accounts with their former "philosophic conscience."[36] To be sure, many of the key concepts Marx had developed earlier retained a position within his transformed problematic: the conspicuous shift in language in *The German Ideology* and after was often purely a surface phenomenon, a strategic move even, devised in part to avoid the willful philosophical misreading Marx felt his articles for the *Deutsch-Französische Jahrbücher* had suffered.[37]

But if many concepts, like alienation, remained, Marx's rejection of philosophical anthropology enabled him to elaborate his ideas in new areas, and to pose them on a new basis. The objective man of 1844 became productive man; the foundation of all higher production was laid by man's production of his means of subsistence. In producing his means of subsistence, the activity of man constituted a "mode of production," a characteristic structure on the basis of which human possibilities were elaborated. "As individuals express their life, so they are." To be sure, Marx's earlier usage of concepts like "human nature" and "species-being" had never simply coincided with Feuerbach's; moreover, any view that described the essence of man as activity and objectification was by intent dynamic and historical, and militated against the hypostatization implicit in the anthropological question, "What is man's nature?"—as if there were self-evidently one. Nevertheless, with the new empirical emphasis of *The German Ideology,* any misunderstanding or reification of the notions "nature" and "essence" became virtually impossible. In this setting, the nature of man became variable, with as many possible meanings as modes of production and forms of life. The essence of man was explicitly linked to the historical conditions under which he produced and expressed himself.[38]

While Marx in effect subjected his own earlier views to scrutiny in *The German Ideology,* he reserved his most caustic jibes for former left-Hegelian colleagues, regardless of their materialist or spiritualist orientation. "Man" had remained an abstraction for neo-Hegelian philosophy; in it, the "human essence," somehow mysteriously incarnate in single individuals, became the conceptual motive force of history, while history itself became the story of the self-estrangement of "Man." But Marx now argued that a philosophically derived essence of man could not be set before the actual relations of men, for it was these latter which sustained all higher human expression, including philosophy. On the other hand, the materialist neo-Feuerbachians, by simply equating essence and existence, equally misunderstood "existing reality."[39] Here Marx argued that the actual relations of men traced out potential avenues for further human fulfillment and expression—but these possibilities were disclosed through historical rather than philosophical understanding.

Marx thus claimed that any social order, when closely studied, revealed a series of repressed or undeveloped possibilities for social and personal development. For example, the existent wealth of wants under capitalism, at least for the ruling class, indicated the objective possibility of a wealth of wants for all men within a society differently structured; or again, the factories and industries that housed the wage laborers of today could be seen as the home of man's communal mastery of nature tomorrow. Every social fact was thus more than it seemed, taken in isolation. When historically grasped, in relation to a wider constellation of other phenomena, a given datum could be interpreted as a negation, privation, or restriction: those conditions currently decried as inhuman suggested a future condition of humanity consequent on their transformation.

Thus "the positive expression 'human' corresponds to the definite conditions *predominant* at a certain stage of production and to the way of satisfying wants determined by them, just as the negative expression 'inhuman' corresponds to the attempt, within the existing mode of production, to negate these predominant conditions and the way of satisfying wants prevailing under them, an attempt that this stage of production daily engenders afresh."[40] The young Hegelians had approached the matter upside-down. Existence could not be deduced from essence: yet the reverse path, from existence to essence, was not only conceivable, but was actually espoused by Marx. Critically comprehended, reality of itself, through the protests of individuals dissatisfied with that reality, pointed beyond the one-dimensional confines of the purely present. As a result, transcendental philosophy had been rendered superfluous: "When reality is depicted, philosophy as an independent branch of knowledge loses its medium of existence."[41]

This new accent on reality obviously had significant ramifications for Marx's theory of individual emancipation. Criticism now became tied to the social relations and norms immanent to a given epoch; communism, previously a social ideal deciphered by philosophy, now became an expression of "the real movement which abolishes the present state of affairs."[42] The social dimension of human existence could similarly be conceived historically, instead of being hypostatized as man's "social being." The development of the individual's social inclinations no longer needed to appear as man's teleological perfection: instead the claims of individuation and communism were both deduced (in theory at least) from the real development of society.[43]

In *The German Ideology*, Marx and Engels thus reposed the question of individual emancipation, on the basis of a new understanding of "materialism." Previous materialists had emphasized the primary reality of physical matter, and the derivation of ideas from sense-data. Marx's novel version of materialism by contrast signified the primacy of "real individuals," not simply as conscious species-beings, but specifically as laboring creatures, producing to satisfy wants, and interacting within historically determinate social relations. For Marx in 1845, the history of productive forces circumscribed the "history of the development of the forces of the individuals themselves." The hitherto incomplete development of humanity and its productive capacities thus helped explain the unavoidable shortcomings of all earlier "conquests of freedom." The communist revolution, however, presupposed a global penetration of advanced productive forces, the merging of local history into world history, and the nullification of parochial barriers to communication and exchange. Modern capitalism had laid the basis for this revolution by placing individuals in "practical connection" with the "material and intellectual production of the whole world"; on this expanding basis of global interdependence, associated individuals, through communal control, might consciously master their powers of production.

To the extent that these productive forces had become global and universal, their appropriation had to be collective and social; any other mode of appropriation would fail to master rationally the historically developed resources. "Modern universal intercourse can be controlled by individuals, therefore, only when controlled by all."[44] Yet the end of such collective action remained individuation. The "reality which communism is creating" was "precisely the true basis for rendering it impossible that anything should exist independently of individuals, insofar as reality is only a product of the preceding intercourse of individuals themselves."[45] The transformation of the capitalist mode of production, through the abolition of private property and the division of labor, formed the material prerequisite for the emergence of fully developed men and women, able to command existent productive forces as "free manifestations of their lives." Particular personal relationships would no longer be subordinated to general class relationships. Beyond the one-sided specialization compelled by the division of labor, a man could "hunt in the morning, fish in the afternoon, rear cattle in the evening, criticize after dinner . . . without ever becoming hunter, fisherman, shepherd or critic."[46]

Marx went so far as to describe a communist form of society as "the only society in which the original and free development of individuals ceases to be a mere phrase." The full range of men's possibilities could thus only be elaborated in the future: for the present, Marx merely affirmed that the individual and his relations would be transformed under communism, that "the individuals' consciousness of their mutual relations will, of course, likewise become something quite different, and, therefore, will no more be 'the principle of love' or *dévouement,* than it will be egoism."[47]

EGOISM

Egoism, indeed, received a good deal of attention in *The German Ideology:* well over half the book was devoted to a critique of Max Stirner, the self-styled egoist and author of *The Ego and His Own*. For Stirner, the ego, which he called a "creative nothing," was the source of all concepts and normative evaluations, although most men, rather than realizing their unique creativity, became "possessed" by commonplace ideals and religious "spooks." Moral conscience hobbled the individual's will: Stirner complained that "the hard fist of morality treats the noble nature of egoism altogether without compassion."[48] He was no less appalled by liberalism; the secular religion of the state dissolved the "bodily, personal, egoistic interests" of each individual in the name of a mythic "general interest of all." By contrast, Stirner's egoist recognized only himself: "All freedom is essentially...self-liberation.... I can have as much freedom as I procure for myself by my ownness." To realize "ownness" in Stirner's terms was to take willful possession of one's fate, and to shape an individualized destiny: "I am my *own* only when I am master of myself, instead of being mastered either by sensuality, or by anything else (God, Man, authority, law, State, Church)."[49] Stirner welcomed the nihilistic implications of his radical egocentrism: "If I found my affair on myself, the unique one, then my concern rests on its transitory, mortal creator, who consumes himself, and I may say: *I have founded my affair on nothing.*"[50]

Since Stirner's theory resembles a primitive brand of existentialism, the commentary by Marx and Engels assumes an added interest. Some of their arguments were predictable: for example, they charged that Stirner's "unique" individual only ideally appropriated the world as his own, while really accepting the world as it already existed. They similarly criticized Stirner for slighting the social and material context that formed the setting for all subjective pursuits, a context that defined the possible forms individuation could take.

Yet Marx and Engels also granted Stirner's egoistic perspective a qualified validity. Engels, who was more enthusiastic on this score than Marx, praised Stirner's book in a letter he wrote Marx in 1844: any effective commitment to social change, remarked Engels, depended on making that cause our "own, egoistic cause." In agreement with Stirner, he argued that the communist desire of returning individuals to their human and social being had, "quite apart from any material expectation," to be interiorized in the desire of the individual ego.[51] While Marx urged Engels to temper his enthusiasm, he could agree with him and Stirner that true freedom entailed "self-liberation." Moreover, while Marx and Engels in *The German Ideology* denied that even bourgeois individuals were the heartless, self-centered egoists that Stirner lauded, they themselves claimed to bring "practical egoism to perfection, precisely by denying the phraseology of egoism — we who are concerned with realising real egoistical interests, not the holy interest of egoism." The communists by no means wanted "to do away with the 'private individual' for the sake of the 'general,' self sacrificing man."[52]

The trouble with Stirner, then, was not his obsession with individuation, but his one-sided abstraction of the individual from physical and social life. The satisfaction of the individual, however, depended "not on consciousness, but on being; not on thought, but on life." If the individual was to be liberated from heavenly ideals and alien authority, the world which "stimulated" his development had to be modified and placed under the control of the individuals themselves. That is why, for Marx and Engels, "the changing of oneself" coincides with "the changing of circumstances."[53]

THE LOGIC OF CAPITAL AND THE LOSS OF AGENCY

As 1848 approached, Marx increasingly devoted his time to political organizing, in conjunction with the Communist League, a London-based federation of exiled German workers. With the outbreak of continental revolution in 1848, Marx returned first to Paris, and then to Cologne, where he assumed editorial responsibilities for the *Neue Rheinische Zeitung*. Throughout the next year, he published a host of journalistic articles, representative of a vocation he pursued intermittently over the next decade, primarily in the *New York Daily Tribune* after 1853. In 1849, with the revolutionaries acrosss Europe in retreat, he was expelled from Cologne; after a brief stay in Paris, he was forced into exile in London, where he set to work on a critique of political economy.

The writings from this period bear witness to Marx's abiding interest in many of the themes first elaborated in earlier manuscripts. "Wage Labor and Capital," for example, described the estrangement under capital of the worker's own "life-activity," which became degraded to an odious means of mere subsistence. Indeed, the modern world appeared, from one perspective, as the alienation of agency, a loss of control. Capitalist society, remarked Marx and Engels in *The Communist Manifesto,* was "like the sorcerer, who is no longer able to control the powers of the nether world which he has called up by his spells."[54] Marx used similar imagery in a speech delivered in 1856: "At the same pace that mankind masters nature, man seems to become enslaved to other men or to his own infamy. Even the pure light of science seems unable to shine but on a dark background of ignorance. All our inventions and progress seem to result in endowing material forces with intellectual life, and in stultifying human life into a material force."[55]

Although Marx did not publish any results of his economic studies until the appearance in 1859 of his little book, *Critique of Political Economy,* his extensive study notes for this precursor to *Capital* have been preserved. Marx had originally envisaged a large six-part work on political economy treating (in order) capital, landed property, wage labor, the state, foreign trade, and the world market: within this plan, the extant four volumes of *Capital* (including *Theories of Surplus Value*) would have constituted only one-sixth of the projected work. Yet in the preface to the *Critique,* Marx claimed that the "entire material lies before me," written "for the purpose of cleaning up these questions to myself."[56] In 1939 and 1941, almost a thousand pages of this work were published in Moscow under the title *Grundrisse der Kritik der politischen Ökonomie (Rohentwurf).* An examination of these manuscripts confirms the fundamental continuity of Marx's work, especially with regard to the question of individual emancipation.

The *Grundrisse* resurrected the Hegelian terms of Marx's 1844 reflections; yet the dialectic of objectification and alienation recurred on a new level, the terrain of his mature comprehension of economics. By focusing on the "logic" of capital, Marx sharply posed the problem of labor as the loss of human agency.

This logic dictated that capital and labor exist as mutually exclusive antitheses. Abstractly considered, capital, objectified wealth, was only capital as nonlabor, while labor, subjective activity, was only labor as noncapital, as the exclusion of objectified wealth. Within the capital-labor relationship, labor found itself divorced from the raw materials, instruments, tools and products necessary for its action—in short, from all the relevant objectivity. Labor as noncapital thus was reduced to its subjective moment: labor not as objective self-expression but rather as the pure potential for objectifying activity. It was this potential that the laborer sold to the capitalist.

Despite the circumstance that labor, within the capital-labor relation, represented "absolute poverty, not as lack, but as complete exclusion of objective wealth,"[57] and was thus devalued, it nonetheless constituted the source of all economic value. Through its separation from capital, it became the abstract, perpetual possibility of activity as the realization of value. Yet this possibility only existed within the production process itself, which temporarily united the otherwise sundered elements of (subjective) labor and (objective) capital. Within the capital-labor relation, this unification of labor with its raw materials and instruments occurred on capital's terms: to the extent that labor entered into its unity, it simultaneously reproduced the disunity, of objectified labor (tools, raw materials), on the one hand, and living labor on the other.

Labor conserved existent value at the same time as it objectified new, or surplus, value for the capitalist. In return for his effort, the laborer received wages, while the capitalist retained a profit; and yet the only productive factor in the capital/labor equation was labor. Just as the substance of value was generally objectified labor, so most components of capital, as products, represented previously objectified labor. The analysis of the capital-labor relation revealed the lopsided contribution of labor, which capital proceeded to usurp. Since labor alone animated the production process, capital could be considered the product of labor, as well as an instrument for labor and a raw material used by it; "we can truly say that capital is not productive."[58]

In modern society, the capital-labor relation, which comprised both a confrontation and exchange between its two elements, had established itself as a force independent of the individual producer. Labor ceased to exist for the worker as "the productive force of wealth," since capital appropriated that force, eventually to counterpose its objectified products to the worker as a hostile power.[59] Worse still, since the laborer produced new or surplus value for capital, he unwittingly reinforced the objective conditions for extracting more such value.

Labor necessarily emerged from the production process poorer than when it entered; its objectified power of creating new value returned to labor, through capital, as its objective powerlessness. "The more labor objectifies itself, the greater will be the objective world of values that faces it in the form of alien property."[60] The past appropriation of labor thus served as the basis for fresh appropriation. Through the production process, labor found itself perpetually alienated from its own proper reality; its objectified traces became a "mere entity of others, or other entity," while its active objectification founded "its own non-being" or "the being of its non-being—of capital."[61]

The laborer consequently faced alienation from his very "manifestation of life," his human agency, which had been ceded to capital in exchange for dead, objectified labor in the form of money. The content of work itself was transformed into an alien object, chosen by the capitalist rather than the laborer. To the extent that the collective power of labor was assembled through capital, this power appeared to the worker as yet another independent force, foreign to his own activity.

The apparently free exchange between labor and capital was thus revealed by Marx as an exchange entailing the alienation and exploitation of labor. The most acute manifestation of this estrangement came in the worker's relation to the machine. By reducing the living activity of labor to a mechanical gesture, the machine reaped the ultimate victory of dead over living labor; rather than labor dominating its own creation, the machine dominated labor. With the machine, capitalist civilization occurred as a nightmare. The continual rise in the productive power of labor itself, the increasing penetration of scientific knowledge into the labor process—all this progress in civilization did not in the first instance enrich labor, but only capital.[62]

HISTORY AND INDIVIDUATION

Marx's early drafts for his critique of political economy contained an abundance of historical illustrations and references. By inserting a lengthy discussion of precapitalist economic formations, he underlined the transience of capitalism itself. Indeed, capitalism was "revolutionary, while all other modes of production were essentially

conservative," Marx wrote in *Capital*. Through historical understanding, capitalism could be seen in terms of the foundations it
already provided for another, more humane form of life.

Capitalism represented a definite progression over previous economic forms. To be sure, at first glance the regime of capital
seemed merely to abolish the old feudal ties to land and lord, only to
erect a new, economic dependence. But capitalism also sought the
complete development of productive forces; by driving labor beyond
the limits of its natural and traditional wants, it laid the basis for a
"rich individuality." While capital fostered a competitive individualism, pitting man against man, the very differentiation of the
individuals thus isolated compelled them to enter into relations with
one another *as individuals*. Not only that: through the exchange of
goods satisfying reciprocal wants, these individuals "stand not only
in an equal, but also in a social relation to one another." In the
marketplace and before the law, capitalism thus in principle established, on the ground of individuation, the abstract equality of all
subjects and also their freedom — achievements anticipated by the
untrammeled circulation of money. Echoing the indifference of
money to personal distinction, exchange encouraged the unfettered
movement of self-seeking egoistical interest. Marx went so far as to
describe the exchange of commodities as the "productive, real basis
of all *equality* and *freedom*."[63]

This account confirmed Marx's materialist approach, in *The German Ideology,* to individual emancipation. In the early writings, the
emergence of the social individual, the "whole man" of 1844, had
marked man's elevation to his essential nature. From this perspective, individuation had appeared not so much an accomplishment
as a given datum of human existence — although the extent and efficacy of the individual's real power naturally varied with his situation.

But Marx in the *Grundrisse* clearly and unequivocally affirmed
that "man is individualized through the process of history."[64] While
man's appearance across history displayed certain constants, these
could only be confirmed through a comparative historical inquiry,
which provisionally determined the nature of man by specifying the
heretofore stable traits shared by all, while anticipating possibilities
for their modification. Man was alienated in modern society, not
from an essence, but from real possibilities for a better form of life —

one that might overcome the dissatisfying disjunction between the constraints imposed by capitalism and the ideals professed by modern culture. Individuation now appeared as one of the foremost progressive achievements — and promises — of modern society.

Capitalism had accumulated wealth, promoted universal exchange, and established a thorough interdependence among producing and consuming individuals. This universal exchange and expanded wealth tended to produce the individual in its own image. He formed the locus of freedom in trade and was guaranteed a certain equality before the law. Any individual might (in theory) develop his labor-power to any end, independently of guild restrictions. Yet ultimately such universality, freedom, and equality encountered immanent barriers to their economic and social elaboration. The freedom of the individual within commodity exchange simultaneously represented a strict limitation or even complete suppression of his actual liberty, insofar as social conditions, such as the division of society into capital and labor, took the form of alien, all-powerful forces governing his life activity. Equality under capitalist conditions of exchange likewise remained a formal endowment confined to the realm of law, or appeared as money, which established its equivalence value only by leveling all distinctions among things and men. [65]

The material liberation of the individual thus required the abolition of capitalist relations of production, even though capitalism itself in large part supplied the social and economic basis to support universal individuation. Through collective production, the associated individuals might consciously appropriate, on a harmonious basis, the extensive productive forces already developed by capital and subordinate them to their own particular aims. Material production would then disappear as an alien compulsion confronting the laboring individual and become instead an objective expression of individual desires satisfied through collective labor.

In broad outline, the *Grundrisse* sketched the stages of human development. The earliest forms of society were marked by restricted relationships of personal dependency. The second form of society by contrast witnessed the establishment of general social intercourse and the expansion of productivity; as a consequence, far-reaching social relations developed among men, individual wants became differentiated, and variable, universal skills in labor were encouraged. Nevertheless, this second form of society, which liberated capital, simultaneously subjected the producers to the caprice of capital; the new independence was confined within a new dependence. The third form of society surpassed such limitations. Marx called this stage, established on the economic basis provided by capitalism, "free individuality." The first form of society explicitly to incorporate individuality as its guiding aim and principle, it was directed toward the further "universal development of individuals and the domination of their communal and social productivity, which has become their social power."[66]

The social individual liberated within Marx's "third form" of society arose as a possibility through the process of history. As Marx remarked in the *Critique of Political Economy,* "We do not proceed from the labor of individuals as social labor, but, on the contrary, from the special labor of private individuals, which appears as universal social labor only by divesting itself of its original character in the process of exchange. Universal social labor is, therefore, no ready-made assumption, but a growing result."[67] Marx now called man a *"zoon politikon,"* not because he was sociable by nature, but rather because he was "an animal which can develop into an individual only in society."[68]

THE SOCIAL INDIVIDUAL LIBERATED

Throughout his later published writings, Marx maintained his interest in individual emancipation. The upshot of world history in *Capital,* as in the *Grundrisse,* was the full development of the particular individual. Modern industry, by the very unstable character of the employment it offered labor, forced the laborer to vary his skills: it replaced the "detail worker of today" with the "fully developed individual, fit for a variety of labor . . . to whom the different social functions he performs are but so many modes of giving free scope to his own natural and acquired powers."[69] In cooperative labor, moreover, the individual "strips off the fetters" of his isolated "individuality and develops the capabilities of his species."[70] Marx indeed was more sanguine about the effects of capitalism on individuality in 1867 than he had been in 1844. The rise of capitalism had definitively shattered the limited economic bases of earlier economic forms, which could only support "the immature development of man individually." The individual in communist society would thus reappropriate "individual property based on the acquisitions of the capitalist era, i.e., on cooperation and the possession in common of the land, and the means of production." The "ruling principle" of communist production was acknowledged as "the full and free development of every individual."[71]

Marx's critique of the Gotha program in 1875 confirmed his commitment to individual emancipation:

In a higher phase of communist society, after the enslaving subordination of the individual to the division of labor, and therewith also the antithesis between mental and physical labor has vanished; after labor has become not only a means of life but life's prime want; after the productive forces have also increased with the all-round development of the individual, and all the springs of cooperative wealth flow more abundantly—only then can the narrow horizon of bourgeois right be crossed in its entirety and society inscribe on its banners: From each according to his ability, to each according to his needs.[72]

Capital and his later writings thus sustained Marx's youthful vision of a society where every individual's capabilities might be freely developed. But Marx had come to view such an emancipation historically rather than philosophically: the social individual was no anthropological a priori, but instead an emergent result of historical tendencies. The institution of communism liberated the individual fostered by the complex of social interdependencies characterizing advanced capitalism. Such men were already social beings in the most profound sense: they could not pursue their lives apart from society. But they were also individuals with livelihoods and identities founded on the elaboration of specialized and particular talents.

The emergence of labor as an abstract, universal, and exploitable potential suggested its liberation as a vehicle of personal expression. The end of individuation then entailed not simply equality before the law, or the bourgeois privilege of eccentricity, but rather the foundation of a society in which, as Theodor Adorno once put it, "people could be different without fear."[73] The material basis of individuation lay in the wealth accumulated by capitalism: upon such a basis, men might be able to objectify themselves with a minimum of material constraints. By placing machinery at the service of the producers and reducing necessary labor time to a minimum, the arena for free human expression could be enlarged.

As free time became available to all, it transformed "anyone who enjoys it into a different person, and it is this different person who then enters the direct process of production."[74] Work, while not becoming play, might then reclaim a lost dimension of creative expression for the individual. The continued progress of productive forces in turn prompted the full development of a wealth of socially acquired wants. Collective production encouraged a "rich individuality, just as universal in production as consumption.... [Its] labor thus itself appears not to be labor anymore, but a full development of activity, in which the natural necessity has disappeared in its direct form, since the place of natural needs has been taken by needs that are historically produced."[75]

The social individual represented a possible future concealed at the heart of a congealed present.

When the narrow bourgeois form has been peeled away, what is wealth, if not the universality of needs, capacities, enjoyments, productive powers, etc., of individuals, produced in universal exchange? What, if not the full development of human control over the forces of nature—those of his own nature as well as those of so-called "nature"? What, if not the absolute elaboration of his creative dispositions, without any preconditions other than antecedent historical evolution which makes the totality of this evolution—i.e., the evolution of all human powers as such, unmeasured by any *previously established* yardstick—an end in itself? What is this, if not a situation where man does not reproduce himself in any determined form, but produces his totality? Where he does not seek to remain something formed by the past, but is in the absolute movement of becoming?[76]

Throughout his life, Marx thus affirmed the end of individual emancipation. Beyond the primarily political and formal emancipation envisaged by liberalism, beyond the purely technical reform of society proposed by utopian socialists like Saint-Simon, beyond the abstractly inward moral metamorphosis espoused by various strains of romanticism, Marx anticipated social conditions that might enable men to become whole, to unite in intention and act, implement and result the reality of their own, particular purposes. Restored to his vital objectivity, the individual might finally begin to elaborate his own world freely, in the inalienable certitude of his acts. Communism would then spell the end of estranged self-expression, as surely as it inaugurated an equitable distribution of wealth. By submitting social institutions to the control of the individuals comprising them, communism returned the individual to society, as its real subject and proper object.

The plausibility of this vision has yet to be demonstrated in practice. Although Marx himself forecast the reconciliation of particular desire and universal interest within a new form of social life, modern history has yet to confirm such expectations. Instead, the emergence of an economy premised on constant growth and geared to the virtually unlimited proliferation of "needs" has called into question Marx's optimistic assessment of the "rich individuality" engendered by capitalism. If Marx's paradigm was the individual as producer, our contemporary problem is the individual as consumer, the object of advertising and market research. Similarly, the rise of a form of life stamped by mass production has tended to liquidate rather than reconcile the distinction between the individual and society: today's social individual increasingly wears the mask of cheerful conformism, while the outsider and solitary thinker, by taking exception to the blandishments of immediate social existence, preserve the possibility of a reconciliation that respects human differences. Marx critically depicted the process of individual emancipation, but he scarcely foresaw the full range of difficulties impeding its realization.

2

The "Real Individual" and Marx's Method

Marx did not limit his interest in individuals to a concern for their emancipation. In fact, throughout his early works he frequently referred to "real individuals" as the basis of social theory. This individualistic accent in Marxian theory strikes an odd contrast to his more familiar social realism, with its emphasis on the command of social and historical conditions over human action; indeed, Marx's talk of real individuals receded in his later works. But it never vanished completely, continuing to play an auxiliary role in his economic theory: The emphasis on individuals served as a reminder that social relations and economic concepts were not static, but developed historically, through the agency of human beings.

THE INDIVIDUAL BASIS OF THEORY: FEUERBACH AND MARX

Marx formed his early methodological perspectives under the influence of Ludwig Feuerbach. In his critique of Hegel, Feuerbach had called for the return of philosophy from the "realm of 'departed souls'" to the "realm of embodied and living souls."[1] Such a return would show the truth of materialism — not the "obtuse" materialism of previous thinkers who had denied the intellect any reality at all, but rather a post-Hegelian materialism that grasped consciousness through an understanding premised on the primacy of sentient human beings and the perceptible world they lived in. According to Feuerbach, Hegel, like all previous rationalists, remained a prisoner of theological abstractions: concepts like "Spirit" were groundless, corresponding to no perceptible or human reality. In his critique of Hegel's *Phenomenology,* Feuerbach traced this groundlessness back to what he took to be Hegel's transcendence of sense-certainty. For Feuerbach, by contrast, sensuous intuition (*Anschauung*) founded all abstract concepts: "Only the intuition of things and beings in their objective reality makes man free, liberated from all prejudices."[2] The highest manifestation of such sensuous intuition of the particular, according to Feuerbach, occurred in loving another human being. In love, the concrete "this" of a specific person acquired an absolute value which could not be conjured away by some dialectical sleight of hand—one reason why Feuerbach called love the "proof" of being.

Despite his unorthodox emphasis on love, the irreducibility of consciousness, and the centrality of the single human being, Feuerbach's doctrine paralleled the materialism of Enlightenment thinkers such as Holbach, who argued that all ideas were based on sentiments and sense-data; like them, Feuerbach attributed reality only to feelings, intuitions, and the consciousness of particular individuals. Similarly, the concomitant of this materialism was a variant on nominalism, the view that concepts represent no objective entities, but instead remain mere names. But Feuerbach's nominalism, like his materialism, harbored ambiguities. According to him, religion formed an essential repository of the self-image of humanity, inverted to be sure, but nonetheless essentially accurate after its materialist reinterpretation. As the metaphors of religion implied, the essence of the human individual was contained in his unity with a community, in the relationship between man and man; in his communal perfection, the individual developed the highest capabilities of the species. He was then no solitary soul, but instead potentially embodied the universal and infinite, which Hegel had mystified as the attribute exclusively of "Spirit" or God. While Feuerbach insisted that the individual could never be *transcended* (by God or by Hegel), he equally insisted that the individual could shed the limitations of his singularity, most critically in the sensuous, loving relationship linking "I" and "Thou." If for Hegel the universal contained the particular, for Feuerbach the particular contained (at least potentially) the universal; to this extent, the universal (such as religious images of God) had a measure of reality.[3]

When Marx came to criticize Hegel in 1843, he adapted Feuerbach's nominalistic method, its ambiguity intact, to his own purposes. Hegel had committed a compound error in his *Philosophy of*

Right, charged Marx: he had abstracted man from his actual life activities and then established the state as the supposedly concrete locus of man's social existence. But the individual, as grasped by neo-Feuerbachian materialism, already, by essential nature, manifested sociable inclinations: the true foundation of politics was not a putatively universal entity, the state, but the individual men whose interaction actually constituted society. In a reasonable society, political institutions would embody nothing but the "modes of existence and operation of the social qualities of men." In his 1844 manuscripts, Marx followed a similar line of argument. Since society consisted of nothing but sociable individuals, there was no need for it to confront the individual as an alien entity. In a communist society, every individual's relations would become an immediate, specific manifestation of "real individual life."[4]

Marx in his early writings thus followed Feuerbach in endorsing a form of *social* nominalism—the view that social groups and institutions have no existence apart from the individuals comprising them. Moreover, Marx in *The Holy Family* also followed Feuerbach in offering nominalist arguments to criticize Hegel's use of concepts. "The main interest for the speculative philosopher is . . . to produce the *existence* of . . . real ordinary fruits and to say in some mysterious way that . . . the apples, pears, almonds and raisins that we rediscover in the speculative world are nothing but *semblances* . . . for they are moments in the life of '*the* Fruit,' this abstract *creation of the mind,* and therefore themselves abstract *creations of the mind.*" Elsewhere in the same work, Marx sympathetically described nominalism as the "first expression of materialism."[5]

The nominalist position proved a useful starting point for the criticism of the left-Hegelians. The greatest enemy of socialism, wrote Marx in 1844, is "speculative idealism, which substitutes 'self-consciousness' or the 'spirit' for the real individual man."[6] Such an idealism construed history as a self-activating train of events, although in fact history was "*nothing but* the activity of man pursuing his aims."[7] Yet Marx's nominalism, like Feuerbach's, remained equivocal. Talk of a human essence and species-being indeed seemed contradictory to the spirit of a thoroughgoing nominalism. And, as subsequent works would make clear, Marx by no means intended to deny the reality of social institutions and relations.

BETWEEN SOCIAL NOMINALISM
AND SOCIAL REALISM

The German Ideology represented the apotheosis of Marx's early neo-Feuerbachian nominalist tendencies, coupled, paradoxically, not only with a critique of Feuerbachian materialism, but also with a growing insistence on the virtually autonomous reality of modern society vis-à-vis any particular individual. Nonetheless, "real individuals" appear prominently throughout the work: "The premises from which we begin are not arbitrary ones, not dogmas, but real premises from which abstraction can be made only in the imagination. They are the real individuals, their activity and the material conditions under which they live, both those which they find already existing, and those produced by their activity. These premises can thus be verified in a purely empirical way."[8] Social theory did not take for granted any philosophical a prioris, humanistic or otherwise; instead, the theorist started from men and the activities they pursued within a specific material and social setting. The emphasis on circumstance and activity underlined the dynamic and intrinsically historical nature of the object the theory described: the individuals it faced underwent a "perceptible process of development" under definite historical conditions.[9]

Yet while Marx here expressed the premises of his materialism in an individualistic fashion, he also emphasized the reality of social classes, and the social origin of religion and philosophy. Typically (in the American sociology inspired by George Herbert Mead, for instance) social nominalism and "methodological individualism" have gone hand in hand with "psychological realism" and a corresponding denial of social reality and "societal facts." But Marx's social-nominalist tendencies consisted only in taking individual acts as the ultimate source of social reality. He nowhere denied the reality of the social realm resulting from the totality of individual acts; he simply denied its independence from human action. Indeed, Marx often insisted that individual beliefs and behavior were critically shaped by such immediately irreducible social phenomena as the rules of exchange and the roles typically assumed within a given social class. Such social objects as class and the division of labor were indubitably real, to the point indeed where they could appear as an independent imposition on the individuals ultimately comprising them.

To be sure, such social structures as class Marx held to be *historically* reducible to the "individual behavior of individuals" at a certain stage of material and social development; it was individuals who "created the existing conditions and daily reproduce them anew."[10] The virtual independence of social relations from the individuals ultimately producing them arose initially from the historical sedimentation of previous human acts, which confronted succeeding individuals as a fait accompli; acts which had once assumed a vital meaning for men left to posterity merely their petrified traces and unintended consequences. Capitalist relations of exchange ratified this reification by vesting control of such institutions as the state and means of production in the hands of a few. A laborer therefore confronted institutions such as the division of labor as alien and rigid, quasi-natural objectivities limiting his own life and its possibilities. Although society consisted only of active individuals who comprised the social order through their relations and practices, the eventual outcome and final totality of these practices and relations eluded the control of any one individual.

While Marx acknowledged the relative autonomy of many humanly created social institutions and relations from the persons entering into and reproducing them, he simultaneously used the "individualistic" premises of his materialism to protest such fixed social relations. By placing social production under the control of the associated producers, communism would facilitate the return of social institutions and relations to the command of the individuals who in fact comprised them. In this sense, the real individual as a theoretical premise helped demystify the social order. Marx's theory then yielded an historical account of the genesis of social relations and institutions, and bore within itself a mandate for the conscious production of history and society by those individuals who had hitherto produced themselves, their society, and their history largely unconsciously.

COMPREHENDING SOCIAL RELATIONS

An emphasis on the activity and intercourse of individuals as the real foundation of society remained characteristic of Marx's thought; yet the later economic works modified his earlier individualism by restricting its role in his social theory. Society had never been for Marx a mere sum of individual acts, but rather a "totality" of interacting individuals, facing one another in various relationships. His later economic works focused precisely on that totality and the economic and social relations which defined it. Modern society did not present a series of simply human relations of man to man, but instead an array of historically specific social and economic relations, such as those of capitalist to worker and landlord to tenant. Such relationships among men appeared determinant only from the standpoint of society; no man was a wage laborer as such. Rather, he could be a wage laborer only "within society and because of it" by entering into a social relation with another individual, in this case a capitalist in search of labor.[11] Modern society embodied "social relations based on the antagonism of classes. These relations are, not the relations of individual to individual, but of workman to capitalist, of farmer to landlord, etc. Efface these relations and you have extinguished the whole of society. . . ."[12]

The individual thus faced a previously established set of social relations outside of his particular control. To this extent, persons entering into them remained unfree. "The social relation of individuals to each other, which has made itself into an autonomous power over them, whether it is presented as a power of nature, an accident or anything else you like, is the necessary result of the fact that the starting point is not the free social individual."[13] In consequence, most men were forced to take on constraining social roles. But "just as it is . . . childish to consider these economic bourgeois roles of buyer and seller as eternal social forms of human individuality, so it is on the other hand preposterous to lament in them the extinction of individuality. They are the necessary manifestations of individuality at a certain stage of the social system of production."[14]

The social interaction of individuals had hitherto occurred within an hypostatized framework that remained virtually independent of the persons involved. Men made their own history—"but they do not make it just as they please, but under circumstances directly encountered, given and transmitted from the past."[15] If society was the historical product of individual acts, *and* a reality virtually independent of such acts, the question of method and the approach of social

theory to its object became acute. Narrative history might emphasize the concatenation of particular actions against a backdrop of
given circumstance; yet political economy approached the backdrop
of given economic circumstance beyond specific individual acts.
How?

Through his study of political economy, Marx came to revise his
earlier neo-Feuerbachian presentation of the methodology and procedures appropriate to social theory. In the process, Marx, while
insisting on the ontological primacy of interacting individuals, disavowed any form of epistemological nominalism. Where Feuerbach
and the early Marx had called the tangible and particular the "concrete," the later Marx followed Hegel in viewing concreteness as an
attribute of theory, a result of a theory's comprehensiveness.

His polemic against Proudhon in *The Poverty of Philosophy* had
previously indicated the course of his development. There he had
unambiguously presented social *relations* as the object of economic
theory. Economic categories merely expressed these relations; to this
end, the categories necessarily ignored particular individuals, just as
any specific social relation qua relation represented something more
than and different from the individuals involved.

Marx's introduction to the *Gundrisse* sketched out in more detail
his mature approach to social relations. As before, the observable
world of individuals producing in society remained the ground of
social theory external to theory itself. But concreteness was now presented as the result and accomplishment of thought itself, "a combination of many determinations, therefore the unity of diverse elements."[16] Such theoretical concreteness led to the conceptual "reproduction" of the observable social world "in the course of reasoning"; but for the first time, it constituted this world as an object of
knowledge by ordering it conceptually.

Marx set out by criticizing previous political economy. He therefore already had a body of abstract concepts before him as his
object. The classical concepts required reformulation because of
internal theoretical contradictions, as well as discrepancies between
the theory and the economic reality ostensibly depicted. For example, Adam Smith had predicted that the free play of self-interest
would generate wealth for all; yet the widespread squalor and poverty endured by the nineteenth-century British worker, documented
at great length in *Capital,* tended to discredit Smith's hypothesis.

The significance of the basic economic concepts lay in their relationship to one another. Fundamental categories like capital remained virtually meaningless without reference to other categories such as labor, value, money, and so on. The increasingly complex articulation of such conceptual relations enabled theory to approximate the real complexity of economic relations, only now comprehended by defined concepts. *Capital* thus moved from abstract notions such as labor, value, and capital toward a presentation of such phenomena as the state and world market. The whole process could be summarized as a movement from real empirical complexity through conceptual simplicity to a conceptually comprehended complexity, a movement which provided the theoretical tools for grasping the initial complexity in its economic dimensions.

Moreover, Marx now implied that the real abstractness and complexity of a phenomenon like the commodity refuted any strictly nominalist perspective. In the first edition of *Capital,* Hegel's logic, for all its absurd inversions, was implicitly vindicated as the method appropriate to an absurdly inverted social reality. In a remarkable reversal of his nominalist critique of *"the* Fruit" in 1845, Marx remarked how, when one commodity, such as gold, functions as a universal equivalent in exchange, "it is as if, above and beyond lions, tigers, hares and all other actual animals which group to form the various kinds, species, subspecies, families, etc., of the animal kingdom, there also existed *the animal,* the individual incarnation of the entire animal kingdom. Such an individual, which includes within itself all actually existing species as the same thing, is a *universal,* like *animal, god,* etc."[17] Yet Marx still preserved a critical distance from Hegel. That he makes his point sarcastically confirms his continuing commitment to demystify apparently abstract social relations, and, ultimately, to return control of society to the individual agency of the associated producers: after all, for Marx in 1867 as in 1845, it was the individual producers who actually created the social wealth abstractly expressed by money.

Marx also differed from Hegel in his historical understanding of the categories of political economy. For him, the map of universal categories and social relations produced by theory in no way replaced the historical world that the theorist started from. The existence of capital, wrote Marx in one of his later notebooks, "is the result of a protracted process in the economic formation of society."

He emphatically added: "At this point it is determined how the dialectical form of representation is only correct when it knows its limits." The historical world of real individuals standing toward each other in specific relations remained independent of theory insofar as the latter did not actively penetrate and transform the world. Marx thus rebuked Hegel for mistaking "the movement of categories for the real act of production."[18]

History entered into economic theory on two levels. First, the social world comprehended by theory remained an historical one, open to modification through human action: theory did not confront a static structure as its ultimate object. On this level, history always posed the possibility of outstripping theory and rendering its key concepts obsolete. Second, social theory had to interpret itself as an historical creation, situated in a particular epoch.

For Marx, the ability to order economic concepts abstractly was itself an historical result. A developed economic system that viewed objectified labor in general as the meaning of wealth comprised the *sine qua non* for conceiving labor abstractly, i.e., in general and without further differentiations. "Indifference as to the particular kind of labor implies the existence of a highly developed totality of different species of concrete labor, none of which is any longer the predominant one."[19] The simple concept of labor thus arose in the most complex social order, where the particularity of work could appear indifferent to the individual undertaking it.

A similar historical perspective modified Marx's insistence that social theory be premised on individuals producing in society. The possibility of such a premise itself appeared now as an historical acquisition. Bourgeois society presented both social interrelations and individual independence at a high stage of development; this historical situation legitimated starting from "individuals producing in society, thus the socially determined production of individuals." Despite its historical genesis, such a formula (like the simple concepts of labor, capital, and so forth) had in retrospect universal validity, thanks precisely to its abstract generality. Human production was always "production at a certain stage of social development, or production by social individuals."[20] Insofar as its elements —man on the one side, nature on the other—remained constant throughout history, "production" could be defined as the "appropriation of nature by the individual within and through a definite form of society."[21]

But the aim of economic theory was not the producing individuals as such, qua their particularity. Rather, theory focused on the social relations that "individuals in the process of reproducing their life" entered into, "under definite material conditions."[22] Although such relations derived from human acts, the problem was precisely to grasp these relations in their reified existence as a second nature, above and beyond the intentions of individual capitalists and laborers. Marx had once defined domination as the "appropriation of another's will"; in this sense, *Capital* sought to unravel the economic forms dominating individual life.

To this end, Marx consistently abstracted from individuals in his economic theory. "Here individuals are dealt with only in so far as they are the personifications of economic categories, embodiments of particular class-relations and class-interests."[23] As the object of theory, the capitalist and laborer were defined strictly by their position within the relations of production; merely as an owner of a factory, the capitalist exercised a definite power over labor, whether he willed it or not. Economic theory construed society as "the sum of connections and relationships in which individuals find themselves"; for theory, "society does not consist of individuals."[24]

Marx had justified such a procedure as early as *The German Ideology*. "The communists in practice treat the conditions created up to now by production and intercourse as inorganic conditions, without, however . . . believing that these conditions were inorganic for the individuals creating them."[25] In the *Grundrisse*, Marx amplified this position. Society, approached as a totality of relationships, as a social process, arises, "it is true, from the mutual influence of conscious individuals on one another"; however, this totality appears to the individuals as an alien and natural objectivity, "neither located in their consciousness, nor subsumed under them as a whole."[26]

Thus despite his methodological abstraction from individuals as such, Marx in his later economic theory maintained his youthful imperatives, as well as the (ontological) premise of (conscious) individuals producing in society. While social *relations* became the primary focus of his theory, he remained cognizant of his original starting point. As the *Grundrisse* put it, even the "simplest economic category" presupposed a population of real individuals, "producing in specific relations." Any category, like any isolated relation, "can never exist other than as an abstract, one-sided relation within an already given, concrete, living whole." The "only subjects" of production are "individuals, but individuals in mutual relationships, which they equally reproduce and produce anew."[27]

The point of conceptual abstraction and theoretical concreteness remained the practical dissipation of reified social relations. "Communism differs from all previous movements in that it overturns the basis of all earlier relations of production and intercourse, and for the first time consciously treats all natural premises as the creatures of men, strips them of their natural character and subjugates them to the power of the united individuals."[28] Long after he had abandoned Feuerbach's nominalist methodology, Marx therefore retained the "real individual" as the critical premise — and ultimate promise — of social theory.

3

Marx's Concept of Labor

We have seen the importance Marx attributed to individual emancipation, and the methodological role he assigned to the "real individual"; but the essential capabilities he ascribed to these individuals remain to be elaborated. Questions, indeed, are raised by some
of his most famous aphorisms. For example, in his preface to the
Critique of Political Economy, he stated that "it is not the consciousness of men that determines their existence, but, on the contrary
their social existence that determines their consciousness."[1] Such
statements seemed to portend a materialist theory of the objective
determination of consciousness, portraying an individual's mind as
the passive object of causal processes purely external to conscious
ness as such. Similar problems were raised by the theory developed
in *The German Ideology,* where Marx and Engels argued that the
leading ideas of an epoch were "phantoms," mere "sublimates" of
empirically verifiable material premises. This approach to ideology
and consciousness implied that the individual's ideas at best submissively reflected the given reality.

Such an account of consciousness in turn raised doubts about the
possible autonomy of the individual: could human beings be emancipated from capitalism only by molding their minds according to
some constellation of external imperatives? Could the intentions of
an individual, even in principle, ever contribute creatively to this
emancipatory process?

These doubts, specifically about the possible importance of consciousness and individual intentions, can be provisionally settled
through an examination of Marx's understanding of labor. For
when he spoke of the determinant force of "social existence," he had
in mind that being which objectifies itself through labor. Even after
abandoning philosophical anthropology as an acceptable basis for

social theory, he continued to maintain a relatively consistent *empirical* anthropology, focusing on *homo faber*—man as a practical animal. Man was inherently active, engaged in shaping a world, and labor became Marx's paradigm for this practical being. By insisting on the teleological element in labor, the projection of an idea to be worked up through the mastery of natural materials, Marx in principle invested individuals, through their intentional agency, with a margin of conscious creativity, a margin which not only separated men from productive animals, but also helped sustain Marx's hopes for communism. That *this* practically oriented human being anchored consciousness hardly entailed an eclipse of individual autonomy. As Ernst Bloch said of Marx's practical orientation, "The concrete idea has never been more highly valued, for here it becomes the illumination for the act; nor has the act ever been more highly valued, for here it becomes the crown of truth."[2]

PRACTICE AND MATERIALISM

Marxist materialism has frequently been distinguished from previous materialist doctrines by its introduction of practice, and, with it, history, into the concept. Auguste Cornu, Marx's biographer, sees this practical perspective as the key to Marx's break with Feuerbach, and his subsequent elaboration of a distinctive theoretical outlook.[3] Yet even before this break, Marx had developed, largely in the 1844 manuscripts, his own concept of labor, derived in part from his critique of Hegel, in part from his readings in political economy.

Marx praised Hegel for making the "dialectic of negativity...the moving and generating principle" of his *Phenomenology*. Because Hegel conceives "the self-creation of man as a process, conceives objectification as loss of the object, as alienation and as transcendence of this alienation," Hegel grasps "the essence of *labor* and comprehends objective man—true, because real man—as the outcome of man's *own labor*." For Marx as well, "The *entire so-called history of the world* is nothing but the creation of man through human labor, nothing but the emergence of nature for man...."[4]

Labor comprised the "life-activity" peculiar to the human species. Since Marx defined the "whole character of a species" by the character of its life activity, the role Marx assigned labor set his interpretation of such Feuerbachian concepts as "species-being" apart from Feuerbach's own. In *The German Ideology* Marx wrote that "men can be distinguished from animals by consciousness, by religion or anything else you like. They themselves begin to distinguish themselves from animals as soon as they begin to *produce*...."[5] But what was unique to man, according to Marx in the 1844 manuscripts, was not mere production, since "admittedly animals also produce"; rather, human production was "conscious life-activity," which "distinguished man immediately from animal life-activity." Only "in creating a *world of objects*, by his practical activity, in *his work upon* inorganic nature" did man prove himself "a conscious species-being."[6]

In short, man effectively distinguished himself as a *conscious* being *through* production. A purely interiorized consciousness remained nothing, unless it was communicated or cast outside of itself, into the objective world. Labor for Marx represented the primary medium of this crystallization of consciousness, an externalization that simultaneously bore witness to its objective existence. When he asserted that "free, conscious activity is man's species character," Marx both offered an abstract description of individual labor as a necessary condition for human survival and proposed a norm of labor as it potentially could appear under unalienated conditions of free and conscious social production.

Because man had a capacity to shape the products of his life activity with a consciousness and a will, men, unlike animals, were capable of producing an infinite variety of objects. An animal produced only what it immediately needed; it reproduced only itself; its products belonged immediately to its body; it formed things only "in accordance with the standard and the need of the species to which it belongs." Man by contrast produced objects even when free from physical need; he produced articles that other men could use; and he produced tools for carrying out production, implements that could be used again. He was capable of reproducing entire aspects of nature; he freely faced the products of his own hand as independent objects; and he could form the world according to an endless variety of standards, including the peculiarly human standard of beauty. Labor as such, considered in abstraction from historically specific social relations, thus in principle comprised a unity of mind and body and creatively realized, by altering the world, the aims, not only of the laboring individual but also, indirectly, of the species. The labor process and its products represented the objective existence of subjectivity and the subjective self-formation of the species: man, by working within the world, "subjectified" the world, by subjecting it to his own ends.[7]

This presentation of labor as a potentially free, conscious, and purposeful activity affected Marx's understanding of human history. If history was the story of humanity's self-genesis through labor, it was also the story of this genesis as "consciously self-transcending." History, like labor itself, never simply unfolded as a one-dimensional succession of happenings, but, additionally, as a series of ideal projects—ones that may not yet have been accomplished. "The entire movement of history is therefore both its *actual* genesis—the birth of its empirical existence—and also for its thinking consciousness the *comprehended* and *known* process of its becoming. . . ."[8] Marx insisted not only on the moment of conscious projection in the labor process: he also defended the intentional projects of men as an essential element of history. In 1844, he even hinted that the aims the communists sought to actualize had their current basis in just such intentions—even more than in the objective reality those intentions, to be effective, had to reckon with.[9]

To be sure, by stressing *labor* as the paradigmatic medium for realizing human intentions, Marx also stressed the importance of anchoring *effective* agency in an objective understanding of the world, in contrast to the Young Hegelians, who preferred to emphasize "pure critique" and the "pure act" to implement it: for Marx, there could be no "pure act," no "pure will." On the other hand, his respect for *purposeful* as well as effective agency served to distinguish his thinking from the materialism of Feuerbach as well as the idealism of the Young Hegelians. In his "Theses on Feuerbach," Marx made explicit his departures from previous versions of materialism.

One of Marx's central objections to Feuerbach concerned his passive portrayal of subjectivity. "The chief defect of all hitherto existing materialism (that of Feuerbach included) is that the thing, reality, sensuousness, is conceived only in the form of the *object or of contemplation,* but not as *sensuous human activity, practice,* not subjectively. Hence, in contradistinction to materialism, the *active* side was developed abstractly by idealism—which, of course, does not know real, sensuous activity as such."[10] This active side entailed for Marx, as for idealism, the conscious assertion of aim. Earlier materialist doctrines had postulated a one-way determinism of circumstances impinging on the individual; but Marx argued classical materialism "forgets that circumstances are changed by men.... The coincidence of the changing of circumstances and human activity or self-changing can be conceived and rationally understood only as *revolutionary practice*."[11]

The touchstone of man's objective existence thus became the practical realization of his intentions through labor. The emphasis of course fell on practice, not consciousness in itself: to the extent that thought was detached from reality, it had not yet even gained the element of its effective existence. "The question whether objective truth can be attributed to human thinking is not a question of theory but is a *practical question*. Man must prove the truth, i.e., the reality and power, the this-sidedness of his thinking in practice."[12]

Marx's analysis of practice in 1844 and the "Theses on Feuerbach" transfigured his materialism in two important respects. The agent discussed was not the solitary *cogito* of contemplative philosophy; instead, through practice, other individuals were experienced, not as objects of thought, but rather as partners in action. As Lucien Goldmann put it, other subjects become "beings *with whom I act in common*. They are no longer *on the object side* but *on the subject side* of knowledge and action."[13] As a consequence, Marx viewed society itself as a collective subject. But this was no transcendental subject whose inert essence would by nature unite the individuals comprising society through a bond of universality; rather the "essence" of man presented an historical accomplishment and objective possibility delimited by the structure of the social whole.[14]

His analysis of practice also enabled Marx to penetrate the circle of passivity erected by previous materialisms. Practice, before actually transforming the world, projected a goal to be realized; to this extent, the cycle of practices was always a cycle of teleological transcendence. The standpoint of materialism incorporating practice was therefore not limited to the immediately given reality, but encompassed as well feasible projects for rationally reforming this reality. Translated into social terms, "the standpoint of the old materialism is civil society; the standpoint of the new is human society, or social humanity."[15] This transcending perspective catapulted materialist theory out of the merely contemplative realm: "The philosophers have only *interpreted* the world in various ways; the point is to *change* it."[16] Feuerbach had wished "merely to produce a correct consciousness about an *existing* fact: whereas for the real communist it is a question of overthrowing the existing state of things."[17]

EXCURSUS ON HEGEL'S CONCEPT OF PRACTICE

Marx's estimation of the labor process and human practice remained a key element in his theory as it evolved into *Capital*. This is not to suggest that no differences exist between *Capital* and the earlier works in their depiction of the labor process. Indeed, the differences might be said (with some exaggeration) to recall those between Hegel's *Phenomenology* and *Science of Logic*. In any event, both of these exercised a considerable influence on Marx's understanding of the labor process. A discussion of Hegel's views on practice can therefore help clarify the status Marx assigned labor.

In the *Phenomenology*, Hegel had described how individuality became actual "in and for itself," through accomplishing works. As he put it, "An individual cannot know what he is till he has made himself real by action."[18] In action, man dissipated the objective situation or original nature he confronted in order to establish a reality formed after his own design. Such action comprised three "moments" or elements in Hegel's account. In the first instance, action presented itself to the individual as a "purpose, and thus opposed to a given reality." In the second, this purpose found its "process of actualization" in a "means," which produced the act's third instance: an object incarnating the original purpose as "brought to light and established as something other than, and external to the acting subject."[19]

On Hegel's account, the means of action recognized, exploited, and finally transcended objective circumstances, adapting them to purposive ends. Man thus came to treat nature as the objective material for actualizing subjective aims. In this sense, the means represented a "unity of inner and outer." Insofar as the essence of the act lay in this unity of the subjective (purpose) and objective (circumstances), the individual's effective act, far from being arbitrary, contained within itself a certain "necessity," which "consists in this, that purpose is directly related to actuality, and the unity of these is the very notion of action...."[20] Hegel valued such action highly for, through work, consciousness learned "the lack of correspondence between idea and reality, which lies in its essence.... In work, therefore, consciousness becomes aware of itself as it in truth is, and its empty notion of itself disappears."[21] At this stage of the *Phenomenology,* as Jean Hyppolite has pointed out, "the objective world and conscious individuality comprise but one concrete reality, and this reality is that of the act."[22]

The convergence of this account with Marx's own is hard to miss; yet even more striking is the correspondence between his analysis of the labor process in *Capital* and Hegel's discussion of teleology and causality in the *Science of Logic.* If there are any important differences to be drawn between Marx's earlier and later works, they would probably involve the relatively greater concern he shows in *Capital* for the objective world and the laws governing it. Hegel's discussion of the act in the *Science of Logic* shared this concern. "Right action is placed in the adherence to objective laws which have no subjective origin and admit no caprice and no treatment which might overthrow their necessity."[23] In this section of the *Logic,* Hegel defined the teleological end as "the subjective notion [considered] as essential tendency and impulse toward external self-positing." To the ends a person pursued were counterposed "Mechanism" and "Chemism," as Hegel referred to the principles of determinism and causality governing the natural world.[24] An activity guided by a purpose or end was related to the Mechanical and Chemical world of nature as "something already given." On this objective basis, man, through teleological (i.e., purposive) action, attempted to transform the natural world and "to posit the object as determined through the [subjective] notion."[25] By realizing his subjective ends, man rendered them objective. The means to the end had necessarily to acknowledge the law-governed objectivity of nature. Through the "means"—the tools and applied knowledge that made work possible—the notion came to have "objectivity as such in itself"; indeed, through the means, the end ceased being merely impulse and tendency, and became activity. There was thus a certain dignity conferred upon the means which a purely utilitarian end might lack: "in his tools man possesses power over external nature, even though, according to his end he frequently is subjected to it."[26]

Hegel's presentation of the intimate relation of the teleological end to law-governed determinism enabled him to overcome the rigid dichotomy subjective idealists like Fichte had established between the human world of voluntary purposive action and the natural world of involuntary causal processes. Hegel, to be sure, had praised the subjective idealists for "giving a correct expression to the nature of all consciousness. The tendency of all man's endeavors is to understand the world, to appropriate and subdue it to himself: and to this end the positive reality of the world must be as it were crushed and pounded, in other words, idealised."[27] But according to Hegel, and Marx after him, human ends governed the laws of nature only as their complement, never as their arbitrary master. The efficacy of subjective purposes rested on a recognition of natural objectivity and its immanent order, distinct from man. To this extent, "mechanical causality" informed effective ends, and eliminated the possibility of arbitrary action, at least where the real transformation of the world was at stake. That Hegel's description of teleological action and Marx's account of the labor process shared an appreciation of freedom within and through necessity is probably not coincidental.

THE LABOR PROCESS IN MARX'S LATER WORKS

Marx's mature discussion of the labor process can be found in the *Grundrisse* as well as in *Capital*. In both, the labor process is accorded a central position: the concept of labor clarified the origin of wealth and provided a paradigm of effective human agency. In *Capital*, Marx described labor as a "natural" condition of all human existence, "a condition of the exchange of matter between man and nature." To the extent that labor was useful, it comprised an "eternal nature-imposed necessity"; by useful labor, Marx meant "productive activity of a definite kind and exercised with a definite aim."[28]

Marx throughout presupposed labor "in a form that stamps it as exclusively human." The labor of men had consequently to be distinguished from the instinctual activity of animals. Here Marx recapitulated the comments on conscious life activity he had first made in the 1844 manuscripts: "a spider conducts operations that resemble those of a weaver, and a bee puts to shame many an architect in the construction of her cells. But what distinguishes the worst architect from the best of bees is this, that the architect raises his structure in imagination before he erects it in reality."

The teleological project that framed the goal of labor itself achieved the dignity of a law in Marx's account—a law that the laborer himself gave to his modus operandi and to which he freely subordinated his will. Marx's description of the labor process in *Capital* left no doubt about the purposive agency of subjectivity; it was precisely by means of this capacity that the individual could effect a change of form in the material on which he worked. "At the end of the labor process, we get a result that already existed in the imagination of the laborer at its commencement."[29] Projective consciousness enabled labor to exist as purposeful activity. When resolved into its "simple and abstract moments," the labor process then appeared as "purposive activity for the production of use values, appropriation of the natural for human needs, the general condition of the metabolism of material between man and nature, and the eternal natural condition of human life, therefore independent of any form of this life, or rather common to all its social forms."[30]

At the same time, Marx's description of the labor process recalled Hegel's discussion of teleology and causation in the *Science of Logic.* Marx, like Hegel, now emphasized the lawfulness of nature as the precondition for effective labor: the worker "makes use of the mechanical, physical and chemical properties of some things in order to set them to work on other things as instruments of his power, in accordance with his purposes."[31] Marx also followed Hegel in dividing the act into three elements: the material worked on (the raw material), the means utilized in work (the instruments of labor), and living labor itself. These elements combined within the labor process to create the product. Labor's object was then twofold: "*raw materials,* i.e., the formless material for the forming, purposive activity of labor, and the *instruments of labor,* the objective means through which subjective activity inserts, between itself and the object, an object as its conductor."[32]

The *essence* of human labor, however, remained its formative power. Labor existed "only as the form external to the material, or it exists itself only materially."[33] The fate of objectified labor was bound to its formed object through a frail and accidental tie, inasmuch as the form of a table, for example, was not the inherent shape of the substance of wood. However, the possibility of the disintegration of the formed object equally signaled the possibility of the mutability of substances for a range of human purposes: "The transitoriness of things is used in order to establish their utility." Marx here confirmed man's creative intervention in the material world of things. "Labor is the living fire that shapes the pattern; it is the transitoriness of things, their temporality, their transformation by living time."[34]

By providing Marx with a criterion of effective agency, the concept of labor fulfilled a critical function throughout *Capital*. In the later chapters of the book, for example, Marx was at pains to refute the individualistic premises and optimistic conclusions of the classical political economists. He discredited their premises by documenting at length the cooperative character of production under capitalism, and the "creation of a new power, namely the collective power of the masses."[35] At the same time, by starting from his own individualized paradigm of labor, which we have just examined, Marx was able to underline to what extent the expansion of productive powers feasible through cooperation benefited, not the worker, but the capitalist: what ought to have been an augmentation of the individual's effective agency appeared instead as an augmentation of the power of others—both men and machines. What he worked on, the pace he worked at, the kinds of tools he used, the variety of tasks he performed—all this was removed from the control of the individuals in cooperative production; "hence the connection existing between their various labors appears to them, ideally, in the shape of a preconceived plan of the capitalist, and practically in the shape of the authority of the same capitalist, in the shape of a powerful alien will, which subjects their activity to its aims."[36] Within capitalist relations of exchange, labor forfeited its effective agency. As Marx put the point in *The Communist Manifesto,* "In bourgeois society, capital is independent and has individuality, while the living person is dependent and has no individuality."[37]

In this context, Marx's "labor theory of value" appears as an assertion of historic right as much as a statement of scientific fact. Inherent in the simple concept of labor as it has developed under capitalism is a claim to effective agency, a claim that each person he enabled to direct his own labor freely and consciously and to benefit fully from it. To deny the value of labor is not merely to condone exploitation, then, but also to disinherit living human agency. For Marx, the integrity of labor became the index of human dignity and true individuality.

Marx's discussion of labor thus supports the interpretation offered in Georg Lukács's last work: "In labor, with the projection of the goal and its means, through a self-guided act, i.e., through teleological projection, consciousness sets out to surpass mere adaptation to the environment . . . by effecting changes in nature which could not originate in nature. When realization becomes a transforming and innovating principle of nature, in contributing impulse and direction, consciousness can no longer exist as an epiphenomenon. This conclusion reveals the distinction between dialectical and mechanical materialism."[38] For Marx, Hegel's restless self-consciousness became restless labor; for both thinkers, reality contained within itself the traces of realized purposes. The human constitution of the world, which Hegel had founded on the achievements of spirit, Marx approached through the accomplishments of labor. While Hegel sublimated actual practice as a formative moment in the self-realization of the Idea through self-consciousness, Marx incorporated consciousness as a formative moment in the self-realization of humanity through labor. He thus viewed each individual as a potentially purposeful and autonomous participant in the transformation of both nature and social relations.

4

Reason, Interest, and the Necessity of History — the Ambiguities of Marx's Legacy

Despite Marx's appreciation of the labor process, his hopes for individuation, and his insistence that social theory be premised on real individuals producing in society—despite all these elements in his own theory, Marxism has nonetheless been predominantly interpreted as a global determinism, a world view potentially inimical to subjectivity and individuality, and minimizing the role of self-conscious human agency.

It is not an accidental interpretation. In *Capital,* Marx himself spoke of natural laws and an inevitable crisis of capitalism. Given such statements, there seems scant room for the voluntary and creative intervention of men in history. History instead appears as an automatic process, governed by immanent laws, moving inexorably forward. Could it be that what he acknowledged as a goal and preserved as a premise—the human individual—vanished or became immaterial within the larger drama of historical development?

In what follows, I will argue that while Marx advocated a deterministic science, as well as a notion of historical necessity, he did not maintain either at the expense of subjectivity, or the subject's creative volition. A closer examination of his treatment of historical necessity and class struggle reveals important nuances in his general conception; taken together with his methodological writings and his treatment of labor, his actual approach to analyzing contemporary history prevents any one-sided reading of Marx as founding a purely objective science. Indeed, I will contend that his outlook on subjectivity, by focusing on the purposive response to circumstances affecting the proletariat, helped found his hopes for a science of society: because men pursued rational projects in their collective interest, a vision of the emergent meaning of history became feasible. Far from crushing subjectivity, necessity in both political economy and history operated only through the rational and purposive acts of men.

As a result, Marx's theory more closely approximates the rationalism of Hegel than the positivism of Comte. Subjectivity, rather than contradicting science, helped establish it. Unfortunately, later Marxists would see the relationship differently, or misunderstand it entirely. By tracing the vicissitudes of the Marxian theory, caught between professions of science and the premise of rational social action, the ambiguities and tensions in Marx's legacy may be clarified.

MARXISM AS A SCIENCE:
THE LAWS OF POLITICAL ECONOMY

As he elaborated the leading tenets of his thought, Marx moved away from ethical entreaty toward historical science. The a prioris of philosophical anthropology still represented (however covertly) a set of universal moral imperatives; the image of the whole man fueled a denunciation of all social situations in which men led a degraded and marginal existence. But Marx persistently strove to harness such indignation with the insight into objective circumstances only science seemed to afford. In place of universal imperatives arose an historically specific sense of real possibilities for a better way of life.

But this development had disquieting implications. Having shunned philosophical reason incarnate in history as an adequate basis for anticipating socialism, Marx swung to another extreme, by seeming to declare social individuation within communism the preordained outcome of economic and technical development. In the *Grundrisse* and *Capital,* history was occasionally portrayed as a movement wherein individuals did not (actively) emancipate themselves, but instead were (passively) emancipated. Historical necessity threatened to liquidate human freedom.

Indicative of the ambiguity in Marx's position on this point was the status of social and economic "contradictions" in his model of capitalist crisis. Most of the contradictions analyzed in *Capital* and the *Grundrisse* can be called "logical": confronting the values professed by classical political economy with the social reality he faced, Marx was able to counterpose claims of equal exchange with the fundamental inequality represented by surplus value. Other contradictions unfolded between socialized production and private ownership, increasing wealth and chronic poverty, between the possibility of expanding free time and the reality of "necessary" labor time. Yet however vividly these logical contradictions illustrated the irrationality and inconsistency of capitalism, they by no means entailed its collapse — even if they did commend its abolition to right-thinking victims of the system.

But at least one dilemma in capitalism appeared to transcend the status of a logical contradiction: Marx's celebrated formulation of the tendency of the rate of profit to fall. His analysis appeared in the third volume of *Capital,* published posthumously by Engels. This account, if correct, indicated an *immanent* contradiction within the movement of capital: increasing productivity led, of itself, to decreasing profitability; the possibilities for economic crisis would forever mount. Marx in the *Grundrisse* had described capital as a "contradiction in action," but in volume three of *Capital* he for the first time analyzed these contradictions as inherently self-destructive. Independently of any human agency, the "law of the tendency of the rate of profit to fall" seemed to guarantee the collapse of capitalism: "The *real barrier* of capitalist production is *capital* itself."[1] Such formulations implied that human agency was incidental to the crisis of capitalism, at most able to intervene and transform the tempo of historical development, without fundamentally affecting its direction.

Similar ambiguities plagued the abstraction from real individuals Marx executed in *Capital.* It made sense that the subject, considered merely as a personified economic category, should be stripped of responsibility and initiative; yet Marx seemed to extend that exoneration to real individuals: "My standpoint," he wrote in the introduction to *Capital,* "from which the evolution of the economic formation of society is viewed as a process of natural history, can less than any other make the individual responsible for relations whose creature he socially remains, however much he may subjectively raise himself above them."[2]

Throughout *Capital,* Marx constantly emphasized necessity and natural laws in a way which suggested he had given an adequate account of a predetermined reality. In his afterword to the second edition, he referred to a "striking and generous" review that described his accomplishment as treating "the social movement as a process of natural history, governed by laws not only independent of human will, consciousness and intelligence, but rather on the contrary, determining that will, consciousness and intelligence."[3] In *Capital* he had elaborated a series of economic formulations that penetrated below surface appearances and intentions; the apparently free exchange of labor for wages turned out to mask the exploitation of labor by capital. The crucial problem was the status he accorded his reconstruction of capitalist relations. Did this reconstruction supplant all subjective accounts, and depict, for the first time, social *reality*, with its specific laws, secretly determining all individual acts? Or was *Capital* a *theoretic* clarification, achieved through a critique of previous political economy and its categories and hence only *indirectly* related to social reality?

At times, Marx endorsed the latter interpretation. Rather than simply dismissing surface appearances as a pure illusion, he was concerned that his model should eventually approximate surface appearances and account for the consciousness of economic production and circulation they fostered. "The various forms of capital, as evolved in this book, thus approach step by step the form which they assume on the surface of society, in the action of the different capitals upon one another, in competition, and in the ordinary consciousness of the agents of production themselves."[4] Similarly, Marx maintained a distinction between theory and the reality it comprehended. Even as a more or less concrete representation of nineteenth-century capitalism, Marx's model could be applied to actual economic situations only with qualifications and emendations. Such classical Marxian "laws" as the falling rate of profit thus became "tendencies" when transferred from the realm of theory to economic reality.[5] The difficulties in applying the economic model to the reality underlined a critical distinction between the two.

Yet Marx himself sometimes blurred that distinction, particularly in his most polemical and prophetic statements. He then claimed that his critique of political economy yielded a system of economic laws governing the development of society. He was not averse to viewing his model as a pure reflection of capitalist realities, offering a causal and comprehensive account—despite the fact that *Capital* contained precious few specific laws. This tendency in turn reinforced Marx's rhetorical penchant for describing the coming collapse of capitalism as ineluctable. Dispossessed of initiative by its bondage to existent economic formations, subjectivity appeared then to become a mere plaything of objective historical forces.

CLASS STRUGGLE AND
THE COLLAPSE OF CAPITALISM

There can be no doubt that Marx viewed the demise of capitalism as necessary, and indeed all but inevitable; but an examination of his views on class struggle suggests that he rested this contention in large part on a practical assumption: that the politically organized proletariat would force the issue and deliver the final blow. If the emancipation of the individual were an automatic gift of history, then his historical relevance would remain marginal, as the ultimate benefactor of the independent motion of history. On the other hand, if a rational outcome of history required the conscious intervention of the proletariat, then individuals, through their purposive action, had an essential role to play in instituting communism.

Marx believed that the political movement of the proletariat provided the foundations for his science, and distinguished his communism from utopianism:

So long as the proletariat is not yet sufficiently developed to constitute itself as a class, and consequently so long as the very struggle of the proletariat with the bourgeoisie has not yet assumed a political character, and the productive forces are not yet sufficiently developed in the bosom of the bourgeoisie itself to enable us to catch a glimpse of the material conditions necessary for the emancipation of the proletariat and for the formation of a new society, these theoreticians are merely utopians who, to meet the wants of the oppressed classes, improvise systems and go in search of a regenerating science. But in the measure that history moves forward, and with it the struggle of the proletariat assumes clearer outlines, they no longer need to seek science in their minds; they have only to take note of what is happening before their eyes and to become its mouthpiece.[6]

A militant class, conscious of its historic vocation and deliberately acting on it, thus appeared a decisive element, both for transcending given social relations and for providing a scientific standpoint for their analysis. In the context of historical development, it seemed transparent that "of all the instruments of production, the greatest productive power is the revolutionary class itself."[7] As a result, Marx devoted himself not only to deciphering the economic laws behind capitalist crises, but also to fostering a militant proletarian movement.

Marx's account of the proletariat and its rise, in *The Communist Manifesto* and elsewhere, underlined the importance he attached to a self-conscious class committed to revolutionary change. Initially, individual laborers had carried on isolated struggles against machinery, the most tangible manifestation of industrial oppression; at this stage, the working-class movement remained parochial, hampered by a nostalgia for the status medieval society had accorded the skilled craftsman. Laborers frequently found themselves in competition with other laborers; and the common causes that might unite them were usually provided by the bourgeoisie, looking for allies in its struggle against the monarchy and feudal institutions.

The proletariat, originally an "incoherent mass scattered over the whole country," only gradually coalesced into a cohesive social grouping. The development of industry altered the circumstances workers lived amid. As the working class grew in numerical extent, it became increasingly concentrated in urban centers, in accordance with the organizational requirements of modern industry. Factory labor became ever more standardized, and distinctions within the proletariat correspondingly declined. Centralized urban areas came to house laborers who increasingly shared the same conditions of life.

Meanwhile, heightened competition among the bourgeoisie rendered the livelihood of the workers ever more precarious. Wages unpredictably fluctuated. Common economic interests began to make their way into the consciousness of the laborers. In short, bourgeois relations of production created social and economic conditions that facilitated the conscious organization of the proletariat as a class militantly pursuing its interests: the rational response to the unstable and oppressive conditions of capital was the political union of the workers. As such combinations arose, and sporadically engaged in disputes, they encouraged imitation and the "ever-expanding union of the workers."[8]

The Holy Family had already forcefully linked the proletariat to the revolutionary breakdown of capitalism. The expansion of capitalist means of production and wealth produced as its antithesis the proletariat, "that dehumanization conscious of its dehumanization, and thus transcending itself."[9] A product of antecedent circumstances, yet already anticipating a more human social setting, the proletariat "executes the sentence" inscribed in the mute contradictions and inhumanity of capitalist relations of production and exchange. The consciousness accompanying this execution was no preordained gift of historical development, but rather a hard-won result, forged through a practical process of struggle. "For the production on a mass scale of this communist consciousness, and for the success of the cause itself, the alteration of men on a mass scale is necessary, an alteration which can only take place in a practical movement, a *revolution;* this revolution is necessary, therefore, not only because the *ruling* class cannot be overthrown in any other way, but also because the class *overthrowing* it can only in a revolution succeed in ridding itself of all the muck of ages and become fitted to found society anew."[10]

Clearly, Marx in such passages assigned a central role to the intentional agency of the proletarians and, implicitly, their teleological anticipation of communist society; without these "subjective" factors, the conflict between labor and capital remained necessarily latent.

Moreover, Marx insisted on the element of *self-emancipation* involved in establishing the subjective conditions of revolution. He maintained a faith in the ability of individual workers to educate themselves, a faith reflected in his circular letter to the German Social Democratic Party, written in 1879.

For almost forty years we have stressed the class struggle as the immediate driving power of history, and in particular the class struggle between bourgeoisie and proletariat as the great lever of the modern social revolution; it is, therefore, impossible for us to cooperate with people who wish to expunge this class struggle from the movement. When the International was formed we expressly formulated the battle cry: The emancipation of the working classes must be won by the working classes themselves. We therefore cannot cooperate with people who openly state that the workers are too uneducated to emancipate themselves and must be freed from above by philanthropic big bourgeois and petty bourgeois.[11]

In his earlier writings, Marx had spoken of the need to arouse "freedom, the feeling of man's dignity. . . . Only this feeling . . . can again transform society into a community of men to achieve their highest purposes. . . ."[12] He also recognized the barrier to arousing such feeling erected by the internalization of bourgeois ideologies. "If Protestantism was not the true solution, it was the true formulation of the problem. The question was no longer the struggle of the layman against the *priest external to him,* but of his struggle against his *own inner priest,* his *priestly nature.*"[13] Marx in his later writings continued to stress the contribution each individual had to make to the emancipatory struggle, a contribution that could not be replaced by the self-conscious agency of a more agile and expert party elite. "Here [in Germany] where the worker's life is regulated from childhood on by bureaucracy, and he himself believes in the authorities, in the bodies appointed over him, he must be taught before all else *to walk by himself.*"[14]

Once a critical consciousness became widespread among the oppressed, their awareness transformed the social situation they faced. Such a teleological and practically oriented awareness helped delineate clearly the social and material conditions which formed a shared way of life: that is why Marx hailed the arrival of class consciousness among the oppressed as a "death knell" for the ruling order.

Nevertheless, his account of class struggle often enough remained equivocal. On the one hand, he granted human agency and class consciousness a pivotal role; on the other, he portrayed them as produced by prior circumstances. Indeed Marx once noted in passing that "objective and subjective conditions" were merely "two different forms of the same conditions."[15] In the *Grundrisse,* Marx observed that "when the worker recognizes the products [of his labor] as being his own and condemns the separation of the conditions of his realization as an intolerable imposition, it will be an enormous progress in consciousness, itself the product of the method of production based on capital, and a death-knell of capital in the same way that once the slaves became aware that they were persons . . .the continued existence of slavery could only vegetate on as an artificial thing. . . ."[16]

In this passage, two elements of Marx's account of human agency and class consciousness intersect. The individual's conscious will is produced by the social relations and mode of production it is situated within; and true consciousness as such comprises a powerful incentive to act, thus promoting the practical dissolution of given conditions. Conscious agency is dynamic, creative, a driving force of social transformation—and such agency is determinate, finite, rooted in a preconstituted social world. This is the authentic Marxian antinomy—one which Marx himself resolved in the dialectic of historical development, conceived as a necessary process.

MARX AND THE CONCEPT OF INTEREST

In his hopes for a communist future, Marx reconciled a doctrine of historical necessity with a notion of active subjectivity: indeed, he held that purposeful human agency at crucial moments *promoted* historical necessity, as his remarks on class struggle and class consciousness show. These two elements in his theory, which have often been considered contradictory, he saw as complementary. But what aspects of human agency enabled it to figure significantly in a history distinguished by its necessity?

We have already gotten a partial answer to this question through an examination of Marx's concept of labor. Yet as we have also seen, his use of labor as a paradigm of agency served to highlight the very *lack* of purposeful mastery under contemporary conditions of production: in other words, the self-constitution of the human species through labor has hitherto largely proceeded unconsciously. The political struggle of the proletariat to emancipate labor, on the other hand, has a different cast to it: here Marx emphasized the contemporary centrality of conscious human agency—and indeed self-emancipation—yet linked it closely to the unfolding of historical necessity. How can these various parts of the Marxist theory be reconciled, and what do they tell us about the sense of subjectivity in Marx?

In what follows, it is argued that Marx's theory rests on the assumption of an abiding rationality in social action. Because men pursued their material concerns rationally, social interaction and, ultimately, historical development could be expected to exhibit a forseeable coherence: the calculated and steadfast response of individuals, and classes, to circumstances, as well as the purposeful mastery that grew naturally out of this response, facilitated a predictive outlook toward human behavior, although that behavior remained voluntary.

In addition to labor, the key concept here is *interest*. If labor supplied the paradigm of effective agency within the world of natural objects, where men mastered material conditions, interest supplied the paradigm of effective agency within the world of human "prehistory," where material conditions still mastered men. Since its importance has not yet been adequately appreciated, the concept of interest in Marx merits an extended discussion.

The term itself is multivalent. In English, interest originally denoted a legal entitlement to something. But in the modern era, it has also come to signify, first, a personal relationship of being concerned or curious about something; second, a preoccupation with one's own well-being (as in "self-interest"); and third, the relationship of a group to matters of common concern (as in the "common interest," the "public interest," or "class interest"). The concept of interest has figured prominently in political thought since the Renaissance, generally as an unclarified and tacit category. Although by the eighteenth century interest had become associated with selfishness, the term was sufficiently elastic to enable Helvétius to proclaim that "as the physical world is ruled by the laws of movement so is the moral universe ruled by laws of interest." In an essay on the rise of interest as a new paradigm of human behavior, Albert O. Hirschman has assessed its importance for the social theorists of the Enlightenment:

Once passion was deemed destructive and reason ineffectual, the view that human action could be exhaustively described by attribution to either one or the other meant an exceedingly somber outlook for humanity. A message of hope was therefore conveyed by the wedging of interest in between the two traditional categories of human motivation. Interest was seen to partake in effect of the better nature of each, as the passion of self-love upgraded and contained by reason, and as reason given direction and force by that passion. The resulting hybrid form of human action was considered exempt from both the destructiveness of passion and the ineffectuality of reason.[17]

Marx was well acquainted with the concept of interest. He would have encountered it, for example, in the *Philosophy of Right,* where Hegel makes interest the *telos* of individuals in civil society: "Individuals in their capacity as burghers in this state are private persons whose end is their own interest."[18] In Adam Ferguson's *Essay on the*

History of Civil Society, which both Hegel and Marx had read, interest is defined in "its most common acceptation" to express "those objects of care which refer to our external condition, and the preservation of our animal nature." Interest is thus implicated in the material conditions of life and the satisfaction of needs; yet as Ferguson added, in man the instinct for survival is "sooner or later combined with reflection and foresight," and it is these rational faculties which "give rise to his apprehensions on the subject of property, and make him acquainted with that object of care which he calls his interest."[19] Once linked to property, as in Ferguson's remark, the category of interest was easily extended from individuals to groups, to denote the concerns common to the owners of similar kinds of property. Adam Smith thus distinguished the interests of the various social orders, and Hegel insisted that "these circles of particular interests must be subordinated to the higher interests of the state."[20]

In Marx's earliest essays, interest was used to describe the behavior of both individuals and social groups. During his investigations of poverty in 1842, he had become perplexed by the relation between private interests in civil society and the presumed universal interest of the state.[21] As he recalled in his 1859 preface to the *Critique of Political Economy,* unraveling the problems posed by these "so-called material interests" gave him "the first impulse to take up the study of economic questions."[22] The centrality of interest for Marx during this period can also be gauged by the fact that his critique of Hegel's *Philosophy of Right* is framed in terms of the problem. Citing Hegel's definition of "concrete freedom" as the identity of particular and universal interest, Marx disputed whether the form of government defended by Hegel could fulfill this definition. A key issue was the role of the executive administration, which Hegel had identified as the "universal estate" responsible for maintaining the state's "universal interest." But Marx mocked Hegel's claim, remarking the dependence of the administration on the monarch, and the emergence of the bureaucracy as a parasitic caste pursuing its own narrow interests. State officials, "commissioned as representatives of *general* concerns . . . actually represent *particular* concerns." A year later, in his 1844 manuscripts, Marx would similarly describe the "contradiction" in the science of political economy as "the motivation of society by unsocial, particular interests."[23]

THE INTEREST OF THE PROLETARIAT

Through this path of questioning, Marx had arrived at one of the key problems in modern social thought, a problem explored by Rousseau, Montesquieu, Tocqueville, and Adam Smith, as well as Hegel: reconciling universal and particular interests, or, alternatively, of demonstrating how the pursuit of private interests conduced to the public benefit. In 1842, Marx had proposed that a free press might serve as an impartial mediator, able to combine reason with a feeling for human suffering, and thus able to evaluate the competing claims of various private interests within society.[24] But he soon dropped this idea, a decision no doubt hastened by censorship of the article in which it appeared. The possibility of a disinterested onlooker, moreover, seemed increasingly incredible, and not only to Marx. In *Democracy in America,* Tocqueville had remarked that since the "period of disinterested patriotism is gone by forever," modern politics had no choice but to "go forward and accelerate the union of private with public interests."[25] While Marx shared Tocqueville's diagnosis, he disputed what form the remedy should take. Where Tocqueville and liberals like John Stuart Mill hoped that increased participation in government would promote a rebirth of civic spirit, Marx looked instead for a social class which already united "private with public interests."

In 1842, he had found such a union in the case of the impoverished: "Private persons who have observed the real poverty of others in the full extent of its development," can see, he wrote, "that the private interest they defend is equally a state interest."[26] Perhaps inspired by Hegel's treatment of the executive administration, Marx now explored the possibility that a truly "universal estate" in fact existed, if not where Hegel had thought. The criteria for identifying any such class crucially involved its social and material circumstances. If civil society was rent by contradictory particular interests, it seemed desirable that a universal class somehow be in civil society but not "of" it; or, as Marx had put it in 1842 while defending the objectivity of a free press, an element was needed "which would be of a *civil* nature without being bound up with private interests."[27] Similarly, if property defined the character of private interests, it seemed plausible that a class *without* property would also be without narrowly defined interests; again Marx had anticipated the implications of this possibility in 1842, when he described the impoverished and their interests as the "interests of those whose property consists of life, freedom, humanity, and citizenship of the state, who own nothing but themselves."[28]

Indeed, once Marx had abandoned all hope of a disinterested mediation between the conflicting private interests within civil society, he had before him, in his writings on the problem of poverty from 1842, and in his criticism of Hegel's *Philosophy of Right,* virtually all the ingredients necessary for his designation, late in 1843, of the proletariat as a universal class, "a class in civil society but not of civil society, an estate which is the dissolution of all estates, a sphere which has a universal character by its universal suffering and claims no *particular right* because no *particular wrong* but *wrong generally* is perpetrated against it."[29] Moreover, when he turned to study *The Wealth of Nations,* he would find his perception of the proletariat at least partially vindicated. According to Adam Smith, "the interest of the second order, that of those who live by wages, is . . . strictly connected with the interest of the society," since there is no order that "suffers so cruelly" from an economic decline—an assessment Marx favorably noted in his 1844 manuscripts.[30]

Thus far, Marx's concept of interest can be seen to have a twofold importance, as a prescriptive as well as an analytic category. It was an essential concept for analyzing the modern state, "based on the unhampered development of bourgeois society, on the free movement of private interest."[31] Interest was similarly a key category for interpreting ideologies: "Law, morality, religion, are to [the proletarian] so many bourgeois prejudices, behind which lurk in ambush just as many bourgeois interests."[32] Finally, interest figured as an important human faculty binding men together: as Marx wrote in *The Holy Family,* "*natural necessity,*" in the form of needs, "the *essential human properties,*" such as sociability, "however estranged they may seem to be, and *interest* . . . hold the members of civil society together."[33]

At the same time, however, interest functioned as a prescriptive category, shaping the ideal of a decent society as well as the practice of the proletarian class that would realize it. The analytic and prescriptive aspects of the category were connected, for "if correctly understood interest is the principle of all morality, man's private interest must be made to coincide with the interest of humanity."[34] Moreover, the discovery of this coincidence within a contemporary class proved a practical precondition for revolutionary transcendence as well: the "subsuming of individuals under definite classes cannot be abolished until a class has evolved which has no longer any particular class interest to assert against a ruling class." Because it anticipated in its own concerns the unity between particular and universal interest, the proletariat could overcome the divisions between countries as well as within nations: "For the peoples to be able truly to unite, they must have common interests. And in order that their interests may become common, the existing property relations must be done away with . . . the abolition of existing property relations is the concern only of the proletariat."[35]

In the present context, it is worth stressing that Marx believed common interests would unite a group without abrogating the particularity of each individual: thus in 1845, he approvingly quoted Bentham's assertion that "individual interests are the only real interests." That is why, on principle, there could be no contradiction, in a properly ordered society, between the general and the individual interest. Unfortunately, the "general interest" has hitherto been defined by a few individuals, to protect privileges which they enjoy in private. "Communist theoreticians," remarked Marx and Engels in *The German Ideology*, "are distinguished precisely by the fact that they alone have *discovered* that throughout history the 'general interest' is created by individuals who are defined as 'private persons.'"[36] The problem with previous theoreticians, including Bentham, was that they either ignored *selfish* individual interests or treated this characteristic of civil society as a fixed facet of human nature. In contrast, Marx anticipated the day when communist society would free individuals from the private pursuit of narrow self-interest as well as those interests common, on the average, to a class, and instead enable them to cultivate their particular concerns as a publicly acknowledged good, in the universal interest.[37]

INTEREST AS AN ATTRIBUTE OF INDIVIDUALITY

The category of interest was thus central to Marx's theory on many levels; it provided insight into present conditions and into their transcendence. In his critique of political economy, to be sure, the category played only a subsidiary role, but in his coverage of contemporary events, interest frequently functioned as an analytic category specifying the motives of actors. Once installed at the heart of the Marxian enterprise as a kind of tacit concept, interest could be invoked whenever the fundamental premises of Marx's theory were at stake.

Proof of the continuing importance of the category for Marx can be found relatively late, in his 1881 notebooks on Henry Sumner Maine's *Lectures on the Early History of Institutions*. At one point in these lectures, Maine rebuked the analytical jurists such as Bentham for treating sovereignty as a question of pure will, rather than acknowledging the limits imposed by "the vast mass of influences, which we may call for shortness *moral*." Marx transcribed Maine's criticism, only to comment acidly that Maine could not see the economic influences behind moral phenomena. Then, in a remarkable passage, Marx attacked the analytical viewpoint of Bentham as well as the conventionalism of Maine. Both missed

the many levels: that the apparent supremely independent existence of the state is only *apparent,* that in all its forms it is an *excrescence of society;* as its *appearance* occurs first on a given stage of development, subsequently fading again, as soon as society has reached a hitherto unattained stage. The first separation of individuality *not* originally from *despotic shackles* (as blockhead Maine understands it), but from satisfying and sociable bonds, the primitive community—therewith the one-sided elaboration of individuality. The true content of the latter is shown when we analyze the contents of the "latter"—*interests.* We find then that interests have become common to social groups, that their characteristic interests have become *class-interests* and thus that this individuality is itself class-etc. individuality, in the last instance having *economic conditions* for a bais. The state is built on this foundation, and presupposes it. [38]

Several aspects of this passage are noteworthy. Marx here underlined the historical specificity of interest, by linking it to the individuality which emerges within civil society after the disintegration of the "primitive community." [39] More important for our purposes, though, is the explicit connection thus drawn between individuality and interest. But what does it mean to call interest the "true content" of individuality? What distinguished interest from other human faculties? Since Marx never explicitly defined the term, we will have to reconstruct his answer from a variety of sources.

We can start with a criticism of Kantian idealism in *The German Ideology*. There Marx and Engels accused Kant of failing to notice that "theoretical ideas . . . had as their basis material interests and a *will* that was conditioned and determined by the material relations of production."[40] The locus of interest that emerges from this statement is indicative: situated between ideas and material circumstances, and tied to a will "conditioned and determined" by social relations, it appears implicitly as an aspect of the individual animated by wants, practically oriented toward satisfying these wants, and rational—even enlisting "theoretical ideas"—in pursuing their satisfaction. That interest transcended the mere instinct for survival was commonly taken for granted: as Ferguson had put it, the interested individual pursued wants with "reflection and foresight." That Marx himself shared this understanding is confirmed by several comments in an 1842 article, where interest was characterized as "crafty" and "keen-sighted," amoral but practical, absorbed in worldly affairs.[41] As Marx summarized his early understanding, "interest has no memory, for it thinks only of itself. And the *one* thing about which it is concerned, itself, it never forgets. But it is not concerned about contradictions, for it never comes into contradiction with itself. It is a constant improviser, for it has no system, only expedients."[42]

While Marx was here condemning that "self-seeking interest which brings nothing of a higher order to realization," it is not impossible to amend this early account with later fragments, and to piece together a description of how the faculty of interest might contribute to the emancipatory process: for it seems only natural that the cooperative pursuit of a social transformation in the universal interest would, in turn, transform the individual faculty of interest. The proletarian, in pursuing his class interest, might then evolve a fraternal solidarity beyond selfish concerns and an abiding rationality beyond expedient cunning. Marx himself held such hopes for the labor movement: "When communist artisans form associations, education and propaganda are their first aims. But the very act of associating creates a new need—the need for society—and what appeared to be a means has become an end." In modern society, however, the preconditions for such a rational solidarity could be found only among the proletarians, who stood to gain "life, freedom, humanity" from pursuing their interests in common. For, as Marx put it in *Capital,* to explain "why capitalists form a veritable freemason society vis-à-vis the whole working class, while there is little love lost between them in competition among themselves," the common interest "is appreciated by each only so long as he gains more by it than without it." In sharp contrast to individual capitalists, all proletarians "have nothing to lose but their chains. They have a world to win."[43]

MATERIALIST PEDAGOGY AND
THE ENLIGHTENMENT OF INTEREST

Marx in any case did not use the notion of interest to denote a static characteristic of human beings and social classes. Indeed, the faculty of interest fulfilled a far from self-evident function even in the case of the proletariat. In *Capital,* Marx himself described "the intellectual desolation . . . artificially produced by converting immature human beings into mere machines for the fabrication of surplus-value."[44] On the basis of similar observations, Adam Smith drew the conclusion that "though the interest of the labourer is strictly connected with that of society, he is incapable either of comprehending that interest, or of understanding its connexion with his own."[45]

Yet for a variety of reasons, Marx maintained a far greater confidence than Smith in the ability of the worker to grasp his situation. One critical factor, certainly, was the inherent reasoning power he ascribed to the faculty of interest: for Marx, unlike Smith, assumed that interest provided a steadfast motive for accurately calculating advantages. (Smith, by contrast, tended to conflate interest with the passions, thus depriving the faculty of any intrinsic link with rationality.;[46] In addition, Marx assumed the importance of consciously *cultivating* an accurate understanding of social concerns. Although the faculty of interest inherently mediated between circumstances and consciousness, its power as an historical force derived from the ability of the interested individuals to perceive common concerns, to act together for mutual benefits, and to acquire an understanding of social relations lucid enough to make such action effective.[47] While Marx believed such an understanding often spontaneously arose in response to circumstances, he also believed such native knowledge could be refined and elucidated through education: this would be the task of a materialist pedagogy aimed at the cultivation of interest.

In *The Holy Family,* Marx had quoted with evident approval several passages from Helvétius and Holbach, both of whom grasped the importance for social change of clearly comprehending one's material interest — unlike the left-Hegelians, who portrayed socialism as an ideal of pure reason independent of reality. "As, according, to Helvétius, it is education, by which he means . . . not only education in the ordinary sense but the totality of the individual's conditions of life, which forms man, if a reform is necessary to abolish the contradiction between particular interests and those of society, so, on the other hand, a transformation of consciousness is necessary to carry out such a reform."[48] Hegel had similarly linked interest and education. In the *Philosophy of Right,* after remarking that the "end" of individuals in civil society is "their own interest," Hegel added that "Individuals can attain their ends only in so far as they themselves determine their knowing, willing and acting in a universal way and make themselves links in this chain of social connexions. In these circumstances, the interest of the Idea — an interest of which these members of civil society are as such unconscious — lies in the process whereby their singularity and their natural condition are raised, as a result of the necessities imposed by nature as well as by arbitrary [i.e., socially generated] needs, to formal freedom and formal universality of knowing and willing — the process whereby their particularity is educated up to subjectivity." For Hegel, "The final purpose of education . . . is liberation and the struggle for a higher liberation still. . . . In the individual subject, this liberation is the hard struggle . . . against the immediacy of desire, against the empty subjectivity of feeling and the caprice of inclination; but it is through this educational struggle that the subjective will itself attains objectivity within. . . ."[49]

For Marx, as for Helvétius and Hegel, the formation process of subjectivity in society was prompted by the "natural" necessity of primary needs, the "arbitrary" necessity of socially acquired needs, and the individual's inherent interest in bettering his condition;[50] moreover, for Marx as for Helvétius, education included "the totality of the individual's conditions of life." The specific shape taken by the educational process, however, depended on the individual's location within society, and the specific social connections he was drawn into and could draw upon.

The situation of the proletarian, for example, facilitated a rough and ready understanding of contemporary social relations and their essentially inequitable nature. According to Engels in *The Condition of the Working Class in England,* an early work that much impressed Marx, "The English working man who can scarcely read and still less write nevertheless has a shrewd notion of where his own interest and that of his nation lies. He knows, too, what the selfish interest of the bourgeoisie is, and what he has to expect of that bourgeoisie." That Marx himself shared this high estimate of the proletariat and its native understanding is confirmed by an article he published in 1844, criticizing the Young Hegelian Arnold Ruge. In an earlier article, Ruge had described the Silesian weavers' revolt of 1844 as the futile gesture of ignorant and desperate men; he recommended that the Young Hegelians help point out the political principles at stake, and impress upon the king the need for reform. Marx, by contrast, praised the "theoretical and conscious character" of the uprising, citing as evidence the "song of the weavers," a popular anthem described by him as a "bold *call* to struggle" which clearly proclaimed "its opposition to the society of private property." In such mundane cultural artifacts—political almanacs and songbooks circulated widely during the popular uprisings of the early nineteenth century—Marx found the rudiments of a civic education. He also saw an eager audience: the German proletariat, argued Marx, had an "educational level or capacity for education" (*Bildungsfähigkeit*) far surpassing that of the timid and narrow-minded German bourgeoisie. Nor did these workers require tutoring in political principles by Young Hegelians like Ruge; indeed, the weavers demonstrated a more realistic understanding of social forces than the latter, with his hopes for benevolent monarchial reform. In this situation, what was needed, according to Marx, was not a patronizing philosophical defense, but instead a clear and accurate description of the Silesian weavers' revolt itself, and an analysis of its context and consequences: "Confronted with the first outbreak of the Silesian workers' uprising, the sole task of one who thinks and loves the truth consisted not in playing the role of *schoolmaster* in relation to this event, but instead of studying its *specific* character."[51]

Marx, like Engels, thus assumed that the proletarians of nineteenth-century Europe were uniquely situated to acquire a clear and lucid understanding of modern social relations; indeed, their personal experience of poverty and exploitation made such an understanding all but imperative. In the words of *The German Ideology*, "The contradiction between the individuality of each separate proletarian and labor, the conditions of life forced upon him, becomes evident to him, for he is sacrified from youth onwards. . . ."[52]

As *The Communist Manifesto* added, the interests of the proletariat were also shaped by the "elements of political and general education" (*Bildungselemente*) bequeathed by the bourgeoisie to the proletariat to enlist its aid in the bourgeois revolutions; as sections of the ruling class subsequently came to defend the interests of the proletariat, they supplied it as well "with fresh elements of enlightenment and progress," and further helped cultivate its interests beyond "the immediacy of desire," to a level of shared insight into historical development and the objective possibilities for freedom it harbored. Thus, as Marx summarized the process in *The Poverty of Philosophy*, economic conditions in themselves helped transform "the mass of the people in the country into workers. The domination of capital had created for this mass a common situation, common interests," but the workers were not immediately aware, either that they shared common interests, or that these interests were implicated in a social *system* which dominated them all: "This mass is thus already a class as against capital, but not yet for itself." However, the native understanding of the worker and the crowded urban conditions of factory labor, coupled with the political education provided by the bourgeois revolutions, gradually brought the workers to the point where they could collectively protest the *social* conditions of an existence they perceived as unjust. The political struggle which followed forced each party to clarify publicly its aims and principles: and it was only in and through this increasingly conscious struggle that the proletariat finally became "united and constitutes itself as a class for itself."[53]

The proletariat's political organization had a critical role to play in this pedagogical process: for if the objective "identity of interests" within a social group generated "no community, no national bond, and no political organization," then this group could prove "incapable of enforcing their class interests in their own name."[54] A political party represented a forum where workers could become aware of common concerns, while party leaders could help transform "the aims of the individual into universal aims."[55] To this end, the new science of society needed to be conveyed to the workers. On the one hand, science, by associating itself with the proletariat, "ceased to be doctrinaire," and became revolutionary; on the other, the proletariat, by equipping itself with a scientific understanding of the laws governing society, ceased to be the passive product of circumstances, and instead became their effective master. It was thus one of Marx's constant concerns to present his scientific findings in a popular form, through speeches and pamphlets like "Wage Labor and Capital." By demonstrating the *systemic* exploitation of labor under capitalism, he hoped to make clear the reasons why a revolutionary transformation was necessary, as well as why such a revolution was in the interest of the workers. However, the ultimate success of this pedagogical task depended on the willingness of workers to educate themselves: "They themselves," declared Marx and Engels in 1850, "must do the utmost for their final victory by clarifying their minds as to what their class interests are," a clarification facilitated "by taking up their position as an independent party as soon as possible."[56]

In the course of the class struggle thus consciously articulated, the proletarians came to understand the discrepancy between reality and the ideals inculcated during the bourgeois revolutions. Moreover, they came to understand this discrepancy as unnecessary and irrational: the technical and economic means for the emancipation of labor and the realization of true liberty and equality existed, as did the cooperative power of the working class necessary to effect such a transformation in their mutual interest. While rooted in the individual and his needs, enlightened interest thus provided a real motive for actualizing such norms as freedom and justice — norms in no way reducible either to the economic demands of trade unionists or to the categorical imperative of the philosphers.[57] Dedicated to making the possibility of communism manifest in just such discrepancies between professed norms and a contradictory reality, the party leaders wanted "the workers to leave the old society alone, the better to be able to enter the new society which they have prepared for them with so much foresight."[58] Yet since the primary role of the party was educational — to form an awareness among workers of the objective possibilities for simultaneously bettering their condition and launching a revolution in the general interest — the party on Marx's account could never assume a "vanguard" role in Lenin's sense, since the success of the party was measured only in terms of the workers it enabled to initiate cooperative action, as well as the enlightened standpoint they took. "It is the business of the International Working Men's Association to combine and generalise the *spontaneous movements* of the working classes, but not to dictate or impose any doctrinary system whatever."[59] Instead, a materialist pedagogy of interest sought to transform the isolated gestures of the "I want" into the effective, organized, and self-conscious agency of the "We need, can and must"—that is, to transform the isolated struggle of the worker for survival into the self-constitution of the proletariat as a class "for itself," practically comprehending the "historical movement as a whole."

The universal interest in Marx, then, was not spontaneously generated through an unintentional "harmony" of interest, as in Smith, nor was it deciphered and imposed from above by a fair-minded elite, as in Hegel's theory of the bureaucracy. Rather, the universal interest in Marx was to be realized through a collective political struggle which simultaneously egendered solidarity among the workers, and, by making them aware of their common interest in a revolutionary transformation, made them aware of their "great historical mission," the emancipation of "the downtrodden millions."[60]

The peculiar features Marx ascribed to interest as a subjective faculty played an essential role in his understanding of this process. As we have seen, Marx, like several theorists before him, portrayed interest as occupying an intermediate region within the panoply of human faculties, partaking of the cunning of reason and the forcefulness of passion, channeling the pressing nature of needs in a rational direction. Individuals could thus be counted on to pursue their interests with some degree of foresight and calculation as well as with steadfastness and perseverance—and it was this constant basis that a materialist pedagogy could build upon.

Let us summarize our findings, then. In Marx's understanding of human prehistory, it was enlightened *interest,* and not consciousness per se, or labor per se, which was the essential aspect of effective human agency. Interest was that critical subjective faculty in Marx's theory that mediated material needs and formative ideals, social conditions and self-conscious historical development, the immanent and the transcendent, the individual and the universal. The class interest of the proletariat within civil society transcended civil society, for the proletariat, in coming to pursue its interests self-consciously, discovered that its particular emancipation entailed universal emancipation: for where all previous political movements were of minorities, "in the interest of minorities," the proletarian movement, in the familiar words of *The Communist Manifesto,* "is the self-conscious, independent movement of the immense majority, in the interest of the immense majority."[61]

HEGEL, SMITH, AND MARX: THE NECESSITY OF REASON

In Marx's theory, only the native rationality of interested human action assured the scientific coherence of social interaction and historical development: an interested calculation heedful of material conditions, like the purposeful mastery of natural means exemplified in free labor, generated forseeable patterns of behavior, and thus facilitated a deterministic and predictive approach to analyzing it. Yet this reconciliation, within Marx's own theory, of a rationally active subjectivity with a scientifically depicted social objectivity marked by necessity was vulnerable to subsequent positivist distortions—a mistaken reading of Marx, to be avoided by reintegrating his work within a tradition of Enlightenment rationalism which includes Smith's political economy as well as Hegel's philosophy. Like Smith and Hegel, Marx depicted a social and historical process marked by necessity, yet incorporating conscious human agency as a causal element in its own right.

In Hegel, necessity had taken the shape of rational dialectic, the "moving soul of scientific progress." Dialectic constituted the principle "through which alone immanent connection and necessity enters into the content of science."[62] For Hegel, "the philosophical approach to history has no other intention than to eliminate the accidental," and, implicitly, present only the necessary.[63]

Hegel's notion of the necessary was unusual, however. In the *Science of Logic,* he argued that "the absolutely necessary is only because it is, and has otherwise neither condition nor ground. But equally it is pure essence; its Being is simple reflection into itself; it is *because* it is."[64] Such an equation of actuality with necessity disarmed the notion of any predictive element: Hegel comprehended necessity retrospectively.

Yet necessity also arose for Hegel in the present, as a sort of "compulsion" exercised by reason itself. In a sense, it could then be considered prospectively as well as retrospectively. In the case of retrospective necessity, knowledge disengaged the essential from the past; in the case of prospective necessity, relative rationality, or reason showing itself in history, actually propelled history forward. In the *Phenomenology,* reason confronted, mediated, and overcame contradictions, such as those between a normative system of beliefs and actual social practices. To the extent that Hegel believed that the rational became actual, the transition from one set of beliefs to another had a certain inevitability conferred upon it; given a contradiction, he frequently spoke as if there were but one rational way to transcend it. As a consequence, sublimation of contradiction appeared in Hegel as a necessary progress in rationality founded on reason itself.

Throughout his works, he proposed a close interrelation between reason, freedom, subjectivity, and necessity. In the *Logic,* he portrayed subjectivity as passive as well as active. As passive, subjectivity subjected itself to "determinate causality," the empirical, natural sequence of causes and effects; as active, subjectivity posited its own identity through a new causality, which represented the subject's own manifestation: "Active substance is manifested in *action* as cause or original substantiality; and action means that it posits itself as its own opposite, which is also the transcendence of its presupposed otherness, of passive substance."[65]

In the course of action, man employed understanding and concepts, faculties which enabled him to comprehend the natural relations of causality he confronted in the surrounding world. By consciously positing his ends via a rational means, man mastered external causality, and shaped himself, as well as circumstances: he attained freedom within and through necessity. Man gave himself his own end "by virtue of the divine in him—that which we designated at the outset as *Reason,* or, insofar as it has activity and power of self-determination, as *Freedom.*"[66] For Hegel necessity accommodated free subjectivity, while subjectivity simultaneously transcended and preserved necessity in its creative acts.

Adam Smith's incorporation of free subjectivity within a necessary social whole not only anticipated but indeed influenced Hegel's philosophy of spirit: the "invisible hand" and the "cunning of reason" are not so dissimilar as might at first appear. In Smith's political economy, atomistic individualism gave rise to a rational and harmonious distribution of economic wealth, beyond the selfish intentions of the acquisitive individuals populating Smith's social world. Free individuality thus participated in a socioeconomic order governed by lawlike regularities.

It was a result facilitated by Smith's assumptions concerning the nature of "economic man." At the foundation of economic order, he placed "the propensity to truck, barter and exchange," which he took as "a necessary consequence of the faculties of reason and speech."[67] According to Smith, self-love and self-interest motivated this propensity, which in the aggregate helped maximize the material goods available to all individuals. The public interest in wealth was served by private avarice; each, by egoistically striving to promote his own material security, unwittingly rendered "the annual revenue of society as great as he can."

But this argument contained as its hidden premise the view that individuals behaved rationally in calculating their interests and undertaking economic ventures. While Smith in *The Wealth of Nations* portrayed avarice as beneficial for the economy, he never argued that private economic folly would lead to public wealth: indeed the economic cunning of reason depended ultimately on the reasoned exercise of cunning, at least in conducting economic affairs. Smith here joined Hegel in affirming (and presuming) the power of reason to order the world, both intentionally and unintentionally. What on a microcosmic level appeared as an anarchic confrontation of interested egos, on the macrocosmic level appeared as a law-governed whole which necessarily satisfied the demand for a reasonable economic order.

Both Smith and Hegel assumed that rationality structured human affairs on both an objective and subjective level. For both, a collective social reason emerged beyond the intentions of the individuals involved; but for both, the exercise by individuals of their reasoning capacity insured, however unintentionally, this reasonable outcome. Both viewed the exercise and outcome of reason as necessary—as necessary as reason itself.

Marx inherited this approach to the problems of necessity and rationality. Like Hegel and Smith, he emphasized the rational outcome of the social and historical process, and he also followed Hegel and Smith in basing this result, however unintended, on the fundamental rationality of human action. Marx of course did not believe men incapable of irrational, shortsighted, or emotional behavior. But he also believed that men were able to calculate their interests, and, at least potentially and in the long run, that they were able to evaluate normative disputes. A history devoid of such forms of rationality could hardly issue in communism; Marx in fact based his hopes for the future on a merger of reasoned class interests (the Smithian heritage) with reasoned progress in superseding obsolete social forms (the Hegelian heritage). The site of this merger, and the contemporary vehicle for progress in rationality, would be the proletariat. Without the rational intervention of the latter, the necessity of history, deciphered by Marx's critical science of political economy, would come to naught.

In short, the hidden premise animating Marxian science was Marx's presumption of the (potential and likely) rationality of social action. His conception of theory could therefore hardly exclude subjective factors, since predictability and hence lawfulness in social theory rested on the anticipation of rational behavior. His science indeed *relied* on this vision of man. By following Hegel and Smith in linking objective necessity with subjective rationality, Marx was able to integrate the "real individual," his potential for conscious agency intact, into a determinate and necessary social universe.

Marx in any case did not elaborate a simple concept of necessity. As in Hegel and Smith before him, at least three different usages of *necessity* can be distinguished, each having a different bearing on the sense of subjectivity.[68]

In the first place, Marx tried to establish a "necessity of events," closely related to the natural scientific concept of determinism. Necessity here defines a result which flows in a predictable manner, independently of human intentions, from antecedent circumstances. Smith believed in this sense that the wealth of nations would be a necessary outcome of free trade, just as Marx believed in this sense that increasing exploitation was the necessary outcome of capitalist relations of production.

Second, a "necessity of means" can be discerned. This necessity represents a method or procedure requisite to attain a desired end and expresses an aspect of instrumental rationality. In this sense, Marx and Hegel both insisted that a mastery of the chemical and mechanical laws governing external nature was necessary to the free exercise of human labor. Engels's description of freedom as insight into necessity bears on this usage.

Finally, there is in Marx a "necessity of ends," where certain norms are deemed essential to being fully human. Freedom could be called a necessity in this sense, as could such other norms as equality and dignity. Indeed, to the extent that they had become universal and apparently self-evident, such values informed the intentional structure of individual action, and thus could be considered practically effective as well as historically specific. Faced with any such "necessity of ends," subjectivity assumed an essentially active role, since it was only through its intentional agency that such "normative necessity" was expressed and fulfilled.

Marx felt communism was necessary in all three senses of the word: the logic of economic events pointed toward and in some sense caused it, the end of rational social planning required it, and, to the extent they desired freedom, men themselves demanded it. Marx's notion of necessity had further affinities with Smith's and Hegel's.

Like Hegel, Marx held that contradictions between a normative set of shared beliefs and social practices would sooner rather than later lead to the establishment of a new set of beliefs concordant with actual practices, or to the transformation of practices to accord with a given normative standard. Such a transcendence of contradiction appeared for both Marx and Hegel as a progress in reason that proceeded with necessity; for both, enlightened subjectivity—in the case of Marx, the class-conscious proletariat—furthered this progress in reason. Marx consequently anticipated the realignment of consciousness during the era of proletarian revolution in a direction favorable to the universalizing social practice already characteristic of capitalism. (Marx and Hegel did not, however, view progress as a unilinear process; on the contrary, for both, reason only emerged in the course of a dialectic marked by setbacks and turnabouts. As the young Marx put it, "Reason has always existed, but not always in a rational form.")[69]

Like Smith, Marx felt confident that individuals and classes were motivated by material interests, and, as Smith put it, a desire for bettering their condition—"a desire which, though generally calm and dispassionate, comes with us from the womb and never leaves us till we go into the grave."[70] Just as Smith's assumption helped him elaborate a deterministic theory founded on free individual acts, so Marx's similar premises enabled him to set the free action of the proletariat within a global historic necessity: the rationality and abiding passion involved in the pursuit of interest facilitated the predictability of social action, as the classical political economists had been quick to appreciate.[71] What Marx basically accomplished in this regard was the replacement of Smith's conception of harmonious egoistic interests with his own notion of conflicting class interests. In both cases, though, interest made possible an ultimately rational and hence necessary social development.

By extending the thesis of interest-governed behavior from individuals to classes, and by combining it with the Hegelian thesis of the enlightenment of consciousness through conflict, Marx was even able to extend the domain of predictability to historical development. But the proletarian on this account was by no means a passive product of history; rather, as a materially interested and increasingly self-conscious participant in history, the proletarian was expected to intervene and transform the direction as well as the tempo of historical development in forseeable ways, through the cooperative pursuit of aims he held in common with others, and through an enlightened understanding of the contradictory forces governing the circumstances he faced.

The role of interest for Marx indeed recalls Hegel's passage on the cunning of reason: "Reason is as *cunning* as she is *powerful*. Her cunning consists principally in her mediating activity, which by causing objects to act and react on each other in accordance with their own nature, in this way, without any direct interference in the process, carries out reason's own intentions. With this explanation, Divine Providence may be said to stand to the world and its processes in the capacity of absolute cunning. God lets men do as they please with their particular passions and interests; but the result is the accomplishment of—not their plans, but His."[72] Lacking faith in divine intercession, a materialist pedagogy by contrast sought intentionally to attune the "particular passions and interests" of enslaved men to their true end and the proper end of history—freedom. But it did so merely by eliciting the interest in universal freedom implicit in the particular interests of each worker and by creating situations where these workers could become aware of their common interest in a revolutionary transformation of society. Without any "direct interference" in the process of historical development, and merely by causing the conflicting classes within civil society "to act and react on each other in accordance with their own nature," the political party of the proletariat helped organize and educate new men consciously dedicated to surmounting the contradictions of capitalism in a more reasonable society. Or, as Marx himself expressed it:

This antagonism between modern industry and science on the one hand, modern misery and dissolution on the other hand; this antagonism between the productive powers, and the social relations of our epoch is a fact, palpable, overwhelming, and not to be controverted. Some parties may wail over it; others may wish to get rid of modern arts, in order to get rid of modern conflicts. . . . On our part, we do not mistake the shape of the shrewd spirit [cf. Hegel's cunning Reason] that continues to mark all these contradictions. We know that to work well the new-fangled forces of society, they only want to be mastered by new-fangled men—and such are the working men. They are as much the invention of modern times as machinery itself. . . . The English working men are the first born sons of modern industry. They will then, certainly, not be the last in aiding the social revolution produced by that industry, a revolution which means the emancipation of their own class all over the world, which is as universal as capital-rule and wages-slavery.[73]

MARX'S RATIONALISM

As should be apparent by now, Marx, like Adam Smith and Hegel, was a rationalist and one of the last radical champions of universal enlightenment. Of course, he was not a rationalist in the sense of a philosopher deducing an a priori metaphysic or regulative ideals of reason; nor did he have much sympathy for the classical rationalism formulated by Descartes, Spinoza, and Leibniz. Instead, Marx was an Enlightenment rationalist in the mold of such materialists as Helvétius, Holbach, and Diderot. These thinkers combined a rejection of innate ideas with a generalizing science of man and were concerned both with the systematic study of society and the enunciation of universal principles of right and justice. As the historian Elie Halévy described him, this type of rationalist "believes in the all-powerfulness of science. . . . Just as science guarantees to man the power to transform physical nature at will and without limits, so also, if it be true to its word, it should guarantee him the possibility of transforming human nature without limits. . . . Education has the faculty of transforming the human character to an unlimited extent, of making all men intellectually equal, and therefore worthy of possessing equal wealth."[74]

Marx, to be sure, would not have recognized himself in this portrait: he was too much the historical realist to place much confidence in universal principles, unarmed science, or educational reforms isolated from the broader context of social development. But *within* this context, in his expectation of capitalist collapse, he anticipated the enlightened practice of new men—politicized proletarians—as surely as his science dissected the destructive laws governing capitalist relations of exchange. At the root of his expectations, moreover, stood an essentially optimistic outlook on the prospects for transforming human character: once the "downtrodden millions" became aware of their stake in changing an exploitative social order, they would surely rise up to act on such rational impulses. To the extent it appeared reasonable, finally, individual and collective action also appeared predictable and hence amenable to scientific treatment.

The extent of Marx's rationalist optimism becomes clear through a comparison with Rousseau. Both Rousseau and Marx felt a legitimate society would be ordered around common interests: as Rousseau put the point in *The Social Contract*, "Unless there were some point in which all interests agree, no society could exist. Now, it is solely with regard to this common interest that the society should be governed."[75] But if Rousseau and Marx agreed about the proper end of association, they disagreed on the means for realizing this end. For Rousseau, the issue was one of properly denaturing men, through a legitimate form of association, which would embody, not just in law, but also in customs and mores, a real commonality of interest; only on this basis might individuals be reconstituted as moral agents and free social beings. The difficulty was that men had already been socialized by the "bad contract" of civil society, which promoted avarice, deceit, and the pursuit of selfish interests. To surmount this substantial difficulty, Rousseau resorted to the fabulous figure of the "Great Legislator," a semidivine public tutor who bestowed just laws and shaped, through a civil religion, the customs and mores of a people; for those used to the luxury and egoism of civil society, there was no other device capable of making them "bear submissively the yoke of the public welfare."[76]

To Marx, by contrast, no such unlikely and drastic device for denaturing men seemed necessary, for the proletariat already implicitly embodied a real commonality of interest. Civil society, rather than being only an obstacle, instead contained many of the elements required for reconstituting individuals as free social beings; what was needed was not a mythic religion to yoke particular interests, but rather a thoroughgoing social science that would clarify the interests defended by the different classes within civil society, and demonstrate the interest of the proletariat in creating a classless society. In this way, Marx's "historical realism" actually reinforced his rationalist optimism.

Marx also believed that the normative elements essential to a good society were already at hand; freedom and equality seemed ideals vouchsafed by the political and economic achievements of the era. As Marx put it in an early essay, "As far as actual life is concerned, the *political state* especially contains in all its *modern* forms the demands of reason," even if these demands remained abstract ideals. Marx made an analogous point in *Capital,* when he remarked that "the notion of human equality has already acquired the fixity of a popular prejudice."[77] The social critic, in short, could count on certain constellations of belief, such as Jacobin liberalism, classical political economy, and Hegelian philosophy, to help orient his practical and theoretical work. And if Marx by no means shared the ahistorical bias of the natural-law theorists of the French and American Revolutions, he did share their view that certain truths were self-evident — even if these were historically developed. It was in this spirit that he could exclaim, in a remarkably concise formulation of his rationalist optimism, "History is the judge — its executioner, the proletariat."[78]

As it affected his understanding of individuality, Marx's own rationalist disposition emerged in his assumption that human beings tended to respond rationally to circumstances and to evaluate shrewdly the advantages afforded by different courses of action. The concept of interest implied a tacit convergence between needs and insight, the passions and reason. Indeed, by taking this convergence for granted, the category of interest minimized the potency of blind inertia, and the possibility of a stubborn discrepancy between understanding and the will to act, between having concerns in the world and caring enough about that world to risk changing it. The concept of labor similarly reinforced Marx's rationalist assumptions. As Marx analyzed it, the labor process resembled a calculated form of instrumental activity, where the materials of nature were modified for coherent ends with insight into the appropriate means. By applying this model of human action to practice in general—by making labor his paradigm of effective human agency—Marx was able to avoid tackling other aspects of human behavior less amenable to rationalist explanation.

Rationalism indeed offered an immanent assurance that Marx's interpretation of history and its ultimate sense would be fulfilled. In his "Toward the Critique of Hegel's Philosophy of Right: Introduction," Marx had aligned the proletariat with (Hegelian) philosophy: the proletariat became the social agent of Reason in history. Although Marx eventually abandoned this essentialist, neo-Hegelian conception, he continued to depict the proletariat as a class driven by rational needs and interests. As Marx's economic works added, the proletariat was also propelled into the foreground of history by the logic of events and institutions; the reign of capital sharpened class polarities and increased the exploitation of labor. Yet even in the later works, subjective needs and interests joined objective events in pushing the proletariat to the point where it had no rational alternative but to revolt: to do otherwise would be an abdication of reason.

As a consequence, capitalism could appear to Marx as a predictable sequence of social situations that necessitated individual actions, in the sense that these situations warranted a foreseeable rational response. The proletariat as a class found itself under the sign of such a compulsion: "The question is *what the proletariat is,* and what, consequent on that *being,* it will be compelled to do."[79]

To be sure, the proletariat had to become aware of its own objective interests, just as the full flowering of man's rational freedom awaited the emancipation of labor. But because Marx held the view that civil society was already held together and driven forward by "natural necessity, essential human properties" and "interest," there was never any serious doubt in his mind that the proletariat would become so enlightened. Indeed, sooner or later it had to, since to remain ignorant of its real interests would be irrational. Marx's rationalist assumptions thus helped guarantee that history would play out the meaningful drama he had deciphered. Within modern history, the proletariat embodied the necessity of reason—a necessity that conferred upon history a teleological coherence.

The removal of the domination of nature over man and of man over man, combined with the dissipation of ideological illusions in the comprehension of a "general mind" employing science, thus seemed to assure human emancipation. The subjective conditions for a proletarian revolution arose necessarily from the proper objective conditions: once the proletariat had entered into an intractable conflict with the bourgeoisie, once traditional ideologies had been dissolved by the advance of capitalist production itself, once a workers' party had indicated to the proletariat where its authentic interests lay, there was little question for Marx that the proletariat would obviously and inevitably act rationally and seek to achieve its authentic class interests with a clear consciousness devoid of ideological contamination. The whole chain leading Marx to anticipate the collapse of capitalism would be unthinkable without the rational response of the vast majority to the rational initiatives of the enlightened organizers of the workers' party.

The rationalist dimension to Marxian theory nonetheless sharply distinguished Marx's outlook on historical necessity from that held by positivism, Comte's in particular. While both Marx and Comte attempted, by analyzing social phenomena, to disclose the laws governing these phenomena, Comte saw society as the ultimate reality and the individual as a mere abstraction. Unlike Marx, who balanced his social realism with an insistence on the ontological primacy of interacting individuals, Comte viewed society as an infinitely greater whole; he claimed that individuals owed their entire development to the larger social organism. The individual for Comte represented a vanishing moment in the forward march of humanity, which, as the higher being of a new positive religion, should be accordingly worshiped. Individuals, stripped of creative will, became the mere objects of the factual investigations and verdicts of positive science.

While Marx's materialism also aimed at a scientific and empirical analysis of social conditions, it did not eliminate the human individual as a factor and force in history. Unlike Comte, Marx incorporated the human subject within the scientifically determinant social object. Indeed, in Marx, it was only the rationality of the social subject which set the final stamp of necessity on the social object.

MARXISM BETWEEN SCIENCE AND REASON

The corpus of Marx's writings represents a synthesis of individualist aims and presuppositions with a scientific and deterministic account of objective social conditions and their historical development. At the heart of this synthesis lay his comprehension of subjectivity as rationally directed interest and causally efficacious labor. It was a synthesis that would eventually collapse under the theoretical pressure of positivism and the practical pressure of revolutionary setbacks and gradualist achievements within the social democratic movement.

Despite Marx's own distance from Comte's positivism, his most "necessitarian" statements came to support a neopositivist orthodoxy within Marxism. Indeed, the focus of Marx's published work on the abstract theory of capital facilitated misunderstanding: by reading into the crisis model of *Capital* a straightforwardly natural scientific concept of determinism, orthodox Marxism relegated his teleological account of the labor process to the margins of the theory. In so doing, orthodoxy obscured the central concepts of reification, alienation, and objectification, none of which could be properly understood apart from his comprehension of labor. Orthodoxy also abandoned Marx's hopes for an indigenous and militant labor movement, its will formed through enlightening the interest in emancipation inherent in each oppressed worker.

Marx himself had envisioned a combination of spontaneous proletarian development and coordinating conscious organization as the twin keys to social revolution. But to the degree that the spontaneous workers' movement failed to meet his original expectations, the emphasis was shifted to organizational questions. Several options were available. German social democracy by the turn of the century had created a huge bureaucratic party structure that could be viewed as paternalistically safeguarding the interests of the proletariat while conditions "ripened." The failure of Marx's original expectations here resulted in accommodation to a political reality seemingly barren of self-generating revolutionary activity.

But a militant wing within the international socialist movement viewed the situation differently. They saw the low level of proletarian militancy as a dangerous sign of bourgeois ideological hegemony and believed the situation could best be corrected by a dedicated cadre of enlightened revolutionaries counterposing themselves to the worker as his true consciousness. The immanent logic of this position pointed in the direction of an elite, possibly conspiratorial party organization; such a party would attempt to wrench the working class into an adequate awareness of its historical mission as defined by Marxian theory.

The most rarely advocated strategic position professed a continuing faith in the spontaneous capacities of the proletariat. This position was generally coupled with an organizational program aimed at encouraging in a revolutionary direction whatever spontaneous workers' movements did arise. Ironically, it was a strategy frequently confused with some heretical variant of anarcho-syndicalism, so complete was the disenchantment of orthodoxy with indigenous working-class activity. Indeed, the widespread preoccupation with organizational issues as a corrective for proletarian lassitude concealed an inability to launch a fundamental reexamination of the subjective premises of the Marxian theory. Marx's assumptions concerning the subjective conditions for revolutions remained a largely unquestioned adjunct to the larger economic edifice.

But the dilemmas and uncertainties surrounding practical questions could not leave the subjective aspects of Marxism unaffected. In fact, in Marx's own formulation, his theory depended to a crucial extent on rational social action if its forecasts were to stand. Marx's understanding of revolutionary possibilities and aims was thus intimately linked with his perception of subjectivity. As a result, the shifting comprehension of practice by Marxists was accompanied by a largely unacknowledged revision of Marx's own comprehension of subjectivity.

Insofar as Marx's optimism concerning the rational capacity of the individuals comprising the proletariat to initiate revolutionary action remained unconfirmed by events, Marxism as a doctrinal system was confronted with several possibilities for reinterpreting or revising Marx's outlook on man. One was simply to hold fast to the rationalist view of man, usually as an unexamined premise, in the face of all historical adversity. In varying degrees, Eduard Bernstein and Rosa Luxemburg, as well as such later neo-Hegelians as Lukács, may be said to have taken this course, which gained some additional credibility with the success of the Bolsheviks in the Russian Revolution.

A second possibility was implicitly or explicitly to empty subjectivity and consciousness of any autonomous force, in favor of a purely objective determinism, that, while externally guaranteeing the validity of Marxism, more resembled a positivistic variant of mechanical materialism than it did Marx's original doctrine. This route was widely traveled in the years after Marx's death; Engels inaugurated the exodus from historical dialectic to positive science as the systematic setting for "dialectical materialism."

Finally, a third possibility lay in the critical reexamination of rationalism as well as positivism. While an altered comprehension of subjectivity would have wide implications for the whole Marxian theory, it might be possible to insert a modified image of subjectivity at the base of Marxism, even if it meant abandoning the primacy of rational interest and labor, and, as a consequence, the necessity of history that Marx had postulated. This infrequently broached possibility was explored at some length in the "existential Marxism" of Maurice Merleau-Ponty and Jean-Paul Sartre.

On the whole however, Marxism has oscillated between the first and second alternatives, between a rationalism based on enlightened subjectivity and a positivism stripped of any reference to subjectivity. In Marx's own case, his tacit commitment to a rationalist view of man, and the degree to which his understanding of history depended on it, was greater before 1848 than after. It is almost as if, after the disappointment of 1848, Marx, whether consciously or not, sought to develop a more objective outlook on history, by focusing on the economic laws which defined the possibilities for social development. To this extent — and despite the fact that Marx never abandoned either an essentially rationalist image of subjectivity, or his insistence that subjectivity must actively participate in fulfilling the meaning of history — the basis for the subsequent elaboration of Marxism as a purely objective positive science was latently contained in his own move beyond the *ratio* of Hegelian Spirit, to economic laws as a principal guarantee of a rational history.

He thus bequeathed to his heirs a legacy charged with ambiguity. Although he himself had insisted on individual emancipation as a cardinal goal of socialism, and valued highly the creative potential of human practice, the understanding he originally elaborated came to be interpreted as a scientific world view of ironclad objective laws. In practice, the goal of individual emancipation faded from view, while in theory, subjectivity and consciousness became epiphemenona of objective material conditions. In Marxism after Marx, the sense of subjectivity was transformed.

PART TWO

From Engels to Gramsci

5

Engels and the Dialectics of Nature

In many ways, the history of Marxist theory is the story of a retreat from Marx's original thinking. Marx himself had premised his understanding on the interaction of real individuals in society: the effective freedom of human agency was his starting point and final hope. Within capitalist societies, he foresaw a rational history unfolding, driven forward by the global development of industrial production and cooperative labor, and, most critically, the resulting conflict between proletarian and capitalist, sharpened and consciously executed along the lines of their divergent interests. Through his original thinking, Marx presented a method of empirical research, an analysis of political economy, and an interpretation of history and its immanent sense—an interpretation that only the political agency of the enlightened proletarians could make meaningful. According to this interpretation, communism appeared as the emancipation of the individual from conditions of alienated self-realization: in addition to abolishing the oppressive property and class relations of capitalism, the individuals within a communist society consummated a transformation in their everyday lives. Through the medium of self-conscious cooperation, society could be restored to the purposeful control of the individuals actually constituting it.

"Orthodox" Marxists after Marx came to ignore or revise many of these aspects of his thought. Confronted with a cautious labor movement, the parliamentary success of socialist parties, and, finally, the victory of revolutionary Marxists in a precapitalist society, the orthodox attempted to consolidate Marxism as a comprehensive world view, capable of dependably orienting action amid the eruption of unforeseen occurrences. In the process, the theory bequeathed by Marx tended to lose the quality of being a mere method and hypothesis about the meaning of history, to become instead a schematic timetable of historical development. Distrusting the uncertainties of human agency, the orthodox justified their theory in terms of predictable natural processes and universally applicable dialectical laws of motion: using this fixed matrix of categories to map the invariant structures of history, they could master unanticipated events by reference to the norm of natural development. What in Marx had been an immanent interpretation, open in principle to modification, became for the orthodox a scientifically confirmed transcendental standard, essentially unaffected by irregular perturbations in the phenomenal world of human affairs. In this context, Marx's own hopes for individual emancipation, the enlightenment of interest, and the practical intervention of men in history were obscured and often altogether suppressed.

ENGELS AND MARX

Ironically, it was Marx's devoted colleague and collaborator, Friedrich Engels, who laid the theoretical foundation for the subsequent rise of orthodox Marxism. A master of popular exposition, Engels's prestige was enhanced by his lifelong association with Marx; in the formative years of Marxian socialism, he played a central role in expounding its "official" theory.

The relation of Engels's theories to Marx's own is complex and ambiguous. By no means a faceless follower, Engels in fact introduced Marx to the study of political economy; he actively participated at many points in developing historical materialism and made original contributions in applying the theory to such fields as politics, anthropology, and military history. Yet his writings frequently seem at odds with Marx, even when they profess to defend the latter's own theory. Never a mechanical expositor, Engels subtly revised entire aspects of historical materialism in the process of popularizing it. His own modesty helped conceal the extent of his contribution to Marxism—a contribution that needs to be distinguished from Marx's own.

In many respects, to be fair, Engels admirably preserved the integrity of Marx's thought. After the latter's death, he consistently disputed any interpretation that portrayed Marxism as reducing all social phenomena to economic causes. "According to the materialist conception of history, the ultimately determining element in history is the production and reproduction of real life.... Hence if somebody twists this into saying that the economic element is the only determining one, he transforms that proposition into a meaningless, abstract, senseless phrase."[1] His intransigent opposition to economic reductionism allowed Engels on occasion to maintain intact Marx's insistence on the contributions of consciousness to history. "In the history of society...the actors are all endowed with consciousness, are men acting with deliberation or passion, working toward definite goals; nothing happens without a conscious purpose, without an intended aim."[2] The task of scientific socialism lay in educating the proletariat to a clear consciousness of the "conditions and nature" of the act "which it is its destiny to accomplish."[3]

Other basic aspects of his thought, however, moved in a direction antagonistic to an appreciation of man's role in history. In attempting to consolidate and codify Marx's theory of history, Engels imposed a systematic schematizing foreign to the former's own approach. Originally a method of historical inquiry, Marx's theory was christened by Engels "historical materialism," a comprehensive world view rivaling (and imitating) Hegel's system in its encyclopedic pretensions. This development was precipitated by a need to provide the burgeoning social democratic movement with a *Weltanschauung* that might supplant the prevalent bourgeois systems. In *Anti-Dühring*, Engels himself virtually admitted as much; impelled by an occasion to prevent further "sectarian division and confusion" from developing within the German socialist party, he had set out to present positively the materialist viewpoint on a wide range of subjects. The result, as against his ostensible intentions, was "modern materialism" systematically developed—yet another world view in the contemporary constellation.

The principle vehicle of this metamorphosis was Engels's expansion of materialism into an all-encompassing cosmology. Marxism was no longer to be confined to the historical domain of human action. Engels indeed claimed that modern materialism, this "simple world outlook," was validated "within the positive sciences." By allying Marxism with natural science, he hoped to lay the basis for a philosophy of nature that could verify and illustrate the dialectical laws which distinguished modern from archaic materialism. While for Marx history, including nature as it appears for man, comprised the field of dialectical understanding, for Engels the laws of dialectic were laws of nature. Nature rather than history became the "test of dialectics."[4] "Dialectical thinking" was in turn relegated to a summation of the results attained by positive science.

DIALECTICS AND DARWIN

Engels reduced dialectics to three laws: the laws of the transformation of quantity into quality; the interpenetration of opposites; and the negation of the negation. He believed these were uniformly applicable to the human and natural worlds. The impetus for this inflation of Marx's naturalism lay in the implicit belief of Engels that if dialectical laws could be verified in nature, then the validity of such laws in history would, as a consequence, have also to be admitted; the truth of dialectics in nature entailed the truth of Marx's concept of history.

Engels's doctrine apotheosized motion. Since "motion is the mode of existence of matter," only dialectics, which was "nothing more than the science of the general laws of motion and development of nature, human society and thought," could fully elucidate matter in its various manifestations.[5] By framing laws of motion, dialectical thought progressively amassed an exact representation of the world. "The dialectics of the brain is only the reflection of the forms of motion of the real world, both of nature and of history."[6]

Marx himself had seen no need for such an external foundation to historical materialism, whether in nature or in general laws of history. In Engels's case, this generalized underpinning of materialism resulted in statements so broad as to be virtually meaningless. For example, he effusively praised dialectics for revealing "the transitory character of everything and in everything; nothing can endure before it except the uninterrupted process of becoming and passing away. . . . And dialectical philosophy is nothing more than the reflection of this process in the thinking brain."[7] Dialectics for Engels came to approximate a cosmic theory of evolution, accounting for the whole of natural and human history. In a speech at his comrade's graveside, he praised Marx's discovery of the "law of development" governing human history, an achievement on a par with Darwin's discovery of the law of development governing natural history.[8]

Indeed, thanks to the example of Engels, orthodox Marxism was eventually based on an evolutionary version of positivism, stressing the primacy of objective laws of development, and dismissing subjective factors as epiphenomenal. Marx had wanted to dedicate *Capital* to Darwin, and Engels, following this lead, eagerly sought to incorporate the latest findings of anthropology into Marxism. On more than one occasion, he compared the findings of Darwin in biology and Morgan in anthropology to those of Marx in political economy and history.[9] The attractions of a neo-Darwinian evolutionary positivism were manifold. Evolutionary positivism promised nothing less than an empiricial explanation of chance and irrationality in the social world. As Engels once remarked, Darwin's discoveries spelled the collapse of metaphysical necessity. Yet Darwin's notion of evolution reinstated a qualitatively higher notion of necessity, incorporating chance. The laws of adaptation and heredity became guiding threads in an evolutionary development eventually issuing in a rational human order.[10] In short, evolutionary positivism could be interpreted as accommodating irrational digressions while guaranteeing rational progress, all without recourse to the subjective presuppositions of Enlightenment rationalism.

The evolutionary thesis thus conveniently accounted for the empirical diversity of man, the influence of accident, and the existence of unreason, at the same time as it preserved values and upheld a teleological end of history. Evolutionary positivism avoided the pitfalls of relativism while affording the prestige of ironclad natural laws. For Engels, it rescued Hegelian dialectic from mystification and delivered it over to natural scientific treatment: "The old teleology has gone to the devil, but the certainty now stands firm that matter in its eternal cycle moves according to laws which at a definite stage—now here, now there—necessarily give rise to the thinking mind in organic beings."[11]

For Engels, precise knowledge resided in a perfect reflection of this world of evolving matter in motion. The "materialist conception of nature" comprised "nothing other than the simple concept of nature, just as it presents itself to us, without any foreign admixture [*ohne fremde Zutat*)."[12] Engels founded the possibility of such a perfectly reflective concept of nature in the very notion of evolutionary materialism. Such a materialism portrayed the universe in its totality as composed of ascending levels of organized matter. "The motion of matter is not merely crude mechanical motion, mere change of place, it is heat and light, electric and magnetic stress, chemical combination and dissociation, life and, finally, consciousness."[13] The dialectical laws framed by consciousness could then appear simply as the emergent reflection of the dialectics objectively present in all matter, from the simplest to the most complex, including consciousness itself. Properly grasped, mind was matter conscious of itself.

SUBJECTIVITY AND NATURE

Engels's desire to ground his materialism in an autonomous dialectic of nature led him beyond Marx. To be sure, Marx, like Engels, had looked forward to a single science of man and nature. But in Marx's synthesis, nature was presented anthropologically: "The *social* reality of nature and *human* natural science, or the *natural science of man* are identical terms."[14] Marx consequently viewed history as the preeminent science: "We know only a single science, the science of history."[15] This divergence between Marx and Engels had implications for other aspects of Marxian theory. Indeed, the doctrine of *Naturdialektik* contradicted not only Marx, but on occasion his own presentation of historical materialism.

In arguing against economic reductionism, Engels had carefully preserved a margin of creativity for conscious agency. Yet the reflective theory of consciousness growing out of his work on the dialectics of nature could only with difficulty sustain an account of individuality that did not render it vacuous and wholly dependent on external circumstance. If consciousness merely reflected the objective world, subjectivity itself could hardly lay claim to any independent contribution to that world. Consistently extended, Engels's *Naturdialektik* suggested that man was always determined, and never determining. His recourse to a dialectics of nature thus helped weaken a significant aspect of Marx's original notion of historical materialism.

Engels was aware of this contradiction. Indeed, his late essay of 1886 on Feuerbach in effect attempted a reconciliation of creative human agency with evolutionary materialism. He avoided an immediate reductionism: "All the driving forces of the actions of any individual person must pass through his brain and transform themselves into motives of his will in order to set him into action." Yet Engels proceeded to argue that the mind functioned as a "conveyor belt" of "driving forces," mediating the objective world and subjective will. As such, the mind had only a formal significance; its content, as opposed to its form, was determined by and derived from the objective world of matter.[16] Mind, as the highest form of matter, thus constituted an irreducible moment of the historical dialectic—but its contribution was purely formal.

Unfortunately, this synthesis, for all its ingenuity, narrowed the scope Marx had granted to human agency in transforming the contents of the material world. Marx had described how the individual could conceptualize an object, and then proceed to materialize that object, a totality of form and content, through labor. But Engels's conveyor belt metaphor undermined this teleological account, which Marx had used to stress the interpenetration of form and content, and to show the possibility of objectifying ideas in reality.

Engels's position indeed raised doubts about some of his own statements elsewhere. As he wrote in *Dialectics of Nature*, "Man is the sole animal capable of working his way out of the merely animal state—his normal state is the one appropriate to his consciousness, *one to be created by* himself."[17] Yet even in his appreciation of human practice, Engels tended to depart from Marx's position. For Marx, labor offered testimony to man's constitutive powers of objectification; the triumph of industry gave evidence of man's human faculties. Marx also used his concept of practice to attack that passive view which portrayed truth merely as a product of verified sense experience; he charged that this view ignored the historical constitution of the objective world by active subjects, and forgot that the very objects of sense-certainty were themselves usually the products of previous acts of individuals.[18] Engels, by contrast, presented practice primarily as an "infallible test" for the correctness of sense perception. In fact he employed the concept of practice in *defense* of the very contemplative understanding of truth that Marx had attacked: "So long as we take care to use our senses properly, and to keep our action within the limits prescribed by perceptions properly made and properly used, so long we shall find that the result of our action proves the conformity of our perceptions with the objective nature of the things perceived."[19]

This realignment of Marx's original appreciation of practice helped attenuate Engels's understanding of the possible creativity of human beings in history. Where for Marx labor was "self-realization and objectification of the subject, therefore real freedom," for Engels labor became "the proof of necessity."[20] On this basis, Engels proffered his refutation of Kant's thing-in-itself, by "practice, namely experiment and industry."[21] Indeed, it may not be purely coincidental that where Engels derived his three laws of dialectics from Hegel's "Objective Logic," Marx modeled his analysis of labor on the treatment of causality and teleology in Hegel's "Subjective Logic." The paradigm of dialectics for Engels was no longer really human practice at all: rather, nature and its inevitable motion provided the new model for Marxian science.

COMMUNISM, CLASS STRUGGLE, AND SCIENCE

Engels did not confine his reinterpretation of Marxism to epistemology and science; he also altered the significance attached to socialism. Marx had portrayed communism as liberating individuals from alienating conditions of self-objectification: on the basis of an equitable satisfaction of wants, a communist society would permit individuals to freely develop their expressive capacities. Engels, by contrast, often presented socialism simply as a kind of efficient technical solution to problems of social engineering: "The government of persons is replaced by the administration of things." The conscious recognition of the social character of production Engels principally saw as a means of averting "disorder and periodic collapse."[22] Socialism then became primarily a promise of hitherto unattainable progress. "Only conscious organization of social production, in which production and distribution are carried on in a planned way, can lift mankind above the rest of the animal world as regards the social aspect. . . . Historical evolution makes such an organization daily more indispensable. . . . From it will date a new epoch of history, in which mankind itself, and with mankind all branches of its activity, and especially natural science, will experience an advance that will put everything preceding it in the deepest shade."[23]

An impoverished concept of freedom accompanied this narrowed vision of communism. According to Engels, "Freedom . . . consists in the control over ourselves and over external nature which is founded on knowledge of natural necessity."[24] Marx by contrast held that this sort of freedom "in harmony with the established laws of nature" always remained confined within the "realm of necessity"; the "true realm of freedom," while it had as its basis the comprehension and control of natural necessity, existed beyond it, in the unfettered "development of human potentiality for its own sake."[25]

Engels's interpretation of communism affected his practical program for attaining it, as did his theory of consciousness. Occasionally, for example, he presented the class struggle as a datum wholly external to individual consciousness. "Modern socialism is nothing but the reflex in thought of this actual conflict, its ideal reflection in the minds first of the class which is directly suffering under it—the working class."[26] Such a conception devalued class consciousness and enlightened interest as constitutive factors of class conflict. Engels insisted that the path to socialism was simply "discovered by means of the mind in the existing material facts of production."[27] These "facts" of production in turn threatened to become reified, self-activating categories in the hands of Engels; he even went so far as to speak of a mode of production "rising in rebellion" against a form of exchange—as if modes and forms were the real actors in history. History thus appeared self-contained and independent of creative human intervention: "This conflict between productive forces and modes of production is not a conflict engendered in the mind of man...it exists, in fact, objectively, outside us, independently of the will and actions, even of the men who have brought it on."[28]

Such comments supported his conception of historical materialism as an objectified schema that, when applied to the appropriate empirical data, automatically dictated correct tactics. "To me the historical theory of Marx is the fundamental condition of all *reasoned* and *consistent* revolutionary tactics; to discover these tactics one has only to apply the theory to the economic and political conditions of the country in question."[29] If modern socialism was merely the accurate reflection in thought of the "real" historical movement, then the collaboration of modern science with socialism might yield a rigorously valid description of history and the laws of development governing it. Together, modern science and socialism verified the laws of dialectic and thus rendered the insights of Marx into the process and stages of historical development self-evident as to their truth. "The more ruthlessly and disinterestedly science proceeds, the more it finds itself in harmony with the interests and aspirations of the workers."[30] With Engels, socialism extended its welcome to the natural scientist as a revolutionary co-worker who would disclose a necessity that, once understood, irrevocably delineated the action of the (essentially passive) proletariat.

Nevertheless, more often than not, Engels in his comments on the actual socialist movement remained close to Marx's own positions. In fact, his thought can be seen throughout as pulling in two different directions simultaneously. On the one hand, Engels sought to secure, consolidate, and codify the theoretical advances inaugurated by Marx in the study of society; at this level, he tried to defend Marx's insights, including the latter's insistence on the importance of class struggle and the irreducibility of subjective factors in the historical process. On the other hand, he attempted to reformulate historical materialism as a sub-discipline within a more inclusive science of dialectics, embracing a dialectics of nature as its ultimate justification; at this level, his own reflex theory of consciousness implied a devaluation of subjectivity, and thus a revision of Marx's original thinking, with far-reaching implications.

Since Engels's commitment to an active pursuit of the class struggle was accompanied by his endorsement of an evolutionary science of historical materialism, his interpretation of Marx proved highly problematic: he raised the ambiguity of Marx's original theory to the level of outright contradiction. Nevertheless, to the extent that proletarians failed to press for a militant and class-conscious politics, the "scientific" side of Engels's outlook, with its promise of a progressive movement of history guaranteed by natural laws, proved an attractive—and authoritative—interpretation of Marx's position. The temptation to extend the dialectical cosmology of Engels into a purely objective (and thus implicitly reductionist) theory claiming the inevitability of socialism became virtually irresistable. Here as elsewhere, Engels, not Marx, pointed the way for orthodox Marxism.

6

The Rise of Orthodox Marxism

Orthodox Marxism attempted to consolidate "dialectical material-ism" as an objective science. While the leading theorists of the Sec-ond International focused on such inherent economic contradic-tions of capitalism as the tendency of the rate of profit to fall, the major party philosophers, including Plekhanov and Labriola, devel-oped Marxism in the direction of a globally explanatory world view. In the process, orthodoxy further sheared Marxism of its subjective components. As socialism became construed simply as an efficient reorganization of the economy harnessed to representative political institutions, problems of individual emancipation also faded from view. Finally, the success of the Russian Revolution established one variant of orthodox Marxism as an institutional dogma; Lenin inherited the objectivistic tradition from Plekhanov and elaborated it in new areas. Within the Soviet Union as well as without, ortho-dox Marxism assumed a quotidian political relevance.

PLEKHANOV AND LABRIOLA: THE AUTONOMY OF HISTORY AND THE PASSIVITY OF PRACTICE

G. V. Plekhanov and Antonio Labriola were almost alone among prominent Marxists in studying the "philosophy" of Marxism during the heyday of the Second International, between 1890 and 1914. Of the two, Plekhanov had the most influence ultimately, thanks to his role as the founder of Soviet Marxism.

Like Engels, Plekhanov presented Marxism as an integrated world view, encompassing a philosophy of nature as well as of his-tory. He also insisted on its philosophical component, and sought to integrate the social theory of historical materialism within a more comprehensive philosophical materialism. He called this comprehensive philosophy "dialectical materialism." According to Plekhanov, a proper understanding of dialectics made Marxism "competent to solve the problem of the rational cause of all that exists."[1] Plekhanov based his understanding of materialism primarily on Engels and on Feuerbach's materialist "correction" of Hegel. Although his own writings concentrated on theoretical problems of history and society, Plekhanov followed Engels in grounding the universal validity of dialectical thought in laws of nature; Engels, he wrote, had "found that the laws of dialectical thinking are confirmed by the dialectical properties of being."[2] Plekhanov also reiterated Engels's view that consciousness merely comprised the highest emergent form of matter, even if it could never be reduced to simple matter. Modern materialism "tries to explain psychic phenomena by these or those qualities of *matter,* by this or that organization of the human, or, in more general terms, of the animal *body.*"[3] Yet despite his doctrinal adhesion to a "dialectics of nature," Plekhanov placed the primary foundation of materialism in epistemology.

Here as elsewhere, Plekhanov largely relied on Feuerbach's example. He believed that Marx's thesis on Feuerbach showed that "man is induced to think chiefly by the sensations he experiences in the process of his acting upon the outer world."[4] Ignoring the fact that Marx had praised idealism for grasping the importance of intentional action and criticized Feuerbach for missing it, Plekhanov interpreted Marx's theses as a "masterly correction" rather than a fundamental critique. He even argued that Marxism could incorporate the essentials of Feuerbach's epistemology as its own. Such a materialist epistemology would take as its guiding theme the determination of consciousness by being.

At the level of social theory, Plekhanov, like Engels, spurned any form of economic reductionism; he granted the self-consciousness of the proletariat a central role in the struggle against capitalism. Both Plekhanov and Labriola advocated a kind of Marxian social psychology to support the Marxist theory of ideology; both also insisted on the interaction of intellectual and material factors. Labriola was particularly emphatic in stressing the importance of consciousness within history. "There is no fact of history which is not preceded, accompanied and followed by determined forms of consciousness, whether it be superstitious or experimental, ingenuous or reflective, impulsive or self-controlled, fantastic or reasoning."[5]

But the attack by orthodoxy on reductionism was blunted by its insertion within an essentially mechanistic model of society. Plekhanov, for example, wanted the prestige of hard science behind modern materialism: "Modern dialectical materialism cannot discover the *mechanical* explanation of history. This is, if you like, *its weakness*."[6] In Plekhanov's schema, the mode of production characterizing a society determined the structure of its economic relations, which in turn determined the psychology and consciousness of the individual men who interacted within society. Despite claims of reciprocal influence, Plekhanov argued that "the psychology of society is always expedient in relation to its economy, always corresonds to it, is always determined by it."[7] In this context, such dialectical laws as the "leap" from quantity into quality only served to render more ironclad what already had been presented as a closed mechanical system.

The orthodox version of historical materialism resulted in the elevation of history into an autonomous process, independent of human intervention. Claiming that progress in history was caused in a fashion wholly external to men and their intentional acts, Plekhanov asserted that Marx "regarded man's nature itself as the eternally changing result of historical progress, the cause of which lies *outside* man."[8] Despite his distinctive emphasis on the role of human insight, Labriola struck a similar theme: "Our aims are rational . . . because they are derived from the objective study of things, that is to say, from the explanation of their process, which is not, and which cannot be, a result of our will, but which on the contrary triumphs over our will and subdues it."[9]

Where Marx and Engels had portrayed history as the result of the collective activity of real individuals, the orthodox Marxists depicted an automatic history which implied the passivity of individuals. As Labriola saw it, the question after the rise of scientific socialism was simply "to recognize or not to recognize in the course of human events the necessity which stands over and above our sympathy and our subjective assent."[10] He felt that what predominated in Marx's practical precepts "was a discipline which had its source in the experience of necessity and in the precise doctrine which must proceed from the reflex consciousness of this necessity."[11] This conception of practice delineated freedom as submission to necessity. Plekhanov, in attempting to find a positive role for the individual within Marxism, suggested another outcome: the glorification of the scientific thinker who adequately reflects necessity. "As human reason can triumph over blind necessity only by becoming aware of the latter's peculiar inner laws, only by beating it with its own strength, the development of knowledge, the development of human consciousness, is the greatest and most noble task of the thinking personality," a *"completely and exceptionally idealistic"* task.[12]

The passive tendency of orthodox Marxism resulted in a practical passivity, most clearly visible in the work of Karl Kautsky. Kautsky agreed with Plekhanov that "modern socialist consciousness can arise only on the basis of profound scientific knowledge." But the average workingman could obviously make no claim to such "profound scientific knowledge"; therefore, "the vehicles of science are not the proletariat, but the *bourgeois intelligentsia.*" It followed that "socialist consciousness is something introduced into the proletarian class struggle from without, and not something that arose within it spontaneously."[13] A passive epistemology here led to the very division of society "into two parts, one of which is superior to society" that Marx had warned against in his 1845 critique of the contemplative bias in traditional materialism.[14] Such contemplative materialism tended to foster a gradualist strategy. Despite his reiterated invocations of revolution and its imminence, Kautsky once confessed that "it is no part of our work to instigate a revolution or to prepare the way for it."[15] Since the socialist revolution was inevitable in any case, practice should focus on moral persuasion and legal reform, rather than direct action.

REVISIONISM, ORTHODOXY, AND THE COMMUNIST PROJECT

Orthodox Marxism conflated the ideal goal of communism with the given movement of empirical history, which scientific socialism presumably reflected. The passivity at the core of orthodox Marxism spelled the elimination of purposeful agency from social theory. By ignoring the teleology inherent in the labor process as Marx described it, and by devaluing the importance of enlightened interest in the class struggle, orthodoxy lost Marx's basis for explaining the teleology immanent to the struggle for communism. Within orthodoxy, the goal of social emancipation rested entirely on the autonomous movement of history, which followed its own laws of development. Plekhanov therefore could not theoretically justify his own remark that "Marx and Engels had an ideal . . . the subordination of *necessity* to *freedom*" — especially when he added, quite properly, that "proceeding from this ideal [N.B.], they directed their practical activity accordingly."[16]

Both revisionist and orthodox Marxists fundamentally agreed that Marxism was an *empirical* science with no normative ethical claims *as science*. In this regard, the Marxism of the Second International reestablished the chasm between "is" and "ought" which Marx had attempted to bridge. As Rudolf Hilferding put it in his preface to *Finance Capital,* "Along with the theory, the politics of Marxism are also free of 'value judgements.' . . . To recognize the validity of Marxism (which implies the recognition of the necessity of socialism) does not at all mean to formulate evaluations or to indicate a line of practical conduct, since it is one thing to recognize a necessity and another to place oneself at the service of the necessity."

Since history according to the orthodox interpretation omitted the purposive intervention of men, any dispute over the actual tendencies of history threatened the socialist project itself. When Eduard Bernstein raised doubts about the empirical necessity of a socialist revolution, he was quickly attacked as a dangerous heretic imperiling the integrity of the Marxist theory. Almost inevitably, his critique of historical tendencies also forced the valuative role of subjectivity to the fore of the debate as well.

Unfortunately, Bernstein only inadequately grappled with the philosophical issues at stake. His alignment of revisionism with the contemporaneously influential neo-Kantian movement in philosophy sanctioned a duality of "is" and "ought," by approaching the goal of communism purely as an ethical issue. The theoretical correlate of an objective social situation where the revolutionary movement seemed quiescent appeared to be a purely subjective moral voluntarism. While Marx had felt that creative human practice unified "is" and "ought," objective causality and subjective teleology, orthodox Marxism banished subjective teleology in favor of a purely objective and necessary history, while revisionist Marxism reinstated teleology on a transcendent moral plane. The impoverished objectivism of orthodoxy produced its obverse in a normative philosophy of ethical socialism.

The most alert orthodox theorists nevertheless recognized the genuine challenge posed by a revisionist ethics, which could present itself, with some justification, as the inevitable complement of the "value-free" Marxist science endorsed by Hilferding. The most subtle attempt to disarm revisionism of its potency in this area was arguably Max Adler's. In response to revisionist objections, he attempted to reintroduce subjective teleology into orthodox Marxism. In Adler's sophisticated scheme, teleology appeared on the immediate level of human reality and practice; from the standpoint of the social actor, teleology was an ineliminable "form of experience." But from the standpoint of the social *scientist,* Adler argued, the influx of individual projects into the social world had to be grasped within a strictly causal nexus; causality was the scientist's ineliminable "form of experience." "The positions of ends...now appears as the *form of experience* through which causality generally unfolds in the particular realm of being that is characterized as social being by its species *consciousness.* Thus the world as deed, human life and action, is grasped in all its powerful vividness without being either degraded to an appearance of free will or cancelled in an illusion of self consciousness; it can only be grasped as the *other side* of causal necessity, that, with its side of [empirical] occurrence, belongs to theoretical observation *at the same time as,* with its side of volition, it belongs to immediate experience.... The fundamental problem of social theory is [in this fashion] resolved.... The relation of personal freedom to social necessity."[17]

Adler's contribution had the advantage of securing a place for creative subjectivity and its practical projects within Marxism, even though his fusion of Kant and Marx left teleology and causality on separate planes of reality. However, Adler remained a lonely figure on the fringes of orthodoxy. Moreover, the convolutions of his position could have been avoided simply by restoring Marx's original comprehension of labor and its unity of teleology and causality.

LENIN AS PHILOSOPHER: REFLECTING NECESSITY

The philosophical contributions of Lenin to these debates would not merit attention, apart from the canonic status his works have since been accorded by communist parties throughout the world. Yet Lenin's writings have assumed an inestimable importance in the development of Marxism as an official dogma. His particular variant of orthodox Marxism has (unfortunately) dominated later Marxist discussions.

Following his teacher Plekhanov, Lenin founded philosophical materialism epistemologically. Man's objective knowledge of the real world was based on sensations, which truly reflected material objects. "For every scientist who has not been led astray by professional philosophy, as well as for every materialist, sensation is indeed the direct connection between consciousness and the external world; it is the transformation of the energy of external excitation into a state of consciousness."[18] Lenin, like Plekhanov, valued practice for the verification it offered of sense-data. He argued that Marx's concept of practice presented "the materialist theory, the theory of the reflection of objects by our mind, with absolute clarity: things exist outside us. Our perception and ideas are their images. Verification of these images, differentiation between true and false images, is given by practice."[19]

However, Lenin soon distinguished himself from Plekhanov by his shrill introduction of party polemics into philosophical discussions. His diatribes against idealism were animated by a conviction that idealism was reactionary, rather than a simply incorrect theory— political reactionaries espoused idealism; therefore it was false. Lenin often seemed most obsessed with the religious delusions idealism allegedly fostered. He categorically denounced religion in a critical approach wholly divergent from Marx's. Marx had remarked that "the religious reflex of the real world can...only...finally vanish, when the practical relations of everyday life offer to man none but perfectly intelligible and reasonable relations with regard to his fellowmen and nature."[20] Lenin however busied himself with detecting dangerous religious ideas within secular philosophy. He valued epistemological materialism as proof positive against any form of transcendentalism that might give comfort to religion. "Once you deny objective reality, given us in sensation, you have already lost every one of your weapons against fideism, for you have slipped into agnosticism or subjectivism—and that is all fideism wants."[21] Here as elsewhere, Lenin conflated metaphysical, epistemological, theological, and political questions.

In *Materialism and Empirio-Criticism,* Lenin painted a picture of the progressive attainment of empirical truth. He assumed that absolute truth was gradually approximated through the accumulating total of relative truths, each of which reflected accurately an independently existing object. The contribution of dialectics lay in its presentation of the "doctrine of development in its fullest, deepest and most comprehensive form, the doctrine of the relativity of the human knowledge that provides us with a reflection of eternally developing matter."[22] For Lenin, "knowledge can be useful biologically, useful in human practice, useful for the preservation of life, for the preservation of the species, only when it reflects an objective truth independent of man."[23]

Lenin did not limit his passive conception of knowledge to the sphere of inanimate objects. The social realm also appeared as an entity entirely divorced from the individual's consciousness of it. Where Marx himself had described conscious and practical individuals, capable of transforming social relations as well as nature through their power of purposeful agency, Lenin insisted that "social being is *independent of the social consciousness of man....* The highest task of humanity is to comprehend the objective logic of economic evolution (the evolution of social life) in its generalized fundamental features, so that it may be possible to adapt *to it* one's social consciousness and the consciousness of the advanced classes of all capitalist countries in as definite, clear and critical a fashion as possible."[24] This orthodox Marxian theme of submission to necessity recurred throughout Lenin's work.

Some of Lenin's writings on organizational and strategic matters seemed nonetheless to contradict the passive implications of the epistemology elaborated in *Materialism and Empirio-Criticism.* In his dispute with the Russian economists, Lenin insisted on the irreducible importance of politics, ideology, and class consciousness to the development of a revolutionary movement; he presented such "subjective" conditions of revolution as "inseparably bound up with the objective condition" of a developed economic structure.[25] After the success of the Russian Revolution of 1917, Lenin similarly insisted on the importance of a "cultural revolution" to complement the political and social one; without such a cultural upheaval, there could be no question of achieving socialism.[26]

Lenin indeed took an activist, almost voluntarist, position as to the role of the Bolshevik Party in organizing the proletariat as a political force. He was hardly content to let events simply take their course, and here he departed sharply from orthodox social democracy. "To say that ideologists (i.e., politically conscious leaders) cannot divert the movement from the path determined by the interaction of environment and elements is to ignore the simple truth that the conscious element *participates* in this interaction, and in the determination of the path. . . . They fail to understand that the 'ideologist' is worthy of the name only when he *precedes* the spontaneous evolution with conscious, evolutionary action."[27] Or, as Lenin asked rhetorically in *What Is to Be Done?*, "What else is the function of Social Democracy if not to be a 'spirit' . . . *raising* the movement to the level of its program?"[28]

But what was the substance of the party's spiritual leadership? In what sense did the communist ideologue precede the spontaneous historical movement and "point out the road"? Lenin's discussion of "trade union consciousness" and his invocation of Kautsky make it clear that for him, as for Kautsky, what was at stake was the inability of the workers' movement to achieve science spontaneously. Social democracy had to assume the role of a spirit, because the workers themselves would remain an incoherent mass without the guiding light afforded by socialist intellectuals: "Class political consciousness can be brought to the workers *only from without,* that is, only outside of the economic struggle, outside of the sphere of relations between workers and employers."[29]

Ironically, Lenin's activist program, rather than wholly contradicting his epistemology, indirectly accorded with it. While Lenin used Kautsky's model of scientific consciousness injected into the class struggle from without for distinctly activist ends, both Lenin and Kautsky treated the proletariat as an inert object which in the first instance lacked any notion of the role cast for it by history, as comprehended by a purely objective socialist science. To paraphrase Lenin, the highest task of the proletariat was to comprehend the objective logic of economic evolution so that it might adapt to it. The vanguard would facilitate this adaptation.

Lenin thus dissolved the unity originally postulated by Marx between a spontaneous socio-historical development and the enlightenment of proletarian interests. The proletariat became a pure object, not only of history, but also of the Communist Party, which claimed a monopoly on adequate consciousness. If in fact the party leaders were the only persons with a handle on the truth, then "amidst the gloom of autocracy," Lenin felt justified in dismissing "'broad democracy' in party organization" as "nothing more than a *useless and harmful toy.*"[30]

To be sure, the initiating role a critical consciousness assumed within the vanguard party indicated that, at least for one sector of society, social being was not independent of social consciousness. In this respect, Lenin's posthumously published *Philosophical Notebooks,* with their clear recognition of the centrality of practice to Hegel's (and Marx's) thought, offered a more consistent underpinning for his theory of practice than *Materialism and Empirio-Criticism.* Although the notebooks in general did not budge from Lenin's reflection theory of knowledge ("Life gives rise to the brain. Nature is reflected in the human brain."), Hegel's remarks on causality and teleology led Lenin to remark that "man's consciousness not only reflects the objective world, but creates it."[31] While cognition remained for Lenin the "eternal, endless approximation of thought to the object," this reflective relation to nature did "not immediately, not simply" coincide with its object.[32] Such epistemological refinements merely rendered Lenin's schema of history more consistent, however; even the activist side of his theory consigned the great majority, including the working class, to a reified passivity and objectivity, which the enlightened communist vanguard investigated and acted upon.

Despite his commitment to a revolutionary strategy, in short, Lenin in his philosophical writings realized the apotheosis of objectivistic Marxism. To his passive epistemology and contempt for democracy corresponded an unannounced eclipse of individual emancipation as a central goal of communism. As Lenin's quip after the revolution that "communism equals soviets plus electrification" implied, communism in Russia came to mean a technical reorganization and modernization of society, rather than a basic transformation abolishing the domination of man by man and of things over men. It was a development presaged by earlier orthodox Marxists. Kautsky's widely read explanation of the Erfurt Program, written in 1892, for example, contained no explicit reference to individual emancipation as a goal in its chapter on "The Commonwealth of the Future." Kautsky instead dwelled on the economic reorganization of society that would enable the "socialist common-wealth" to "outshine in moral greatness and material wellbeing the most glorious society [Greece] that history has thus far known."[33] Here as elsewhere, Lenin summarized theoretically the movement of orthodox Marxism. Thanks to his unwavering practical commitment, he also established it in power.

ORTHODOXY AND THE LIQUIDATION
OF SUBJECTIVITY

Lenin, Kautsky, and Plekhanov all shared a devotion to a materialist world view that specified general dialectical laws of human history, developing out of, and verified by, general dialectical laws of nature. History and nature together comprised an evolutionary system issuing ultimately in communism, that social order incarnating man's rational mastery of natural necessity through its recognition. For orthodox Marxism, the attainment of this benign state increasingly was posed as a technical problem of economic reorganization and social planning. The early successes of socialist revolutions in underdeveloped countries such as Russia and China naturally reinforced such technical tendencies: when it is a matter of preventing starvation and death, the quest for the whole man tends to become a marginal concern.

Long before Stalin's dictatorship over the proletariat, the individual had vanished from orthodox Marxist theory. The leading Marxist philosophers of the Second International had each consolidated the objectivistic implications of Engels's dialectic of nature. As Louis Althusser has pointed out, the thesis of a dialectics of nature "has the polemical meaning that history is a *process without a subject*"; Lenin followed Engels in attempting "the elimination of the category of the Subject (whether transcendental or otherwise)."[34] Instead of placing man at the foundation of history, orthodox Marxism held that history itself created subjectivity. As Plekhanov remarked, "Man becomes a *'subject' only in history.* . . . 'Economic' materialism is the reply to the question of . . . how the *subjective side of history* comes about."[35] From the orthodox understanding, history simply made men, rather than men also making history, as Marx had emphatically added. The dialectical materialism of orthodox Marxism thus became a one-sided dissection of the undeniable power of objective circumstances in human affairs. Unfortunately, it remained incapable of consistently explaining how these circumstances arose in the first place.

This inability to comprehend origins was simultaneously an inability to grasp transcendence. Orthodox Marxism found itself in the embarrassing position of being unable to account theoretically for the revolutionary project. By presenting labor merely as the active verification of sense-data, orthodoxy ignored the idealistic aspects of practice in its teleological projection of an idea to be realized. Where for Marx practice had represented a creative unity of teleology and causality, for orthodoxy, practice simply confirmed causality: freedom as submission to necessity. The practice of the revolutionary movement was thus, by extension, prohibited from any creative mastery of historical possibility; orthodoxy consigned political practice to trail after empirical history, reflecting more or less adequately its autonomous imperatives (which supposedly pointed toward socialism).

The orthodox theorists thus consecrated Marxism as a purely objective dialectic in an attempt to secure its theoretical validity. Marx's original theory had rested on his optimistic expectations for the proletariat: the proletariat, in rationally acting on its interests, would emancipate the whole of society and institute communism. By the turn of the century, such expectations had come to appear highly questionable and even utopian. The proletariat, although increasingly organized in large political parties in Germany, France, and elsewhere, displayed little of the combative militancy so crucial to Marx's original conception. Faced with this failure of the subjective conditions for socialism, the orthodox Marxists responded by excising those conditions as necessary to communism. Socialism came to appear the inevitable result of an autonomous technical and economic evolution, governing the direction of historical development. Orthodoxy cast off the subjective aspects of Marx's rationalist legacy and instead solicited the support of natural science. In effect, the theory of orthodox Marxism liquidated the creative human subject. Its determinism offered the scant consolation of a mechanical guarantee.[36]

7

Revolutionary Rationalism—
Luxemburg, Lukács, and Gramsci

Despite a tenuous consensus among orthodox theoreticians within the Second International, several independent Marxists refused to ratify the standard interpretations of historical materialism. Rosa Luxemburg, for example, retained a basic confidence in the revolutionary potential of the proletariat; in this regard, she remained faithful to Marx's original understanding. As the reformist implications of orthodoxy gradually became apparent, Luxemburg and other revolutionary theorists on the left wing began to elaborate their own reading of Marx. The outbreak of world war and the Russian Revolution of 1917 finally combined to shatter the outlook of orthodox social democrats, the former by undermining their gradualist and internationalist program; the latter by rekindling revolutionary aspirations.

In the years immediately succeeding the revolution, Marxist philosophy underwent a renaissance and a metamorphosis, bolstered by a renewed hope for imminent social change. The leading figures in the revival of Marxist philosophy in the West—Georg Lukács, Karl Korsch, and Antonio Gramsci—had in common an acquaintance with the Hegelian sources of Marxian thought and a dissatisfaction with the evolutionary positivism of orthodoxy. Spurred on by the practical example of Lenin as a resolute revolutionary, Lukács and Gramsci proceeded to redraw the boundaries of Marxian theoretical discourse.

ROSA LUXEMBURG AND THE
NECESSITY OF SOCIALISM

Rosa Luxemburg stands as the key transitional figure between orthodox Marxism and later theorists like Lukács. Although she joined Kautsky in attacking the revisionists at the turn of the century, she eschewed orthodoxy to develop an independent perspective, rooted in a relatively sanguine assessment of the proletariat and its potential for militantly pursuing its true class interests. In opposing neopositivist and neo-Kantian versions of Marxism, Luxemburg reaffirmed Marx's original rationalism within a new historical setting.

Unlike Plekhanov, Rosa Luxemburg viewed Marx's theory primarily as supplying a "method of investigation," rather than a system of unimpeachable categories. Her Marxism always remained open-ended and tentative: "It is not true that socialism will arise automatically and under all circumstances."[1] For her, as for Marx and Engels, history did not comprise an entity independent of consciousness and practice, but instead the field of subjective intervention through action. Socialist theory disclosed and analyzed historical and economic tendencies leading to the collapse of capitalism; yet without the contributions of an ongoing class struggle, these tendencies remained barren of real meaning. Where Plekhanov had claimed that the cause of historical progress "lies *outside* man," Rosa Luxemburg asserted that "only the working class, through its own activity, can make the word flesh."[2]

Luxemburg perceived the primary task of socialism as the return of the human world to conscious control. The central mystery of economics for her revolved around the rise of hypostatized social structures: how did a fixed social order develop in opposition to human intentions and volition? "In this manner the problem faced by scientific investigation becomes defined as the lack of human consciousness in the economic life of society."[3] The vitality of any social institution rested on the "active, untrammelled and energetic" participation of the "broadest masses of the people." The lack of such conscious participation condemned not only the alienated objectivity of capitalist social relations but also any political movement that shunned democracy.

If the proletariat was in fact to break the spell of blind necessity, then a central task of socialist theory and practice had to be the development among proletarians of an understanding of their common interests and the possibilities for a more equitable world. Social democratic leadership ought to enable the proletariat to "learn to take hold of the rudder of society, to become instead of the powerless victim of history, its conscious guide."[4] It was a task dictating a persistent struggle against bourgeois patterns of thought within the proletariat. Particularly after experiencing working-class chauvinism during World War I, Luxemburg refused to presume an innate proclivity toward socialism on the part of the proletariat. "The immediate mission of socialism is the spiritual liberation of the proletariat from the tutelage of the bourgoisie, which expresses itself through the influence of nationalist ideology."[5] Yet Luxemburg, unlike Lenin, refused to vest the fate of the proletariat in the hands of an enlightened vanguard. The struggle for socialism depended on the conscious spiritual commitment of each individual proletarian. "Socialism must be created by the masses, by every proletarian. Where the chains of capitalism are forged, there they must be broken. *That is socialism.*"[6]

In advancing such views, Luxemburg rejoined Marx's original position on the centrality of proletarian commitment and class struggle to the attainment of communism. At the same time, she emphasized the necessity of history: again like Marx, she combined hopes for the creative intervention of men in history with a deterministic theory of the tendencies to crisis and collapse inherent in capitalism. She shared with Marx the belief that the revolutionary initiatives of the proletariat flowed necessarily from its rational reaction to the contradictions of capitalism. Yet precisely because she retained Marx's rationalist and deterministic framework, it is interesting to note her reaction to World War I and the dissolution of the Second International.

Despite the cosmopolitan and antimilitarist line taken by the Second International, the German Social Democrats failed to resist the furies of nationalism unleashed by the onset of World War I. The extent of chauvinism among the working classes of Europe indeed suggested that the subjective conditions for socialism might be far more problematic than previously suspected. Such doubts concerning the eagerness of the proletariat for an international socialist revolution in turn threw into question the strict necessity of socialism, since in Luxemburg's eyes socialism was inevitable only insofar as the subjective condition of militant class struggle could be fulfilled. Her writings during the war urgently expressed her mounting uncertainty, as well as her unshakable conviction that a socialist society, in spite of setbacks, remained imperative.

While she still foresaw the inevitable collapse of capitalism, Luxemburg now defined two competing historical outcomes, both of them in some sense necessities, one leading to socialism, the other to barbarism. The individual thus was confronted with a choice. "The world rule of imperialism is a historic necessity, but likewise its overthrow by the proletarian international. Side by side the two historic necessities exist in constant conflict with each other. And ours is the necessity of socialism. Our necessity receives its justification with the moment when the capitalist class ceases to be the bearer of historical progress, when it becomes a hindrance, a danger to the future development of society."[7]

It is an odd necessity that requires ulterior justification; and it is an odd necessity that needs to be chosen to become necessary. But then, what was only implicit in Marx's synthesis of reason and necessity becomes explicit in Rosa Luxemburg's last writings: the "historic mission" of the proletariat was precisely "to transform historical necessity into reality."[8] Without a conscious political struggle waged by committed workers, socialism remained not merely devoid of content, but, so to speak, unnecessary. Ironically, in proportion as she admitted the possibility of barbarism, Luxemburg increasingly insisted on the necessity of socialism, if civilization was to avert catastrophe. "Socialism has become necessary not merely because the proletariat is no longer willing to live under the conditions imposed by the capitalist class but, rather, because if the proletariat fails to fulfill its class duties, if it fails to realize socialism, we shall crash down together to a common doom."[9] A new historical situation thus revealed that any Marxist version of historical necessity which incorporated men at its foundation had to be radically different from the orthodox understanding of necessity, with its reassuring but arid laws of historical development.

GEORG LUKÁCS: THE REIFICATION OF SUBJECTIVITY

The Russian Revolution transformed the practical context of Marxian theory. Socialism no longer appeared a distant goal; militant action no longer seemed futile; the gloomy urgency of Rosa Luxemburg's wartime essays was replaced by a new spirit of combative optimism. With the end of the war and the collapse of social order in Germany and Hungary, a fluid historical situation emerged, foster-

ing apocalyptic hopes. Revolutionaries could believe in the "imminence of world revolution and the total transformation of the civi-
lized world," as Georg Lukács has recalled.[10] The example of Lenin
himself fueled such hopes. Against Marxist gradualism, with its cautious evolutionary positivism, Lenin epitomized the primacy of
human action; this radical figure who had seized history by the reins
attracted a new stratum of Western intellectuals to Marxism. Such
communists as Lukács, Antonio Gramsci, and Karl Korsch brought
to Marxism a fresh set of theoretical perspectives, coupled with an
activist orientation.

The subjective and spiritual dimensions of Marxism slighted by
orthodoxy were suddenly revived. Theorists expressed renewed
interest in the nature of class consciousness and a refurbished faith
in the revolutionary capabilities inherent in the proletariat. Events
now suggested that Marx's original prognosis of proletarian militancy was not wholly mistaken. Socialism could appear plausibly as
the inevitable rational goal of modern history: not coincidentally,
the Marxist revival coincided with a Hegelian revival in several theoretical circles.

Lukács, a thinker influenced by Max Weber and Georg Simmel
as well as Hegel, stands at the beginning of the contemporary renaissance of Marxist philosophical studies. In *The Theory of the Novel*,
his last major pre-Marxist work, Lukács had described the modern
era as "an age in which the extensive totality of life is no longer
given, in which the immanence of meaning in life has become a
problem, yet which still thinks in terms of totality."[11] When Lukács
transported this aesthetic yearning for wholeness into Marxism, he
resurrected Marx's own hopes for a qualitatively new form of life.

He also briefly resurrected Marx's rationalist optimism, a rebirth
vividly conveyed in his first Marxist essays, collected in *Tactics and
Ethics* and published in 1919. The messianic significance of the
Russian Revolution decisively colored his prose: "The message of
reality," exclaimed Lukács, "Marxist reality, the unity of the historical process, is quite clear: *the revolution is here.*" The imminence of
revolution invested the situation of the proletariat with an extraordinary moral urgency. Every proletarian, he asserted, was impelled to
attain a clear sense of his true class interest, which necessarily surpassed the "merely given" to comprehend a "world-historical mission." While only Marxism could provide "intellectual leadership"

in this ongoing process "of making social development conscious," the inner essence and momentum of history seemed relatively unambiguous: for Marx had properly perceived world history "as a homogenous process, as an uninterrupted revolutionary process of liberation."[12]

The temper of these essays was impatient, impetuous, demanding, of a piece with a romantic reading of Lenin's accomplishment: "*Decisions, real decisions, precede the facts.*" One telling indicator of Lukács's optimism at this stage was his doctrine of the party. After describing orthodox socialist parties as the "external organizational expression" of the proletariat's immaturity, its "inability to impose its will and its interests on society," he proceeded to praise the Bolsheviks for dismantling the traditional party organization, and enabling "the proletariat to take all power into its own hands. . . . *The parties have ceased to exist—now there is a unified proletariat.*"[13]

The illusion of a revolution without political parties quickly dissipated, however: rationalist optimism gave way to rationalist pessimism. Under the impact of revolutionary setbacks in Hungary and Italy in 1919, and confronted with Lenin's critique of his position as "ultra-Leftist" in 1920, he was driven to reformulate his outlook and specifically to reconsider his position on the party. By 1923, when *History and Class Consciousness* was published, additional reasons for a reassessment could be found in Lukács's own theory of reification. The importance of this book was twofold. Not only did he analyze the formation and function of class consciousness, he also sharply posed the problems involved in liberating men from fixed and falsifying forms of thought. The rationality of the proletariat — its understanding of its "world-historical mission" — could no longer be taken for granted as an emergent result of historical development.

His theory of reification took as its starting point Marx's discussion in *Capital* of commodity fetishism. The development of capitalist society had created "the fetishistic character of economic forms, the reification of all human relations, the constant expansion and extension of the division of labor which subjects the process of production to an abstract, rational analysis, without regard to the human potentialities and abilities of the immediate producers; all these things transform the phenomena of society and, with them, the way in which they are perceived."[14] Under the reign of capital, society was mobilized for the accumulation of surplus value, rather than the cultivation of human capacities—an omission which took its toll on the victims of the system and their understanding of their situation. Here Lukács invoked Max Weber as well as Karl Marx: within modern society, most men had become prisoners of bureaucratic routine and instrumental manipulation, creatures of closed categories. The reification represented in commodity exchange thus infected the subjects of exchange: the worker, enmeshed in unthinking activities overseen by the capitalist, was in thrall to bourgeois forms of thought.

For Lukács, as for Marx, the individual in a commodity form of exchange was immediately confronted with a "fantastic relation between things," rather than the actual relation between men which produced this appearance. One of Marx's main tasks in *Capital* had been the penetration of appearances such as the "free exchange" of wages for labor power to reveal the exploitative logic of capital. He also seemed to follow Marx in deriving fetishistic forms "from the primary forms of human relations."[15] But he refused to join Marx in premising theory on the concrete activity of real individuals. Instead, he asserted that "no path leads from the individual to the totality."[16]

Indeed, by 1923 Lukács felt that the prevalent reification of bourgeois society had prevented most individual workers from acquiring a "true, concrete self-knowledge of man as a *social being*." The categories of bourgeois consciousness presented, not the reality of domination, but the unreflected appearance of free exchange. Marxist theory thus decisively outstripped proletarian practice: "We must never overlook the distance that separates the consciousness of even the most revolutionary worker from the authentic class consciousness of the proletariat."[17] Lukács thus reserved the possibility of true consciousness for classes alone; only a class as a whole could attain a "total point of view," and grasp the essential social relations. Sundered from Marx's original premise of individuals producing in society, and questioning the capacity of even the most enlightened individual workers for self-emancipation, his theory proceeded to present modern history as an ongoing struggle, not between interested individuals involved in antagonistic class relations, but between two conceptual entities, the proletariat and the bourgeoisie.

The conceptual proletariat, catalyzed by a true class consciousness, became the general subject of a true history in his eyes. But the empirical proletarians did not immediately coincide with their conceptual essence— a situation which only the enlightened efforts of the Communist Party could rectify. He thus assigned to the party the sublime role of bearing the authentic class consciousness of the proletariat, the "consciousness of its historic vocation," although he departed from Leninist orthodoxy by emphasizing the cultural and pedagogical aspects of the party's mission.[18] Nevertheless, for Lukács as for Lenin the concrete subjects of history—*these* particular proletarians—were deemed incapable of educating themselves, of acquiring a proper grasp of the social totality. Like the Great Legislator in Rousseau, the party in Lukács appeared a slightly fabulous creature—as if only the gnosis of the party's illuminati, by divining the "final goal," could rescue workers from the falsifying forms of thought typical of bourgeois society. Moreover, since Lukács tended to portray the subject of history ideally, as a collective "we," the individual workers threatened to become relatively inconsequential elements in a rigidly teleological movement governed by the party's interpretation of history and its "objective possibilities." Perhaps this is the real meaning of Lukács's remark that reification "over-individualizes" men: the quest for a unified totality here led, first, to the abandonment of real individuals as an ontological premise of theory, and then to an attenuation of individuation as a goal of communism.[19]

But these were not the critical aspects of his contribution. Instead, subsequent Marxists fastened on his understanding of class consciousness, and his insights, however problematically linked to a defense of the Leninist party, into the importance of a materialist pedagogy able to raise interests to the level of rational action. As the foremost philosopher of a genuinely dialectical theory of history, Lukács stimulated a new concern with the subjective aspects of Marxist theory, while redirecting attention to the human basis of revolutionary practice. If his own theory in *History and Class Consciousness* veered toward conceptual rigidity, perhaps this was but a by-product of his steadfast adherence to Marx's original rationalist hopes in an increasingly unpromising situation.

GRAMSCI: SOCIALISM BEYOND THE NECESSITY OF REASON

Despite his heresy in treating authentic class consciousness as the demiurge of a true history, Lukács, like Rosa Luxemburg, retained Marx's necessitarian language. While he insisted on the importance of purposive action by the proletariat, he also presumed a rational end of history, which established the "concrete meaning" of each prior historical stage: "The objective evolution [of the economy] only gives the proletariat the possibility and the necessity [sic] of changing society. But this transformation itself can only come about as the — free — action of the proletariat itself."[20] Both Lukács and Luxemburg thus advanced a concept of necessity that protected the proletariat's freedom to act; yet neither seriously doubted that when the proletariat finally did act, it would do so rationally, and thus bear out the necessity of communism. Here, as elsewhere, they preserved and extended Marx's rationalist understanding, although in Lukács's case only through the medium of an enlightened vanguard party.

Against this backdrop, Antonio Gramsci's studies assume a special significance. Like Lukács, Karl Korsch, and the Council Communists (particularly Anton Pannekoek), Gramsci was sensitive to the subjective aspects of social theory, what the Council Communists called its *geistige* factors. Gramsci, again like Lukács, came to Marxism indirectly, through the philosophy of Benedetto Croce and the Italian Hegelians, and under the influence of Georges Sorel and, later, Henri Bergson. In 1919, at a point when he was already committed to socialism, Gramsci had declared that "man is above all else mind, consciousness," and he greeted the Russian Revolution accordingly, as "The Revolution Against *Capital.*" "The Bolsheviks have denied Karl Marx, and they have affirmed by their action, by their conquests, that the laws of historical materialism are less inflexible than was hitherto believed."[21] Gramsci never abandoned his interest in the *geistige* elements of society, an interest he brought to Marxism in the form of such concepts as "consent" and "intellectual and moral leadership."

The Marxism of Gramsci's notebooks, compiled while he was imprisoned under Mussolini's regime, differed from the Marxism of Lukács and Luxemburg. Unlike these predecessors, Gramsci assigned the labor process a central significance for elaborating the philosophy of historical materialism. As a consequence, Gramsci insisted on the inseparability of *homo faber* from *homo sapiens;* he also portrayed individuals, via labor, as actively shaping a world of objects and norms. "Ever man, in as much as he is active, i.e., living, contributes to modifying the social environment in which he develops . . . in other words, he tends to establish 'norms,' rules of living and of behavior."[22] His eloquent appreciation of the individual's creative efficacy in labor permitted Gramsci to restore "individuals producing in society" at the basis of Marxian theory.

One must conceive of man as a series of active relationships (a process) in which individuality, though perhaps the most important, is not, however, the only element to be taken into account. . . . The humanity which is reflected in each individuality is composed of various elements: 1. the individual; 2. other men; 3. the natural world. . . . Each one of us changes himself . . . to the extent that he changes . . . the complex relations of which he is the hub. . . . If one's own individuality is the *ensemble* of these relations, to create one's own personality means to acquire consciousness of them, and to modify one's own personality means to modify the *ensemble* of these relations. But these relations, as we have said, are not simple. Some are necessary, others are voluntary. . . . It will be said that what each individual can change is very little, considering his strength. This is true up to a point. But when the individual can associate himself with all the other individuals who want the same changes, and if the changes wanted are rational, the individual can be multiplied an impressive number of times, and can obtain a change which is far more radical than at first sight seemed possible. . . . Up to now the significance attributed to these supraindividual organisms [that the individual is related to] (both the *societas hominum* and the *societas rerum*) has been mechanistic and determinist; hence the reaction against it. It is necessary to elaborate a doctrine in which these relations are seen as active and in movement, establishing quite clearly that the source of this activity is the consciousness of the individual man who knows, wishes, admires, creates . . . and conceives of himself not as isolated but rich in the possibilities offered him by other men and by the society of things of which he cannot help having a certain knowledge.[23]

Gramsci also diverged from Lukács and Luxemburg on the issue of necessity in history. Instead of preserving Marx's deterministic rhetoric, Gramsci openly challenged causal explanation in social theory. His interest in Bergson and Sorel facilitated his elaboration of a Marxism critical of its own rationalist premises. Earlier in the century, Sorel had criticized Marxism for relying on an unprovable notion of progress in rationality; Marx, he charged, had covertly assumed the Hegelian notion of a *Weltgeist* guiding history toward socialism. However useful as myth such a notion might be, it had nothing to do with science; the socialist revolution would be absolutely unpredictable.[24] Gramsci took over and refined such skepticism.

He pointed out the intimate connection between necessity and rationalism in social theory. "It would appear that the concept of 'necessity' in history is closely connected to that of 'regularity' and 'rationality.'"[25] Not only did necessity depend on rationality, the rationality of social acts depended on their "necessity," on their predictable and regular occurrence. "If social facts cannot be predicted, and the very concept of prediction is meaningless, then the irrational cannot but be dominant."[26]

Gramsci thus faced a series of dilemmas. Predictability averted irrationality, but was prediction possible? How could such prediction proceed? What did it involve? Gramsci dismissed making mechanically objective laws the basis of social predictions. Such laws inappropriately excluded the subjective factor from history. "Objective always means 'humanly objective' which can be held to correspond exactly to 'historically subjective.'"[27] He rejected most "so-called laws of sociology" as having negligible value: "They are almost always tautologies and paralogisms."[28] In the realm of human affairs, Gramsci in fact denied the possibility of any "purely 'objective' prediction." "Anybody who makes a prediction has in fact a program for whose victory he is working, and his prediction is precisely an element contributing to that victory. . . . If one excludes all voluntarist elements, or if it is only other people's wills whose intervention one reckons as an objective element in the general interplay of forces, one mutilates reality itself."[29]

But rather than simply discarding the concept of social prediction as meaningless, Gramsci reinterpreted it. He argued that prediction could be viewed as a practical act, instead of a mechanical accounting of some quasi-natural and purely objective causality. Prediction would then so thoroughly involve subjective factors that a primary guarantee of the truth of a prediction would lie in the practical resolve of the predictor to make it true. "One can 'foresee' to the extent that one acts, to the extent that one applies a voluntary effort and therefore contributes concretely to creating the result 'foreseen.' Prediction thus reveals itself, not as a scientific act of knowledge, but as the abstract expression of the effort made, the practical way of creating a collective will."[30]

As a result of his investigations, Gramsci abandoned entirely the concept of prediction applied to history. While the theorist still investigated "how in historical evolution relatively permanent forces are constituted which operate with a certain regularity and automatism," Gramsci's Marxism ignored any misplaced imperatives to construct a closed causal system of general laws.[31] He also refused to take the rationality of human action for granted; the problem was precisely to cultivate a rational subject, dedicated to realizing the goals of communism. This interest animated all of his investigations into ideological hegemony and intellectual leadership.

Communists had, as their crucial task, "to demonstrate that the necessary and sufficient conditions already exist to make possible, and hence imperative, the accomplishment of certain historical tasks." The accomplishment of these tasks was imperative not because they were "historically inevitable" but rather "because any falling short" would increase "the necessary disorder" and prepare the way for "more serious consequences."[32] In other words, Gramsci posed again Rosa Luxemburg's alternatives: socialism or barbarism. Action oriented toward the progressive end of history, communism, laid the grounds for a creative politics that might "dominate and transcend" given conditions, even as "one still moves on the terrain of effective reality."[33] Gramsci, like Lukács, thus restored to Marxism its pedagogical concerns and teleological dimension; the achievement of communism required the purposeful intervention of enlightened proletarians.

Although Gramsci's thought remained incomplete, what fragments do survive in his prison notebooks suggest that Gramsci had a sharper understanding than his contemporaries of the inadequacies of Marxism, both as a necessitarian outlook, and as a theory presupposing a rationalist view of man. With Gramsci, Marxism began to appear more as a political art than a natural science: there is something of Machiavelli's *virtù* and Bergson's intuition in his description of the great political leader. After his own fashion, he anticipated a sense of subjectivity new to Marxism, beyond either positivism or rationalism.

PART THREE

Existential Marxism

8

The Prospects for
Individuation Reconsidered

Marxism came of age in a philosophical atmosphere dominated by evolutionary positivism. To be sure, the prevalent strains within the Marxian philosophy were occasionally opposed by recourse to neo-Kantianism (Bernstein) and, after World War I, neo-Hegelianism (Lukács). More rarely, so-called "irrationalist" tendencies figured tangentially in Marxian discourse—for example, in Gramsci's appreciation of Bergson and Sorel. Yet neither a refurbished rationalism nor an historicized evolutionary positivism proved capable of unraveling the complex of theoretical problems surrounding the presentation of subjectivity, human practice, and historical necessity in Marxism. On the one hand, the orthodox Marxists contradicted Marx's own insistence on the centrality of class struggle, and his own comprehension of purposive labor, by reducing consciousness to a reflection of external conditions. On the other hand, an optimistic assessment of man's inherent responsiveness to enlightened interest no longer provided any convincing guarantee that historical truth might triumph, especially with the shadow of fascism falling across Europe. When they were discussed at all by Marxists, the issues of subjectivity and historical necessity too often remained confused, or the object of merely suggestive marginalia.

The philosophies of existence which had grown up in the meantime offered a different perspective on these issues, one rarely explored in prewar Marxist discussions. Contemporaneously with Marx, Kirkegaard had argued, against Hegel, for the insurmountability of the suffering human subject; when dialectical thought lost this anchor, it lost its authentic opening onto religion and ethics, areas which Hegel had treated from the lofty standpoint of Absolute

Knowledge. Later in the nineteenth century, Nietzsche had dissected human dependence, self-deception, and the solace of unfreedom, arguing against purely external, deterministic theories of bondage. Both Kierkegaard and Nietzsche interpreted human life as a perpetual process, falsified when conceptually hypostatized, whether through necessary categories of reason, or a positivist determinism, both mythical guarantors of a counterfeit certainty. At the turn of the century, Wilhelm Dilthey took a parallel route, arguing that the special character of cultural meaning, and its foundation in "the enigma of life," dictated an interpretive logic peculiar to the "human sciences," such as history and philosophy.

Contemporary social theorists shared a similar range of concerns. Democrats were alarmed at the emergence of the modern party as an hierarchical institution, confounding earlier hopes for enlightened emancipation through increased participation in politics; conservatives were similarly alarmed by the rise of the masses, and suggested that the rational pursuit of interest disappeared in an emotional contagion whenever groups of men acted in a revolutionary situation. Bureaucratic strangulation, passions unhinged from reason, blind submission to authority, the suffocation of creative innovation — such were some of the themes explored by thinkers like Max Weber, Robert Michels, Georg Simmel, Gustave LeBon, and Sigmund Freud. Although not all of them were equally concerned about the implications of their insights for Marxism, most of them had something to contribute to the debate over the role of human agency in history and the outlook for individuation. The implications were not reassuring.

The best of twentieth-century Marxist thought attempted to confront these implications. The ambiguous — and frequently barbaric —chronicle of socialism in this century in itself has warranted a radical rethinking of the entire Marxian project, while the challenge mounted by philosophers as diverse as Nietzsche, Husserl, and Heidegger sooner or later had to enter into the discussion, if only to be criticized rather than merely ignored.

NIETZSCHE'S CHALLENGE

Although several nineteenth-century thinkers had questioned the rationalism and idealism of the Enlightenment, none had quite the impact of Friedrich Nietzsche. As Max Weber put it after World War I, "One can measure the honesty of a contemporary scholar, and above all, of a contemporary philosopher, in his posture toward Nietzsche and Marx."[1]

In the present context, Nietzsche's thought assumes a special significance, since his starting point is the reflective individual. With Nietzsche, subjectivity claimed not just an epistemological priority —"the subject alone is demonstrable"—but also the dignity of a duty: "We, however, *want to become those we are*—human beings who are new, unique, incomparable, who give themselves laws, who create themselves."[2] On the other hand, Nietzsche, like Marx, acknowledged individuation to be an historical result, calling the "sovereign individual" the "ripest fruit" of "this tremendous process." This meant, as Nietzsche admitted, that "the 'subject' is not something given, it is something added and invented."[3]

While he promulgated an important series of affirmative doctrines, such as the will to power and eternal recurrence, his decisive significance for social theory derives not so much from his positive ontology, which valued whatever enhances life, as from his negative teaching, and, above all, his insight into the modern epoch. Nietzsche's basic assessment of his age is clear enough: "Disintegration characterizes this time, and thus uncertainty: nothing stands firmly on its feet or on a hard faith in itself. . . . Everything on our way is slippery and dangerous, and the ice that still supports us has become thin: all of us feel the warm, uncanny breath of the thawing wind; where we still walk, soon no one will be able to walk." The image of foreboding is indicative: modern men confronted a chaos of "very diverse value judgements," none of them compelling or essential any longer as "the basis, 'the condition of existence.'" Recognition of this situation engendered what Nietzsche called a "radical nihilism."[4]

Previously, societies, through their conventions, traditions, and religions, had provided an objective pattern which the individual could follow. But just as Nietzsche believed that the chaos of the modern era betrayed the arbitrary and insubstantial artifice of all normative order, so he believed that the contemporary epoch, by throwing the individual back on his own resources, revealed the fragility and insubstantial artifice of all psychic order. In the past, "to be alone, to experience things by oneself, neither to obey nor to rule, to be an individual—that was not a pleasure but a punishment; one was sentenced 'to individuality.'"[5] Even in the modern era, individuation proved a fate most men would prefer escaping. The realization, through the dissolution of all objective norms, of a limitless individual freedom seemed more frightening than liberating—in direct contradiction to the expectations of the Enlightenment. Why this fear? Primarily because the solitary ego, despite the assurances of modern philosophy, afforded no more substantial foundation than objective norms for the orientation of life. According to Nietzsche, the individual intrinsically embodied little more than a number of ceaselessly demanding drives and impulses.[6] The challenge was to govern this unruly subjective commonwealth and to forge a unique psychic order without resorting to the discredited customary fictions.

But most people declined the challenge to become truly unique individuals; the way was difficult, the rewards uncertain. Instead, they devised strategies for escaping the "prison" of individuality. One could blindly reaffirm old faiths, for example, and Nietzsche charged that most modern world views simply resurrected the "Christian moral hypothesis" of man's dignity and perfectibility in various new disguises. Nietzsche himself, by contrast, welcomed the chaotic conflict of contemporary life, even if he doubted the capacity of most men to withstand the ambiguity and tension such ethical pluralism entailed. The collapse of traditional moral codes, and above all the decline of Judeo-Christian monotheism—the "death of God"—created a situation of unprecedented possibilities which he described in such hopeful imagery as a "new dawn," an "open sea" permitting "all the daring of the lover of knowledge."[7]

In the prologue to *Thus Spoke Zarathustra*, Nietzsche expressed the central tension in his thought between hopes for a rebirth of creative vitality and fears of a totally pacified existence:

And thus spoke Zarathustra to the people: "The time has come for man to set himself a goal. The time has come for man to plant the seed of his highest hope. His soil is still rich enough. But one day this soil will be poor and domesticated. . . .

"I say unto you: one must still have chaos in oneself to be able to give birth to a dancing star. I say unto you: you still have chaos in yourselves.

"Alas, the time is coming when man will no longer give birth to a star. Alas, the time of the most despicable man is coming, he that is no longer able to despise himself. Behold, I show you the last man. . . .

"The earth has become small, on it hops the last man, who makes everything small. His race is as ineradicable as the flea-beetle; the last man lives longest. . . ."[8]

Nietzsche's social thought reflected his fears. While he formulated the ideal of an individuated existence, he restricted its enjoyment to those few noble souls able to form and follow their own laws. Most of the "rabble," on the other hand, remained servants of circumstance, bound to routine and unquestioned conventions. At best, he hoped for a "new nobility," appreciative of each other's creative exploits, able to promulgate new values and new polytheistic myths, perhaps even capable of rescuing modern life from the aimless drift that might otherwise result from democratic mediocrity.

A more direct assault on the value of universal enlightenment can scarcely be imagined. Not only was the "truth" to be conveyed called into question; the human subject of enlightenment, deprived of any necessary interest in rationality and freedom, and described as the locus of conflicting drives and appetites, also became a questionable medium for coming to understand any truths whatsoever. Moreover, if all the conceptual paraphernalia of our thinking, be it scientific, religious, or moral, was purely conventional, did not the quest for truth lead not necessarily to liberation but perhaps also to a destructive skepticism, a paralyzing doubt?

Nietzsche's challenge to Marxism grew out of this ambivalent outlook on enlightenment. Marx, as we have seen, relied on an understanding of history and human agency that linked the pursuit of material interest with the ideal of individual emancipation. Nietzsche, by contrast, portrayed human beings as creatures driven, for the most part, by *fear:* fear of reasoning, of freedom, of truth, or novelty, of individuation, of the tensions created by a multifaceted personality. Interest, one of the key faculties Marx believed operative in social action, Nietzsche dismissed as relatively unimportant: "Man is an indifferent egoist: even the cleverest thinks his habits more important than his advantage."[9] Most individuals, left to their own devices, craved security, order, certainty, the familiar, tried-and-true routine that seemed to provide a steady foundation for life. Nor did discomfort and material distress necessarily dissolve such patterns of behavior: "In an age of disintegration...happiness appears...in agreement with a tranquilizing...medicine and way of thought, pre-eminently as the happiness of resting, of not being disturbed."[10]

Nietzsche also viewed with suspicion any theory of history as a purposeful progression, in large part because he suspected these theories of mollifying the fears of the craven. A philosophy of history like Marx's appeared primarily as one more ideological avenue for escaping the perils and promise of the current era: "One wants to get around the will, the willing of a goal, the risk of positing a goal *for oneself;* one wants to rid oneself of the responsibility (one would accept fatalism)." Moreover, because he feared that a pacified existence was what most men wanted, Nietzsche was doubly disturbed by the "economic optimism" animating the democratic credo of the socialists: "Once we possess that common economic management of the earth that will soon be inevitable," wrote Nietzsche in a note dating from 1887, "mankind will be able to find its best meaning as a machine in the service of this economy—as a tremendous clockwork, composed of ever smaller, ever more subtly 'adapted' gears; as an ever-growing superfluity of all dominating and commanding elements; as a whole of tremendous force; whose individual factors represent *minimal forces, minimal values.*"[11] Along this path lay not Marx's social individual but Nietzsche's last man, as ineradicable as a flea-beetle.

PHENOMENOLOGY AND THE QUESTION OF INDIVIDUALITY

The reconsideration of subjectivity and the fate of the individual took several divergent and even contradictory forms in twentieth-century European philosophy. One of the most influential approaches was phenomenology, the philosophical discipline founded by Edmund Husserl. Where Nietzsche had given a stormy diagnosis of the modern world and its ills, Husserl, who was primarily interested in logic and epistemology, soberly inventoried the ego's constitutive capacity, its ability to invest a world with significance.

In his *Logical Investigations* of 1900, he had attempted to establish the objectivity of logical categories through an analysis of the invariant aspects of subjective experience. Despite its demonstration of an objective logic, the phenomenological method of "direct intuition" and insight into "essential structures" led naturally over the following decades to a broader exploration of the "stream of consciousness," and, in Husserl's case, to a form of transcendental idealism; by the time of the *Cartesian Meditations* of 1930, he was claiming that "all that exists for the pure ego becomes constituted in it itself."[12] Nevertheless, through the key concept of intentionality, Husserl's phenomenology pointed beyond the strict subject/object dualism characteristic of Cartesian rationalism. By "intentionality," Husserl meant to specify consciousness as an inherent relation to an object: consciousness was always consciousness *of* something, and that in a specific manner. For example, one might doubt, surmise, hope or fear, judge, approve, or merely be presented with, an object. The notion of intentionality suggested that consciousness gained its element of intelligibility through a double relation, to the world of objects, which could appear under a variety of different aspects, and to the world of subjective acts, which could apprehend the world of objects in a number of different ways, and with different aims in mind. Husserl thus described a more or less stable structure of objectivity, grasped through the fluctuating relations of a dynamic subjectivity.

Although Husserl's focus on logic largely removed history from his purview, the rise of fascism led him to a reconsideration of the foundations of philosophy. *The Crisis of European Sciences and Transcendental Phenomenology,* published posthumously, but written between 1934 and 1937, raised the question of a crisis as to the meaning of man. At a time when political philosophers were advocating a return to natural law (legal positivism seemed the unwitting ally of fascism), Husserl resurrected the Kantian notion of a teleological Idea of humanity. Humanity, according to Husserl, had forgotten its proper goal, the attainment of rationality and freedom, and had thus betrayed the essence of the meaning of man.

The crisis in science alluded to in Husserl's title concerned not the methodology of the objective sciences, such as physics, but rather the illicit importation of natural scientific method into the sphere of human life itself. In lieu of a reasoned reflection on man's meaning, science provided a ready-made human self-understanding. But this objectivistic self-understanding created a crisis in human existence, for "men treated as facts become facts,"[13] and a fact could hardly be expected to comprehend its own transcendental essence. Under the sway of universal objectivism, the tasks of rationality and freedom had thus been displaced by mathematical-physical knowledge, a critical human accomplishment to be sure, but one that increasingly had forgotten its *human* origins. Phenomenology's role in this situation became the restoration of the teleology immanent in subjectivity to its proper place. By demonstrating the grounding of any human logos, including the *mathesis universalis* of physics, in transcendental subjectivity, phenomenology uncovered the teleological Idea of man as an historical goal still outstanding.

Rationality in the *Crisis* thus became a task to be accomplished, rather than an innate endowment of the transcendental ego. Moreover, Husserl insisted that rationality, properly understood, transcended the narrow *ratio* of mathematical-physical objectivism, encompassing as well man's autonomous freedom to shape himself and his environment.[14] Only philosophy—only phenomenology—provided an adequate *ratio* for the self-reflection of mankind. Through a "bracketing" of the account of the world given by natural science, phenomenology reached the "life-world," that mundane environment of human existence, where Husserl already discovered the ongoing teleological accomplishments of subjectivity, filling the world with meaning, prior to objective understanding. Whether this life-world, precisely distinguished by him as the pregiven foundation of all higher theory, could be reconciled with his previous idealistic theory, which insisted on the transcendental constitution of the world by the ego, remained unresolved at his death. What Husserl himself desired is less debatable: "I want to establish, against mysticism and irrationalism, a kind of super-rationalism [*Überrationalismus*] which transcends the old rationalism as inadequate and yet vindicates its inmost objectives."[15]

Husserl left a varied legacy to future philosophers; realists and existentialists as well as idealists could find support in some stage of his elaboration of the phenomenological method. But the relevance of phenomenology for social theory first became clear not through his own work, but through that of Max Scheler, and particularly through Martin Heidegger's *Being and Time,* published in 1927 in Husserl's *Jahrbuch fur Phänomenologie und phänomenologische Forschung*.

Being and Time had an immediate impact. On a purely philosophical level, the book criticized traditional metaphysics from Aristotle to Hegel in the name of a truly "fundamental ontology" that overcame the traditional equation of being with substance. Confronting such forebears as Kant and Descartes, Heidegger set out to destroy previous ontologies, in preparation for posing anew the question fundamental to his own thought: "What is the meaning of Being?" Yet *Being and Time* also contained a detailed analysis of *human* being: by proposing a novel interpretation of what being human meant, he linked the ontological dispute over substance to an indictment of everyday life in the modern world. The potential for human excellence was being diminished while life was leveled down to dull uniformity: this was one message clearly transmitted through an elaborately technical philosophical prose.

Like Husserl in the *Crisis*, Heidegger in *Being and Time* wished to retrieve the capacity for transcendence inherent in human existence from its fixation within a deceptively self-evident world of objective entities. To this end, he distinguished between "authentic" (*eigentlich*) and "inauthentic" ways of being human. Where the inauthentic person assumed the world he inherited as a given, the authentic individual confronted this world as a set of possibilities grasped through his own decisions, acts, and commitments. To be sure, Heidegger, like Nietzsche, presumed that most people would forfeit the creative powers and freedom inherent in being human, preferring instead the anonymous security afforded by the conformity and stereotyped possibilities of "the crowd" (*das Man*). To cast one's lot with the crowd was to abdicate individuation to interchangeability: "Everyone is other and no one is himself."[16] Heidegger also drew a sharp distinction between the "concern" (*Besorgen*) with which a person pursued his everyday life, and the "care" (*Sorgen*) with which an authentic individual resolved on a unique (*eigenst*) way of being. In his concern with daily affairs, a person could disburden and literally lose himself in mundane matters. By contrast, in caring about his world, the authentic individual realized and acted upon his inherent capacity to form his own (*eigen*) life, by choosing among the factual possibilities disclosed by his thoughtful resolve.

But what led a person to care about his world? What aspects of human existence could potentially break the spell of everyday life and its seductive concerns? On Heidegger's account, the crucial moments came in fleeting moods, in nagging fears—in anxiety, in the sense of impending death, ultimately in the "call" of conscience. Where everyday life preoccupied, the thought of death disturbed: and in the experience of anxiety before death as a person's ultimate possibility, Heidegger detected the voice of conscience, calling the individual to care about his world, and to accept responsibility for his own life. By setting a final limit to the possibilities of existence, the anticipation of death also revealed the finitude and temporal unity of a person's life span. The authentic individual faced the future knowing it was finite, and yet grasped the past as something to be assimilated in the present, through a free choice among possible ways of being.

While the anticipation of death thus individualized a person and disclosed authenticity as an essential possibility of being human, the authentic individual returned to a public world of shared endeavors, where he fashioned a unique historical "fate" for himself. Indeed, this unfolding of the individual's "finite freedom" finally overcame the powerlessness of an isolated witness before death only by submitting to the shared "destiny" of a people, a power liberated "in communicating and in struggling." Only with historical destiny on the horizon did the authentic individual become empowered with a firm resolve that confirmed his own commitments; only by "surrendering" his isolatated individuality could a person "win" himself as an "authentic self."[17]

The implications of *Being and Time* were far-reaching. In addition to discarding the Cartesian dualism dividing mind and body, Heidegger was concerned to show the formative significance of states of mind, such as moods, emotions, fears; instead of assuming rational judgment as a distinctive and universal human attribute, he presented it as merely one mode of existence, one way of approaching the world. In opposition to any transcendental idea of Reason, Heidegger substituted an interpretation of human beings as the sole source of reasons: through their own transcending freedom, by the ways of being human they chose, it was men alone who brought reason to life.[18]

Despite the conservative implications of his understanding of historical destiny, the importance of Heidegger's philosophy for radical theory was undeniable, although few Marxists of the period were prepared to acknowledge it; Lucien Goldmann has even argued that *Being and Time* contains a covert response to, and hidden affinity with, Lukács's *History and Class Consciousness*.[19] By suggesting that a practical concern with worldly affairs only obstructed caring enough about the world to risk changing it or making it one's own, Heidegger implicitly called into question the convergence of inter-

est, labor, and insight Marx had assumed, as well as the individuat-
ing tendencies Marx had found at work in modern society. Moreover, by pointing out the consolations a person derived from forfeit-
ing his distinctiveness, Heidegger challenged the Marxist understanding of alienation: what in Marx represented primarily dispos-
session, in Heidegger appeared as "tranquilization" as well.[20] To the
extent that anonymity and unfreedom appeared comforting, while
individuality and freedom appeared burdensome, the understanding of individual emancipation had to be revised.

Whatever difficulties fundamental ontology as a whole confronted, in all these particulars Heidegger helped redraw the boundaries for theoretical discussions within the human studies. He also
transformed their style. If positivism had imported a dry factuality
into Marxism, Heidegger's philosophy would impart a flavor of
ontological salvation. The promise of authentic Being, wed to revolutionary Marxism, produced an aura of messianic hope that
attracted neo-Marxist thinkers as diverse as Maurice Merleau-Ponty
and Herbert Marcuse.

THE POSSIBILITY OF CRITICAL THEORY

The implications of the new philosophies of subjectivity and individuality were infrequently explored within most Marxist circles.
Yet they played an important role in shaping contemporary social
theory and psychology. Freud's psychoanalysis, for example, paralleled Nietzsche's philosophy in its exploration of the chaotic
impulses animating the psyche and the ways in which the ego could
harness the instincts; through his therapy, Freud tried to equip
patients with a rationality flexible enough to withstand the tensions
and anxieties endemic to the godless world Nietzsche had described.

Nietzsche's thought also had a crucial impact on the sociology
elaborated by Max Weber, who felt that the value of modern progress had been decisively thrown into doubt. Scientific mastery entailed what Weber called "the disenchantment of the world," the
obliteration of the last bases of transcendental belief alongside the
rationalization of world views. At the "end of this tremendous development," Weber concluded, no one can know "whether entirely
new prophets will arise, or there will be a great rebirth of old ideas

and ideals, or, if neither, mechanized petrification."[21] Ironically, for Weber as for Neitzsche, the triumph of scientific rationality starkly illuminated the irrational aspects of human existence. Weber felt it illusory to interpret history using a purposeful model of agency: "The action of men is *not* interpretable in such purely rational terms," for "not only irrational 'prejudices,' errors in thinking and factual errors but also 'temperament,' 'moods' and affects disturb his freedom." Weber also cautioned against any one-sided recourse to the category of material interest: "Interests (material and ideal ones), not ideas, determine the actions of men directly. The *Weltbilder* that were created by 'ideas,' however, very often were the switchmen who determined the lines alongside which the dynamism of interests pushed human action onwards."[22]

For both Weber and Freud, the new philosophies of subjectivity implied a new skepticism in theory, and stoicism in practice. Like Nietzsche, Weber saw contemporary society as a battleground for conflicting values, with no hope for a scientific mediation among them: "Fate, and certainly not 'science' holds sway over these gods and their struggle." "Chained to the course of progress," the social theorist in Weber's view could only catalog the forms of fate: "What is hard for modern man is to measure up to *workaday* existence" — a sentiment Freud shared.[23] The difficulty, as Freud and Weber both well knew, was to accomplish this submission to fate without sacrificing all sense of personal worth and responsibility: the autonomous individual, where he survived at all, became for Freud and Weber the shrewd banker of an increasingly scarce resource — the rational understanding of reality.

As elucidated by psychoanalysis and interpretive sociology, the implications of the new philosophies of subjectivity scarcely seemed reassuring for Marxism. Yet Lukács, as we have seen, felt able to surmount Weber's stoicism from the practical standpoint of the proletariat, which dissolved skepticism by deciphering an immanent meaning of history. From this vantage point, Weber's former colleague explained the rationalization of life as a transient phenomenon engendered by the reification of commodity exchange under capitalism.

This resolution of the dilemma proved attractive for those few Marxist thinkers alive to the implications of the new philosophies. In the thirties, the most important such thinkers were the exponents of "critical theory," Max Horkheimer, Theodor Adorno, and Herbert Marcuse. Marcuse had studied under Heidegger, and briefly proposed a merger between Marxism and fundamental ontology, while Adorno devoted early studies to Kierkegaard and Husserl. Indeed, while Communists such as Lukács had their interest in the new philosophy censored by the orthodoxy imposed under Stalin, the critical theorists, as independent Marxists, were able to devote considerable attention to contemporary developments in philosophy and social theory; they were also forced to confront a rapidly deteriorating political situation in Europe that created further difficulties for a Marxist rationalism presumably rooted in the real tendencies of history.

In the new metaphysics, Horkheimer found first of all a response to the ethical pluralism depicted by Nietzsche and Weber: "Now that faith in the absolute validity of any developed system had disappeared, the whole series of cultural forms, their rhythm, independence and regularities, became the instrument of intellectual formation."[24] With relativism an apparently accomplished fact, and the individual assumed as a primordial given, philosophers turned to such primitive general categories as life and existence to unify and evaluate the competing cultural forms. But Horkheimer, in a line of argument recalling Marx's critique of Max Stirner, assailed the preoccupation with existence for "belittling the importance of a theoretical comprehension of social processes" and for validating the narrow individualism generated within bourgeois society. In this respect, the new metaphysics served a social function: in his dreams of authenticity, "the isolated, insignificant individual can identify himself with superhuman forces, with omnipotent nature, with the stream of life or an inexhaustible world-ground"; the monadic individual could thus, in imagination, surmount the obstacles imposed by an uncongenial world. The "freedom of the personality" promised by the new metaphysics thus acted in private life "as an opiate; in society, as a fraud"—for a society of authentic ones would leave the objective forms of domination untouched.[25] As Adorno put it, the obsession with authenticity was "nothing other than a defiant and obstinate insistence on the monadological form which social oppression imposes on man."[26]

Horkheimer and Adorno were nevertheless ambivalent in their assessment of existentialism and the philosophies of life. Adorno, for

example, praised Nietzsche as a philosopher "whose reflection penetrated even the concept of truth," while Horkheimer esteemed Husserl as the "last genuine theoretician of knowledge." "What is true in
the concept of existence," wrote Adorno in *Negative Dialectics,* "is
the protest against a condition of society and scientific thought that
would expel unregimented experience — a condition that would virtually expel the subject as a moment of cognition." Moreover,
Adorno vindicated some of Nietzsche's most troubling insights:
"The individual's rational economic behavior undoubtedly derives
from something more than economic calculation and the profit
motive. . . . *Fear* constitues a more crucial subjective motive of
rationality."[27]

Perhaps because he dreaded the total eclipse of the autonomous
subject, Adorno developed a particularly nuanced understanding of
individuation and its problems. Within bourgeois society, individuation occurred as isolation from other human beings; "the capacity
for seeing them as such and not as functions of one's own will
withers, as does that, above all, of fruitful contrast, the possibility of
going beyond oneself by assimilating the contradictory." But the
cult of authenticity expressed in the philosophy of Heidegger ironically obscured this constriction of individuality, in part by ignoring
the extent to which "the individual owes his crystallization to the
forms of political economy." Thus the new philosophies of subjectivity did not always grasp the ambiguities of individuation: "Within
repressive society, the individual's emancipation not only benefits
but damages him. Freedom from society robs him of the strength for
freedom." The individuals in contemporary society, reduced to
"monadological individual interest and its precipitate, character,"
quickly capitulate to dictatorship, "the moment organization and
terror overtake them." Adorno thus claimed to uncover a hidden
link between a fearful individualism and fascism. The autonomous
individual was nevertheless an important, if precarious, sanctuary
for critical thought: what remained, for Adorno as for Marx, was to
restore individuation to its proper social context, and thus to "make
an end of the fatality which individualizes men, only to break them
completely in their isolation."[28]

The rise of fascism in the thirties forced the critical theorists to
reassess the basis of their hopes for a more rational society. The cre-
dos of the Enlightenment had been called into question by the very

process of historical development: "As industrial society progresses and is supposed to have overcome its own law of impoverishment, the notion which justified the whole system, that of man as a person, a bearer of reason, is destroyed."[29] But if "man as a bearer of reason" was destroyed, how could hopes for a communist society be sustained? In an early essay on "Philosophy and Critical Theory," Marcuse had called reason the "fundamental category of philosophical thought," and asserted that in critical theory "the philosophical construction of reason is replaced by the creation of a rational society."[30] But what if, Marcuse asked, "the development outlined by the theory does not occur?" What if the proletariat failed to fulfill Marx's expectations? Moreover, if "man as a bearer of reason" seemed an increasingly endangered species, what warrant was there for believing the "development outlined by the theory" ever would occur?

Horkheimer at first held fast to the theory of knowledge and history defended by Lukács in *History and Class Consciousness:* critical theory was inherently historical and derived the "idea of a reasonable organization of society" from an analysis of the "goals of human activity." The road leading to the future signified for Horkheimer as for Lukács a "concrete historical" as well as a "logical" process. Since the truth value of the theory hinged on its practical realization, the theorist of necessity addressed himself to "the development of the masses. . . . The theoretician and his specific object are seen as forming a dynamic unity with the oppressed class."[31] Critical theory thus aimed at enlightening the "right interest" of the oppressed.

The rationalist assumptions behind this model of interest and class consciousness, only implicit in Lukács and Marx, became explicit at several points in Horkheimer's essays from the thirties. Once dialectical thought has integrated the "empirical constituents" of a situation into a "structure of experience" which can inform "the historical interests with which dialectical thought is connected," Horkheimer seemed to feel confident that any man could become a "bearer of reason": "When an active individual of sound common sense perceives the sordid state of the world, desire to change it becomes the guiding principle by which he organizes given facts and shapes them into a theory. . . . This, in turn, discloses both his sound common sense and the character of the world. Right thinking

depends as much on right willing as right willing on right thinking."
Despite his appreciation of the new situation in theory and practice,
Horkheimer thus remained tied to the rationalist tradition he had
inherited from Marx through Lukács: against the prevailing stupe-
faction of the spirit, he could only offer the hope of a subjectively
inherent *ratio*. "The thrust towards a rational society, which
admittedly seems to exist today only in the realm of fantasy, is really
innate in every man."[32]

Yet by linking the validity of critical theory to concrete historical
factors, he left open the possibility that its hopes might prove
groundless. And indeed, confronted with the events of World War II
and its aftermath, Horkheimer became extremely pessimistic: "To
protect, preserve, and where possible, extend the limited and ephemeral freedom of the individual in the face of the growing threat to
it is far more urgent a task than to issue abstract denunciations of it
or to endanger it by actions that have no hope of success."[33] Faced
with an apparently docile proletariat in the West and Stalinist
regimes in the East, other critical theorists looked elsewhere for support. Herbert Marcuse, for one, elaborated a psychoanalytic variant
on philosophical anthropology, focusing on man as a creature of
repressed innate needs; on this "biological basis," Marcuse ultimately rested his hopes for a revolution driven by "the vital need to
be freed from the administered comforts and the destructive productivity of the exploitative society."[34]

Theodor Adorno, by contrast, forthrightly faced the implications
of the practical impasse in critical theory: grounded as it was in history, the theory could claim no transcendental foundation. Rejecting the pursuit of First Philosophy, specifically in the Heideggerian
form of fundamental ontology, Adorno in *Negative Dialectics*
denounced the spell of identity theory on philosophy: "Dialectics is
the consistent sense of nonidentity. It does not begin by taking a
standpoint." Enduring the vertigo such a position implied, Adorno
depicted the theory as a revolving series of critiques, based only on
relative standpoints which reflected the disintegration of modern
life; the possibility of transcendence was now locked in "the fragments which decay has chipped, and which bear the objective meanings." The concept of freedom, for example, "can be defined in
negation only, corresponding to the concrete form of a specific unfreedom." As for historical materialism, and hopes for a communist

future, they are reduced to an imageless desire for "the resurrection of the flesh. . . . The perspective vanishing point of historic materialism would be its self-sublimation, the spirit's liberation from the primacy of material needs in their state of fulfillment."[35] Adorno thus conceded Marx's practical concerns to the realm of utopian imagery: a critical philosophy—and in this respect, Adorno and Horkheimer agreed—lived on only in the immanent critique practiced by those thinking individuals still committed to reason.

The unflinching loyalty of the critical theorists to a Hegelio-Marxist form of rationalism helped keep a critical Marxist philosophy alive throughout the thirties and forties. At the same time, though, their allegiance, however qualified, to Hegelian modes of thought, as well as their apparent belief that Freud had essentially solved "the problem of the subject," helped limit their philosophical reconsideration of subjectivity.

Instead, the most sustained encounter between Marxism and the new philosophical understanding of subjectivity unfolded in the thought of Jean-Paul Sartre and Maurice Merleau-Ponty, who were unaware of the critical theorists. Both Sartre and Merleau-Ponty had been educated in the phenomenological tradition of Heidegger and Husserl, influenced by the renaissance of French interest in Hegel in the thirties, and shaped by the experience of the French Resistance during the forties.[36] Philosophically, they were committed to "existentialism," a term they used to define a historical movement (involving Kierkegaard and Heidegger, among others) and to describe their own efforts at illuminating the structure of human existence—a structure encompassing irrational inertia as well as the possibility of rational action. Politically, however, they maintained a lively interest in socialism, although both kept their distance from socialist politics, although both also preserved a distance from orthodox Marxism. Despite shortcomings and flaws, their social theories remain the most provocative examples of a Marxism built on new subjective foundations.

9

Sartre—The Fear of Freedom

The chief proponent of an "existential Marxism" has been Jean-Paul Sartre, novelist and playwright, polemicist and philosopher. Despite a relatively late conversion to Marxism, in the early fifties, Sartre has created one of the most idiosyncratic bodies of contemporary Marxian literature, while providing a paradigm of the politically engaged philosopher.

He differed from his colleague Merleau-Ponty not only in his attempt to reconcile existentialism and Marxism systematically but also in his insistence on man as a creature of passions, often fearful of freedom, and distrustful of reason. While Merleau-Ponty, by virtue of his philosophy of perception, was led to abandon Marxism as a deterministic science or a rationalist philosophy, he maintained a fundamental trust in men's sociable and rational inclinations. Sartre, by contrast, thanks in part to his philosophy of interpersonal relations and doctrine of absolute freedom, discarded the relatively sanguine outlook on human proclivities traditionally held by Marxists. More than a vessel of ambiguous meaning and situated freedom, the human being was also an agent who frequently forfeited creativity and freedom of choice in favor of familiar habits. In such circumstances, neither rationality nor freedom could necessarily be accounted a universal desideratum.

In formulating his existential Marxism, Sartre started from the philosophical anthropology he detailed in *Being and Nothingness*. By painting man as a basically solitary and antisocial animal, in search of a substantial and unyielding identity, Sartre was led to portray social life as an incessant series of conflicts, each threatening to deprive the individual of a hermetically secure sense of self and to limit his access to scarce resources. Such an understanding added some curious twists to Sartre's phenomenology of the social world in the *Critique of Dialectical Reason*, where he attempted to vindicate Marx's dialectical understanding by tracing the rise of social forms from individual interaction.

Yet despite his inclination to an almost Hobbesian view of human nature, a view sharply at variance with Marx's own, Sartre has nonetheless illuminated several areas of Marxian social theory, not so much in his explicitly Marxist works as in his essays, biographies, and early philosophy. By analyzing the individual in "bad faith" as averting freedom and rational reflection, he has clarified some of the most important implications of Nietzsche's and Heidegger's philosophies, while by posing the problem of an authentic individuality as a precondition of enlightened social action, he has also attempted to surmount one of the most difficult dilemmas disclosed by their thought.

The individual, raised within a context of inherited norms and habitual expectations, can either creatively shape his own identity or seek solace in previously defined roles. In shirking the task of genuine self-definition, the individual, suggested Sartre, in effect passively supported the prevailing social reality; by refusing to depart from established patterns of behavior, the individual necessarily failed to reflect on inherited norms critically. Similarly, if the individual were to transform society, he would also have to transform himself, by overcoming feelings of inertia and fear and asserting his own transcending freedom. Sartre here contended that the individual, susceptible to a reified yet comforting vision of personal possibilities, could not be presumed a rational agent; rather, rationality itself appeared as a disposition chosen and acted upon, sometimes at great risk to the individual's routinized sense of self.

Despite such hints at a Marxism critical of rationalist assumptions, Sartre's work has vacillated between modest accomplishments and portentous failures. While from a Marxist perspective, his *Critique of Dialectical Reason* represents the most striking fruit of his intellectual odyssey, the structure and distinctive concerns of the *Critique* cannot be properly assessed without examining his original philosophy. It was on this basis that he formulated his critique of rationalism, his theory of "the Other," and his program for an "existential psychoanalysis"; and it was from these sources that he derived the most provocative, as well as the most problematic, aspects of his later social theory.

FREEDOM AS FOUNDATION AND PROBLEM

The touchstone of Sartre's original philosophizing lay in his concept of freedom. It was the freedom of others that enslaved Sartrean man; it was his own freedom that plunged that man into anguish; it was freedom that he fled; it was freedom that ultimately reduced his hopes for a stable identity to nothingness. His early defense of absolute ontological freedom would eventually force Sartre to a consideration of the social world — especially since the evidence of empirical social bondage seemed a persuasive argument against innate human freedom. Sartre's concept of freedom thus formed the key link between his early and later philosophy. If man was by nature free, why did he everywhere appear in chains?

Sartre originally asserted a pervasive human freedom in *Psychology of Imagination,* published in 1940. There he inquired into the conditions that made imagination as a phenomenon possible. If man existed totally immersed in a world that determined his every response, it was difficult to account for the origin and place of imagination, that human capacity for elaborating ideas not directly derived from the perception of existing objects. If man were free by nature, however, the grounds of imagination would be secured; and Sartre himself argued this case. "It is because he is transcendentally free that man can imagine."[1]

This line of argument, which Sartre elaborated in *Being and Nothingness,* derived from the rationalist and idealist traditions in modern philosophy. In his essay on imagination, he explicitly linked the problem of doubt with that of imagination, thus rejoining the Cartesian deduction of man's power of doubting from the primary datum of free will. The modern tradition inaugurated by Descartes had portrayed man as innately free, at least in his soul (or in the noumenal realm beyond empirical appearance). Simultaneously, however, thinkers within this tradition distinguished inner freedom from external necessity. In Kant's account, for example, while man always remained inwardly free, he was compelled to act in a phenomenal world governed by natural laws. Idealism thus tended to approach freedom both as an end yet to be empirically attained, as well as an innate endowment of the human spirit.

On several occasions, Sartre presented himself as the heir to this tradition. He tellingly praised Descartes for realizing that "to be free is not to be able to do what one wants, but to want what one can."[2] Indeed, he found many points of contact between existential phenomenology and the rationalist heritage; after all, had not Heidegger himself spoken of freedom as the "ground of all grounds"?[3] In claiming that man provided the grounds for his own behavior by freely assigning himself intentions and motives, Sartre adapted an amalgam of rationalist and Heideggerean positions. Nothing external made a man be what he was: rather, man's essential freedom forced human reality "*to make itself* instead of *to be*."[4]

Yet this synthesis threatened to rob the concept of freedom of its traditional force in criticizing unnecessary external constraints. In *Being and Nothingness,* Sartre defined consciousness, or the "for-itself" of human being, in terms of freedom and transcendence: in his consciousness and his action, the human being was inherently free. On this basis, he claimed that causes could only have an effect on action thanks to the meaning assigned them within a purposive plan devised by a conscious actor: "No factual state whatever it may be (the political and economic structure of society, the psychological 'state,' etc.) is capable by itself of motivating any act whatsoever."[5] The implications of this position were sometimes startling. For example, Sartre argued that a man remained free even when in chains — and not simply because any man was free by definition. Since the prisoner could always choose to accept his condition, according to Sartre, a free choice could always remove from the chains the significance of obstructing freedom. Of course, to note that the prisoner endowed his chains with an oppressive significance by thinking of escape did not mean that the prisoner *chose* these chains, or brought them into existence. Yet while he granted the independent existence of factual barriers to the expression of free will, Sartre minimized their importance, by emphasizing the role of a person's intentions in defining what counted as a barrier. In some passages of *Being and Nothingness,* he verged on an extreme form of subjective idealism: "Since human reality is act, it can be conceived only as being at its core a rupture with the given. It is the being which causes *there to be* a given by breaking with it and illuminating it in the light of the not yet existing."[6] Given such formulations, it is not surprising that by the end of *Being and Nothingness,* he was finding freedom everywhere.

Ironically, Sartre's greatest early contribution to the critique of rationalism stemmed precisely from his revision of the traditional notion of freedom. By finding freedom everywhere, he also uncovered the fear of freedom. Enlightenment rationalism and its German idealist executors had presumed that freedom formed an obvious human good, desired by all; it represented an end in itself. As Hegel put it, "Freedom is itself its own object of attainment and the sole purpose of Spirit. It is the ultimate purpose toward which all world history has continually aimed."[7] The contrast with Sartre's philosophy could hardly be more striking. Early in *Being and Nothingness,* Sartre described the consciousness of freedom as anguish: "In anguish I apprehend myself at once as totally free and as not being able to derive the meaning of the world except as coming from myself."[8] Far from being an unqualified good, freedom in Sartre's world imposed a crushing burden of responsibility. The attempt to escape from freedom, through what Sartre called "bad faith," thus became a central theme of *Being and Nothingness.*

In bad faith, the individual denied his inherent freedom and tried instead to act like a thing with a fixed and unchanging essence. To use his terms (borrowed from Hegel), the "for-itself" of human being aspired to the substance and unproblematic identity of the "in-itself" of nonconscious being. In fact, Sartre suggested that *every* man desired the self-sufficient transcendence which Hegel had attributed to God, the "absolute Being" of the "in-itself-for-itself": "The supreme value toward which consciousness at every instant surpasses itself by its very being is the absolute being of the self, with its characteristics of identity, of purity, of permanence, etc., and as its own foundation."[9]

Several avenues of flight from freedom were open to the individual in bad faith. The individual, as a "being-for-others," appeared in public as a personality with certain habitual traits: in the eyes of a friend, he *was* somebody, had a familiar past, and sustained a recognizable character. In a quest for stable identity, the individual in bad faith might therefore try to assume the fixed image others had of him. Values afforded another avenue of escape. By assigning a person a raison d'être, traditional religious and moral codes provided an impersonal standard to orient the individual's treadmill transcendence and to underwrite its significance. Finally, social institutions also offered a refuge from freedom, in the shape of social roles and functional involvement in collective projects. By playing out a role, the individual might fleetingly attain a "repose in self." But all these attempts at flight eventually had to fail. Consciousness for Sartre embraced the paradox of "being what it is not and not being what it is." Because it was defined by transcendence — and was thus inherently free — consciousness could never completely coincide with itself, as the individual in search of a fixed identity wished. As a result, "human reality" was "by its nature an unhappy consciousness with no possibility of surpassing its unhappy state."[10]

For Sartre, the desire for freedom thus became a problem rather than an assumption. As his accounts of man's flight from freedom indicate, he abandoned the supposition that freedom formed a self-evident end in itself. In bad faith, the individual freely attempted to alienate his own inalienable freedom. Yet even here, and despite his heterodoxy, Sartre ultimately remained true to the program of Enlightenment rationalism. While the willingness of man to accept fully his ineluctable freedom appeared problematical, Sartre never doubted that genuinely accepting responsibility for one's self, and acting consciously in freedom, represented the hallmarks of human beings beyond bad faith. For him, as for the rationalists, men only became truly human when they recognized, affirmed, and purposefully realized their own freedom.

AUTHENTICITY AND MAN'S SOCIAL SITUATION

Sartre approached the individual's genuine "self-recovery" and appropriation of freedom through the concept of authenticity, a term borrowed from Heidegger. In *Being and Time,* Heidegger used the word *authenticity (Eigentlichkeit)* to denote the recovery by a human being of its self as its own (*eigen*). Rather than losing itself in anonymous social roles, or falling heedlessly into the ephemeral interests of everyday life, a human being in authentically existing recalled its own transcendence, and how this transcendence imbued a world of factual entities with significance. In authentic resolve, the individual acknowledged the world given him as essentially his *own,* to be assimilated and made over through his *own* projects, his *own* choice among the possibilities contingently open to him.

Because Sartre objected to the ethical aura of the term in *Being and Time,* as well as to Heidegger's focus on death as the most unique possibility of a person, the concept of authenticity did not play a prominent role in *Being and Nothingness.* Yet the notion nonetheless assumed some importance in Sartre's account as a marginal concept. At the conclusion of his analysis of bad faith, he remarked in a footnote that "it is indifferent whether one is in good or bad faith; because bad faith reapprehends good faith and slides to the very origin of the project of good faith, that does not mean that we cannot radically escape bad faith. But this presupposes a self-recovery of being which was previously corrupted. This self-recovery we shall call authenticity, the description of which has no place here."[11]

Despite this disclaimer, *Being and Nothingness* did provide some clues as to what an authentic "self-recovery of being" might involve for Sartre. Two complementary components of being appeared crucial to such a "self-recovery." On the one hand, since the individual existed in a world populated by other people, he encountered interpretations by other people of his behavior, present and past; such interpretations comprised a public persona the individual could never wholly ignore or disown. On the other hand, the individual maintained this public self only by freely choosing it; his social persona never subsisted as an immutable datum, like the qualities of a rock.

These two aspects of Sartrean selfhood suggested that any authentic "self-recovery of being" had to affirm the individual's being someone, as well as his being free. The individual had to assume freely what he was in the mode of not being "it." As Sartre expressed the thought, "I can neither abstain totally in relation to what I am (for the Other)—for to *refuse* is not to abstain but still to assume—nor can I submit to it passively (which in a sense amounts to the same thing). Whether in fury, hate, pride, shame, disheartened refusal or joyous demand, it is necessary for me to choose to be what I am."[12] Any such choice involved a "project of myself toward the future," so that for Sartre, as for Heidegger, the self-recovery of a human being as transcendence was oriented toward the future. Authenticity thus entailed a fundamental choice of being—a way of being that neither fled the subject's freedom, its past, or its being-for-others.

Sartre's main discussion of authenticity occurred not in *Being and Nothingness,* but in an essay on the Jewish question published in 1946. Even here, Sartre only outlined the concept briefly. "If it is agreed that man may be defined as a being having freedom within the limits of a situation, then it is easy to see that the exercise of this freedom may be considered as *authentic* or *inauthentic* according to the choices made in the situation. Authenticity, it is almost needless to say, consists in having a true and lucid consciousness of the situation, in assuming the responsibility and risks that it involves, in accepting it in pride or humiliation, sometimes in horror."[13]

Such a concept of authenticity implied the possibility of distinguishing authentic from inauthentic choices made within a social situation. An "authentic" choice would somehow evince a "clear and lucid consciousness" of the social situation, although how an authentic choice might so distinguish itself remained ambiguous. But an individual's lucid recognition of his social situation might not be accompanied by a recognition of his freedom, or of his past; since authenticity for Sartre apparently depended on a recognition of the subject's freedom *and* its past *and* its being-for-others (its social situation), authenticity could not be attributed to the individual solely on the basis of a "clear and lucid" recognition of his social situation. Moreover, he failed to offer any hints as to what recognition might entail in this context, apart from a purely subjective witness.

Such difficulties cast considerable doubt on any declaration of authentic behavior. Yet the concept retained a certain measure of plausibility in Sartre's hands, since far fewer problems attended the identification of inauthenticity. Here, one had only to show that an individual was *not* recognizing either his freedom *or* his past *or* his being-for-others; failure and flight in any one area sufficed for a verdict of inauthenticity. Although even such negative assessments were tricky, Sartre proceeded in his essay to construct a brilliant and nuanced argument about the patterns of Jewish behavior in the face of anti-Semitism. The subtlety of his essay did not, however, resolve the difficulties surrounding its central critical concept.

Although Sartre's concept of authenticity faced grave problems in its empirical application, the real value of the concept might lie in the ethical realm: perhaps Sartrean authenticity was best understood as a prescription for action, rather than an analytic tool. He hinted at such an ethical application in the 1946 essay, when he wrote that "the choice of authenticity appears to be a *moral* decision."[14] He made this claim with the knowledge that authenticity could not be considered a political or social decision, inasmuch as his own essay revealed a lack of specific political or social content pertinent to the choice of authenticity—a lack of content recalling Kant's formalization of morality through the categorical imperative. Indeed, if authenticity could be considered a moral concept, then it had to be one of uttermost inwardness, all talk of "social situations" to the contrary. While authenticity enjoined the subject from certain modes of behavior, on Sartre's own admission it did not prescribe any specific alternative course of action. But this meant that, even speaking ethically, he lacked concrete criteria for prescribing as well as identifying authentic acts.

Despite the difficulties surrounding the concept, the notion of authenticity fulfilled a critical function in Sartre's thought. His early writing approached freedom as a problematic endowment to be "worked through" and struggled with, rather than simply taken for granted as a desirable good; the notions of authenticity and inauthenticity tried to clarify the terms of this struggle, by critically classifying the various modes of fleeing as well as facing freedom. In elaborating these concepts, Sartre was also forced to reconsider the relation of social existence to freedom. Once again, his philosophy encountered the social realm through its own immanent exposition.

His descriptions of authentic behavior repeatedly suggested that the individual's past and publicly recognized self situated the individual's freedom. Yet this tendency in Sartre's thinking seemed to contradict the claims of absolute freedom defended in *Being and Nothingness*. To be sure, even in his essay on the Jewish question, he spoke of anti-Semitism as a "free and total" choice of oneself. On the other hand, *Being and Nothingness* had already contained passing references to the indissolubility of constraints in the external world: the *"fact* of my condition . . . is what causes the for-itself, while choosing the *meaning* of its situation and while constituting itself as the foundation of itself in a situation, *not to choose* its position."[15] Sartre's two tendencies were incompatible. Either the individual made a "free and total choice" that "caused there to be given" reality, or the individual faced a *limited* choice among possibilities forced upon him by his situation.

In his essay on the Jewish question, Sartre undertook a preliminary clarification, by restating his concept of "situation."

For us, man is defined first of all as a being 'in a situation.' That means that he forms a synthetic whole with his situation—biological, economic, political, cultural, etc. He cannot be distinguished from his situation, for it forms him and decides his possibilities; but, inversely, it is he who gives it meaning by making his choices within it and by it. To be in a situation, as we see it, is *to choose oneself* in a situation, and men differ from one another in their situation and also in the choices they themselves make of themselves. What men have in common is not a 'nature,' but a condition, that is, an ensemble of limits and restrictions: the inevitability of death, the necessity of working for a living, of living in a world inhabited by other men.[16]

This account implied a modification of Sartre's previous position. If he was to reconcile successfully the two tendencies of his thought, he had to moderate his doctrine of freedom sufficiently to admit a moment of passivity into consciousness and the for-itself: the voluntary had to accommodate the involuntary. Naturally, any such accommodation would compromise the radical ontology of freedom that dominated *Being and Nothingness,* unless Sartre could somehow derive the dependency of the for-itself from the free acts of that for-itself. The *Critique of Dialectical Reason* in fact attempted just such an ontological derivation. But in the meantime, his developing social thought was left to oscillate uneasily between admissions of situational dependency and assertions of absolute freedom. This was the ambiguous orientation Sartre brought to Marxism.

REVOLUTION AND TRANSCENDENCE

According to Simone de Beauvoir, Sartre evinced a sympathy for the oppressed long before he actively adopted any form of radical politics. Even such early works as *Being and Nothingness* contained passages on the proletariat marked by indignation, if not Marxist theory. But Sartre's explicit commitment to a socialist politics developed only gradually, as did his interest in Marxist philosophy. His ontology of freedom, as well as his experiences with the Resistance during World War II at first led him to maintain a politically ambiguous philosophy of engagement in the immediate postwar period. Based on the notion of man as perpetual free action, his primary political strictures centered around the view that a humane politics should maximize individual liberty. Only a democratic order could allow man to express fully his intrinsic freedom.

His role in *Les Temps modernes* brought him into close contact with postwar French political arguments. These debates, conducted at first in a hopeful atmosphere of open possibilities, encouraged optimism among the noncommunist left, at least until the onset of the cold war helped dash the aspirations of independent radicals like himself. By making the strategic position of noncommunist leftists virtually untenable, the cold war cast a pall over independent left-wing political thought. In a situation of oppressive adversity, a realistic politics seemed to force a choice either for or against Communism—but surely nothing in between. Nevertheless, in 1948 Sartre helped found the one political party he has unconditionally supported, a short-lived grouping of democratic leftists called the Rassemblement Democratique Revolutionnaire; at the time, he wrote that "our aim is the integration of the free individual in a society conceived as the unity of the free activity of individuals."[17] Both Sartre and Albert Camus contributed to the party's journal, *La Gauche,* but by 1949 the Rassemblement had collapsed for lack of popular support.

The dissolution of the Rassemblement, coupled with the outbreak of the Korean War, inaugurated Sartre's drift toward the French Communist Party. Although he never joined the party, he did for a while become one of its most outspoken fellow travelers. By 1952, he was arguing the need to support Communist policies, since the party represented the only viable vehicle of revolutionary practice in a period of cold war. Nevertheless, Sartre claimed the right to support the party for his reasons rather than theirs, and at no point did he ratify the party's sanctioned version of dialectical materialism. As a result, the Communists remained cool toward Sartre.

After Russia crushed the Hungarian uprising of 1956, Sartre assumed an increasingly critical stance toward institutionalized communism, although he steadfastly refused to embrace any form of anticommunism. He was one of the first prominent European intellectuals to speak out strongly against European colonialism, and during the sixties he bestowed his sympathies on the various new left groups dotting the French political landscape. But through it all, he reserved for himself a critical distance, the final luxury, perhaps, of the self-consciously *declassé* intellectual.

Sartre's attitude toward Marxism as a social philosophy can be separated into two phases. In the first, prior to 1950, he attacked Marxism while generally exempting Marx himself from his critique; in the second, he associated Marxism with his own reading of Marx and declared that *this* Marxism possessed a vantage point superior to all other current forms of philosophy. At no point, however, did he drastically modify his own basic outlook on human existence; indeed, his original criticisms of (orthodox) Marxism became the basis of his own (existential) version. The difference lay in his attempt, after 1950, to rescue what he found true in Marxism by suggesting what it *ought* to be—an attempt that culminated in his *Critique of Dialectical Reason.*

Sartre's first important essay on Marxism was "Materialism and Revolution," an attack on orthodox Marxism from the perspective of existentialism. Published in 1946 in *Les Temps modernes,* this essay outlined his objections to philosophical materialism—objections never withdrawn. He focused his criticism on crude materialism, which he took to embrace three central claims: neither God nor any other form of transcendence existed; mind could be reduced to matter; and the world, including subjectivity, could be reduced to a system of objects connected by universal law-governed relationships. Sartre pointed out that these materialist theses involved a metaphysic, despite claims to the contrary by orthodox Marxists. The main trouble with this materialist metaphysic, at least as a philosophy of revolution, was its inconsistency with the phenomenon of revolutionary action itself: philosophical materialism could not properly interpret revolutionary behavior.

Dialectical materialism ascribed the development of revolution to a state of the world; yet it failed to explain how a revolutionary transcendence of a given social order could possibly emerge from a state of things. A revolution represented a movement of *human* transcendence, aiming purposefully beyond a given social situation toward another end, that of the classless society, for instance. Things themselves, Sartre argued, could never intend or accomplish such a teleological end; only human beings could bring transcendence, a meaningful project, and the leverage of freedom to the world of things.

Only men, not things, could comprise a revolutionary transcendence. As Sartre dryly remarked, "A state of the world will never be able to produce class consciousness."[18] Insofar as Marxism embraced philosophical materialism as its ideology, it became a contradiction in action, a theory unable to account for its own practice.

Sartre concluded that revolutionaries should abandon materialism in favor of a "philosophy of transcendence." Only such a philosophy could correctly interpret revolutionary practice, which displaced the reigning "society of laws" by a "community of ends." A revolutionary philosophy of freedom would meet the following requirements: (1) show that men laid the contingent foundation of all transcendent values; (2) assume that any set of values could be overthrown in favor of new values; (3) illuminate how any set of values formed part of a social order and tended to preserve it; (4) suggest that any social order was mutable, even if the expression of new values had to be invented in practice, through the very effort of transcending given values.[19] In all these particulars, Sartre suggested that his own existentialism just might be the philosophy to replace a discredited materialism.

As he made clear, adopting a philosophy of transcendence as the foundation of revolutionary theory entailed an abandonment of causal thinking. He drove this point home by examining the labor process. If the worker "discovers the relation between cause and effect," he argued, "it is not by submitting to it, but in the very act which transcends the material state...toward a certain end which illuminates and defines this state from within the future."[20] At the level of human affairs, causality was subsumed under freedom, for it was the free project which illuminated the law-governed nature of the world. The revolutionary dynamic of history similarly resided, not in laws of nature, but in human transcendence. Sartre never surrendered this perspective. As he argued in the *Critique of Dialectical Reason,* dialectic is not a determinism.

THE WILL TO REVOLUTION

In opposition to deterministic explanations of revolutionary behavior, Sartre offered his own interpretation of the genesis of revolutionary practice. His alternative account first appeared in *Being and Nothingness,* in the context of his discussion of freedom. He there tried to show that the individual's relation to his historical environment was precisely the opposite of that usually assumed by materialism. Taking the worker's experience of hardship as his example, he argued that such suffering, far from causing indignation, was only meaningfully established qua suffering through the worker's free projection of an alternative way of life, beyond hardship. To be sure, from the standpoint of the present historical situation, hardship was an inherent aspect of the worker's existence, rather than a contingent misfortune that could be ignored. But the *intolerability* of such suffering only appeared in the light of a project aimed at changing this situation.

"Materialism and Revolution" expanded this interpretation of revolutionary action, although Sartre insisted more strongly than before on the objective, situational components that defined a revolutionary. According to him, a revolutionary had to be a worker who was oppressed by a dominant class; still, such social attributes remained insufficient in themselves to make anyone a revolutionary. Rather, a revolutionary was always characterized in addition by his "*going beyond* the situation in which he is placed," toward a "radically new situation"; the revolutionary comprehended his situation as mutable precisely through his project for the future.[21]

The truth of Sartre's point concerned the teleological character of practice: any attempt to reshape the world always involves a meaningful project, irreducible to antecedent conditions. But his doctrine of freedom complicated the argument. In *Being and Nothingness,* he often implied that being anything—a revolutionary or a waiter—not only involved transcendence, but also could be *reduced* to transcendence; "being a revolutionary" would then involve a freely assumed attitude. In "Materialism and Revolution," he countered this implicit bias by stating explicitly that freedom, properly grasped, merely provided a "necessary condition" of intentional action.[22] Without some such proviso, revolutionary practice would resemble a pure act dictated by conscience, rather than a creative but objectively circumscribed response to a given social situation.

Sartre, however, was not entirely consistent in elaborating a social theory and his own version of Marxism. In *The Communists and the Peace,* originally published as a series of essays in *Les Temps modernes* between 1952 and 1954, he apotheosized "the act" and "praxis" as the tangible signs of human freedom. In these articles, he defended his decision to support the Communist Party, claiming it was the only realistic vehicle of French working-class aspirations. Simultaneously, he tried to buttress this political position with his own philosophical arguments. The idiosyncratic result satisfied neither the Communists nor the independent left—and with good reason.

According to Sartre in *The Communists and Peace,* refusal—a negation of the given reality—stood at the core of all revolutionary behavior. The worker's "human reality is. . . not *in what he is,* but *in his refusal to be such.*" Sartre linked this refusal to a projectively oriented revolutionary élan, "which postulates [its] ends all at once in order to call for their immediate realization."[23] These theses, familiar from *Being and Nothingness,* now came to define Marxism according to Sartre's version. The meaning of communism for him became, as Merleau-Ponty accurately described it, "the categorical will to bring into being what never was."[24] In his own works, Merleau-Ponty insisted upon the relative permanence of institutions and social conventions; the individual's choice of action did not spring purely from the future, but also—and perhaps even more importantly—gestated in a personal and social past. Sartre by contrast spoke primarily of refusal, rupture, and violence; he abandoned the Marxian/Hegelian synthesis of realism and idealism in favor of the subjective gesture of defiance, which constituted the Sartrean revolutionary.

For this philosophy, action became the touchstone of human freedom, the forceable evidence of transcendence. The individual's action ratified his decisions and committed him to his choices. The Sartrean act indeed assumed the dimensions of an absolute: "Everything which is *praxis* is real" exulted Sartre at one point in *The Communists and Peace.* But action also fulfilled more mundane functions in his world; for example, through action the worker came to believe in the communist project: "Action is in and of itself a kind of confidence." Sartre's worker "*does not decide* to act, he acts, he *is* action."[25] In this perpetual practice and restless freedom, Sartre discovered the image of proletarian upheaval.

IN PRAISE OF LENINISM

So far, *The Communists and Peace* might merely seem an extreme paean to human freedom and subjective volition, little different from earlier Sartrean fare. But Sartre's essay also attempted to harness his existential philosophy of freedom to claims of Communist political supremacy. It was a curious spectacle.

Indeed, what really distinguished his argument was the deceptive ease with which he banished by one assertion what he seemed to grant with another. Thus he refused the individual worker any genuine capacity to choose freely the "right" transcendent project (communism), even while claiming that the essence of the revolutionary act resided in a free choice. The worker's social situation at one point was declared powerless to motivate the worker in any way; at another point it virtually consumed the worker's own initiative. Although Sartrean freedom, as an ontological structure of human being, might have been thought inalienable, in *The Communists and Peace* Sartre suddenly discovered the social alienation of freedom. Clearly, his new apologetics faced several theoretical difficulties, centering on the relationship between ontological freedom and the limits imposed, on consciousness as well as on action, by a person's social situation.

Presumably Sartre was speaking about a factual circumstance when he wrote that "the historical whole determines our powers at any given moment, it prescribes their limits in our field of action and our *real* future; it conditions our attitude toward the possible and the impossible, the real and the imaginary, what is and what should be, time and space. From there on, we in turn determine our relationship with others, that is to say the meaning of our life and the value of our death...."[26] Yet the situational bounding and determination of human action described in this passage conflicted with the claims of freedom and refusal found elsewhere in *The Communists and Peace*. Even more clearly than Sartre's essay on anti-Semitism, this work displayed a barely contained tension between assertions of ontological freedom and descriptions of factual unfreedom. Could it be that Sartrean man freely chose his own social bondage? Sartre himself at one point seemed willing to argue as much; when the worker "makes himself [N.B.] the agent of production, he feels himself acted upon; in the depths of his subjectivity, he experiences himself as an object.... He takes refuge in passivity because he has been deprived of all [N.B.] initiative."[27]

This statement, proffered in support of a Leninist version of Marxist politics, was extraordinary coming from Sartre. After a career of ferreting out freedom in every nook and cranny of human endeavor, he apparently found no great contradiction in asserting that "the masses are the object of history; they never act by themselves. . . ."[28] The political conclusion was inescapable. If the working class could not attain its own freedom, it had to be led to it: by the Communist Party, of course. "The inertia of the masses . . . is such that movement comes to them from outside."[29] Moreover, only working-class confidence in the party's leaders could assure the proletariat of "coherence and power."[30] How could it be otherwise? Especially when Sartre declared that "all objective structures of the social world present themselves as an initial confusion to the worker's subjectivity."[31] The end result was an odd amalgam of existentialism and Leninism that raised more questions than it answered.

In *The Communists and Peace,* Sartre reduced the proletariat to a passive objectivity, a precipitate reduction that his own thought should have warned him against. At one point he remarked that "the proletariat as subjective experience is identical [N.B.] with the process of production unwinding in the ideal milieu of subjectivity."[32] Yet *Being and Nothingness* had denied the very possibility of so identifying objectivity and subjectivity. While *The Communists and Peace* quite legitimately attempted to incorporate the experience of subjective dependency and inertia into Sartre's thought — a crucial extension if he was to make any philosophical sense out of Marxism — the work's involved argument, now asserting ontological freedom, now claiming social dependency, served as a cover for bad philosophy and bad politics. The evidence of Communist brutality in the Hungarian revolt of 1956 soon turned Sartre away from apologies for institutionalized communism. But *The Communists and Peace* remains his unique contribution to that strain of Marxian literature which lumps together the proletariat, the Communist Party, and the party's leaders in One Big Happy Family: Father knows best.

Although Sartre's early Marxism left a host of philosophical issues unresolved, *The Communists and Peace* reaffirmed the ontological primacy of human freedom, even as it portrayed an objective human realm with the power to eclipse human freedom. As he wrote at the time, "Intentions without consciousness, actions without subjects, human relationships without men, participating at once in material necessity and finality: such are generally our undertakings when they develop freely in the dimension of objectivity."

He now faced the prospect of squaring such observations of unfreedom with his assumptions about the freedom innate in being human.

He had several options. He could have consistently claimed that social unfreedom was itself freely chosen by the individual; while there seemed to be some warrant for this move in his previous account of bad faith, it was not the kind of argument he could rest content with. Then again, he could have dropped one pole of his thought, either the ontological or the social; yet abandoning one aspect would have spelled the ruin of Sartrean ontology, or the collapse of Sartrean social theory — neither a palatable prospect. A more arresting option lay in a systematic attempt at reconciliation, consisting of a demonstration that the ontological freedom of human beings constituted contingent social arrangements that, once fixed, factually limited the freedom of human beings. Human freedom itself would then be revealed as the ontological foundation of human unfreedom. This approach to the problem could also claim the dignity of elaborating Marx's own implied resolution of the dilemma.

EXISTENTIALISM AND MARXISM

Sartre approached the *Critique of Dialectical Reason* from two interrelated but distinct perspectives. On the one hand, his philosophy of absolute ontological freedom had in some manner to accommodate the fact of social unfreedom. On the other, orthodox Marxism in his eyes labored under an unsupportable doctrine of philosophical materialism; Marxism itself had to be restored to its true roots in a dialectic which incorporated human agency as its ineliminable basis.

In 1957, responding to an invitation from a Polish review, Sartre published an essay on "Existentialism and Marxism," later titled *Questions de méthode* (*Search for a Method* in the American translation), and eventually reprinted as the first part of the *Critique*. This concise and provocative essay clarified Sartre's intentions as thoroughly as the 600-odd pages of the *Critique* obscured them. It also introduced his thematic reflections on Marx as a thinker, a topic his earlier polemics had largely avoided.

In *Search for a Method* he argued that Marx should properly be seen as the true successor to Kierkegaard as well as Hegel. Hegel had correctly presented the totality of human Spirit as forming the coherent context and ultimate reference point of human meaning; unfortunately, Hegel had conflated this insight with the notion of an infinite Absolute Spirit (i.e., God), and had falsely promised an ultimate reconciliation of knowing and being at the end of history. Kierkegaard by contrast properly insisted on the individual living person as the ultimate source of all transcendent meaning, which in any case could never assuage the suffering, pain, and finitude inseparable from individual existence. Unfortunately, where Hegel's thought evaporated in a universal infinite Spirit, Kierkegaard's compressed into an ineffable subjectivity. If Kierkegaard reinstated the perpetual incommensurability of knowledge and being, Hegel just as surely established the dependence of human intelligibility on objectivity.

According to Sartre's interpretation, Marx had resolved the Hegelian/Kierkegaardian antinomies. While Marx agreed with Hegel that human beings were essentially objectifying, *objective* and social, he also agreed with Kierkegaard that this objectivity could never surpass incarnate subjectivity and the real individual at the base of a still incomplete yet universal history.[33] Unfortunately, latter-day Marxism had fallen away from Marx's original synthesis. The subjective pole had been abandoned in favor of the false idol of a purely natural dialectic. But this fall suggested that Marxism required restatement, especially to the extent that Marx himself had become implicated in the objectivistic misunderstanding.[34]

Because it represented the living conscience of Marxism's suppressed subjective pole, existentialism maintained its philosophical rights independently of Marxism, at least for the time being. But the contemporary task of existentialism lay in dissolving itself as a particular philosophy. Since Marxism, properly understood, was "the unsurpassable framework of knowledge" for our time, existentialism ought merely to amend Marxism, and recall it to its original intentions. An existentially refounded Marxism would provide a viable "theory of consciousness," and ground Marxism in a dialectic of living, sentient individuals.[35]

The first of these aims Sartre accomplished by importing his own theory of consciousness into Marxism via the interpretation of praxis. Praxis he understood as the general process of human action, including the labor process; it involved the exteriorization of subjective meanings through projects, as well as the interiorization of objective conditions through situations. Consciousness and transcendence were essential to praxis: "In relation to the given, *praxis* is negativity. . . . In relation to the object aimed at, *praxis* is positivity, but this positivity opens onto the 'non-existent,' to what *has not yet* been. A flight and a leap ahead, at once a refusal and a realization, the project retains and unveils the surpassed reality which is refused by the very movement which surpassed it. Thus knowing is a moment of *praxis,* even its most fundamental one."[36]

Sartre's other task proved more formidable. Given his interpretation, Marxism had to be rigorously reconstructed as a "dialectical nominalism" if Marx's claim that history always represented the collective interaction of real individuals was to be taken seriously. Calling Marxism a "dialectical nominalism" indicated that the social whole only subsisted through a multiplicity of "totalizing singularities," or individuals engaged in specific meaningful projects.[37] "There is then no ontologically communal *praxis:* there are practical individuals who construe their multiplicity as an object starting from which each fulfills his task in the freely consented heterogeneity of the communal function, i.e., by totalization-in-course."[38] For Sartre, "The only practical and dialectical reality, the motor of the whole, is *individual action.*"[39]

THE PHENOMENOLOGY OF THE SOCIAL WORLD AND THE PROBLEM OF "THE OTHER"

Sartre's point of departure in the *Critique* was thus the individual. As he put it in *Being and Nothingness,* "The sole point of departure is the interiority of the *cogito.* We must understand by this that each one must be able by starting out from his own interiority, to rediscover the Other's being as a transcendence which conditions the very being of that interiority."[40] The whole of existential phenomenology pointed toward subjectivity as the fulcrum of logic, meaning, and, ultimately, science; Sartre's aim in the *Critique* was the disclosure of a similarly founding role for subjectivity in the specifically social realm. He thus set out to derive the objective social order, and its evident unfreedom, from the subjective individual order, and its primordial freedom. Setting out from consciousness, existential social thought took as its object "life," the objective being of the subject in a world; from this starting point, the subject's own understanding "must lead to the denial of its singular determination in favor of a search for its dialectical intelligibility in the whole human adventure."[41] In other words, a comprehensible path had to link the conscious individual to transindividual social structures that in effect constrained and limited the individual.

Tracing this path would comprise nothing less than a phenomenology of the social world, where phenomenology was understood simultaneously in its Husserlian and Hegelian senses: Husserlian, because Sartre's method supposedly remained immanent and descriptive; Hegelian, because Sartre's method supposedly proceeded historically and dialectically. Like Hegel, Sartre equated science with the genetic totality disclosed at the end of phenomenology; however, his basic point about this genetic totality remained Husserlian: science had to account for its own existence, which (for Sartre as for Husserl) ultimately led philosophy back to the *cogito* and conscious life.

Unfortunately, Sartre's social phenomenology faced a tough hurdle from the outset, namely, how to cope with "the Other," as he labeled fellow human beings. In *Being and Nothingness,* he had criticized Hegel, Husserl, and Heidegger for mistaking the nature of our "being-for-others." Sartre himself used the "look" as his descriptive key for approaching the experience of another person. When another person glanced at an individual, the latter could feel his "being-an-object" under the other's gaze. The basis of this being-as-object, however, lay in the individual's apprehension of the other person in his being-as-subject: "Through the look I experience the Other concretely as a free, conscious subject." On the other hand, any direct confrontation with the other person immediately dissolves his subjectivity under the individual's own gaze, which now grasps the Other as an object. Sartre thus implied that another person could only be experienced obliquely, through the individual's sense of "being-an-object" for another. While other people incontrovertibly *existed,* the respective meanings two people projected upon one another could never be reconciled through mutual recognition. Instead, the one's freedom ratified the other's alienation, and vice versa. It was no wonder, then, that Sartre proclaimed conflict to be "the original meaning of being-for-others." As he confided elsewhere in *Being and Nothingness,* "We can consider ourselves as 'slaves' in so far as we appear to the Other."[42]

In his early Marxist essays, such as *The Communists and Peace,* Sartre used this concept of the Other to analyze class struggle. Since the worker, from his first day of labor, was beholden to the Other as a hostile power which exploited him, the Other (presumably the bourgeois Other) precipitated the worker's revolutionary will. As Sartre put it, the worker "cannot 'restructure' his work without putting down at once the desire to seize power from the Other."[43] While some of Sartre's notions appeared compatible with Marxism—he did insist on the primacy of class conflict, after all—Marx himself had never placed an insurmountable conflict between individuals at the heart of history. For one thing, Marx spoke of *social* and institutional conflicts; for another, Marx attempted to expose these conflicts as transitory. Moreover, Sartre's manner of rephrasing Marxism left unresolved such questions as the possibility of genuinely cooperative action and the feasibility of communal freedom. As Alfred Schutz once remarked, apropos of *Being and Nothingness,* "Mutual interaction in freedom has no place within Sartre's philosophy."[44] Indeed, it is hard to see how a social philosophy premised on a model of incessant interpersonal conflict could ever adequately account for such an important social phenomenon as trust.

At first glance, the *Critique* seemed to modify Sartre's outlook on sociability significantly. Conflict no longer was presented as an ontological given, and social units were no longer portrayed as phenomena marginal to individual action. Instead, Sartre introduced the notion of social being from the outset, by describing a spectator who observed two men working together. Such a third party ascribed an objective meaning to the acts of these men; through the meaningful relationship he established between them, the third party also constituted these subjects as a coherent social unit, at least in his own interpretation. Social being was thus depicted as an essential human possibility. Given Sartre's professed admiration for Marx, it no longer seemed absurd to hope for an eventual reconciliation of conflicting claims among individuals and classes.

Yet a closer look at the *Critique* raises doubts about these apparent modifications in Sartre's outlook. Despite a metamorphosis of language, the *Critique* betrays a fundamental continuity with *Being and Nothingness* in its concerns and concepts. Starting from the individual and his praxis, Sartre incorporated his earlier use of "the project" to define human action. Where ontological nothingness sired the project, empirical needs such as hunger engendered praxis; in both cases, a lack compelled the human subject to act. In Sartre's present account, man (the for-itself), through praxis (the project), conferred meaning on the "inert," as nonconscious being (the in-itself) was sometimes referred to in the *Critique*.

But what, then, had become of the interpersonal conflict he had previously found at the core of the human condition? The answer seems to be that he translated the outlook of his earlier ontology into a new, sociological vocabulary. Thus conflict, banished as an onto-logical given, returned as man's fate, the inevitable result of mate-rial scarcity. In the *Critique,* Sartre found scarcity at the heart of human endeavor in history. Unfortunately, if there existed a scar-city of resources essential for human survival, then every man became a potential enemy, capable of limiting the possibilities of another. As Sartre put it, "Scarcity realizes the passive totality of the individuals within a collectivity as an impossibility of coexistence."[45] Pending a revolutionary transformation—and the final subjection of nature—any social order had to contend with the prospect of a primordial war of each against all. Through the category of scar-city, Sartre thus supplied a factual foundation for his earlier onto-logical vision of hell as other people.

To be sure, scarcity did not preclude the possibility of genuine community: but it did render precarious the preservation of any such community. It is also worth recalling that Sartre had already admitted the possibility of a genuine community in *Being and Noth-ingness*. There the "We-subject" (a group of individuals cooperating to realize some common project) was revealed on the basis of an "Us-object" (a collection of individuals observed by a spectator). Indeed, he argued that a "We-subject" was effectively forged *only* in the cru-cible of class conflict: in such a situation, a collection of individuals might be impelled to take over their previously established status as an "Us-object" for some Other group. Thus, "The primary fact is that the member of the oppressed collectivity . . . apprehends his condition and that of other members of this collectivity as looked-at and thought about by consciousnesses which escape him. . . . The oppressed class finds its class unity in the knowledge which the oppressing class has of it, and the appearance among the oppressed of class consciousness corresponds to the assumption in shame of an Us-object."[46]

Sartre followed a similar line of argument in the early pages of the *Critique,* moving from the being-for-others suggested by individual praxis driven by need, to the being-with-others suggested by warlike competition over scarce resources, to the Us-object suggested by the spectator's gaze that initially constituted a social unit. The implications of these parallels with *Being and Nothingness* become even clearer when Sartre's classification of social forms in the *Critique* is considered.

HUMAN COLLECTIVITIES:
FROM THE GROUP TO THE SERIES

The *Critique* described two fundamentally different types of human ensemble. One Sartre called the "series," a term designating a lump sum of objects, each interchangeable with the other, interrelated through a negative bond of reciprocal indifference: in short, an atomistic assemblage of sovereign Sartrean egos. The other type of collective he called the "group," a genuine unity of subjective wills bound together by common interest and a common project. The relative importance of these two fundamental types of ensemble proved asymmetric: "The group carries a destiny of seriality from the moment of its practical totalization."[47]

The bulk of the *Critique* was devoted to analyzing the permutations and combinations of the group and series, borrowing concepts and illustrations from sources as diverse as Georges Lefebvre and Robert Michels. Sartre's main sociological points about the group and series were simple enough. The genuine "We-subject"—the group capable of acting in concert and forging individuals into a social unity expressive of real subjective freedom within the group— was an historical anomaly that briefly fluttered across the stage of history, only to collapse in the wings, exhausted. In its wake—and without going into all the intermediary social structures conceivable —arose that indifferent conjunction of hostile egos Sartre called "seriality." He expended a great deal of subtlety and space classifying the various intermediary forms, ranging from the "pledged group" (what the "group-in-fusion" — the authentic group — became when its spontaneous action was formalized through conscious promises, pledges, laws, mutual terror, and so forth) to the "institutionalized apparatus" (what the pledged group became when its original common action evaporated, leaving behind a skeleton of promises, pledges, laws, and other structural bric-a-brac).

According to Sartre, the group-in-fusion, his term in the *Critique* for an authentic "We-subject," only arose at times of *haute temperature historique,* such as the storming of the Bastille, to take his own example. But what (if any) prior conditions attended the formation of the group-in-fusion? "In order for the city or sections [of Paris] to make of themselves a totalising totality [i.e., a group] — when the same realities [such as hunger and exploitation] are lived as 'collective' [i.e., serially endured] under other circumstances — it is necessary that they [the city or sections] be constituted as such [as a group] by the external action of another organized group."[48] In other words, an "Us-object" logically preceded the "We-subject"; or, to use the terminology of the *Critique,* a "third party" unified the multiplicity of individuals into a group. Moreover, as Sartre's own example suggests, the most intense articulation of community occurred only through an awareness of mutual animosity and conflict. Now this description certainly captures an essential aspect of group action in revolutionary situations: most of Sartre's points had been anticipated by Georges Lefebvre, the great historian of the French Revolution. Relating real or imaginary threats to the ebb and flow of the Revolution, Lefebvre interpreted the latter as a series of "defensive reactions." Both Lefebvre and Sartre underlined the centrality of fear and terror in revolutionary group action.[49]

But the group-in-fusion functioned as something more than an analytic category in the *Critique.* It also functioned as an archetype of social freedom: as Sartre put it, "The essential character of the group-in-fusion is the abrupt resurrection of liberty." In this context, Sartre's category raises some questions. Is it reasonable to erect the action of revolutionary groups in a civil war as the sole paradigm of communal freedom? Is it accurate to imply that communal freedom can only flow from social conflict? If conflict is the precondition of true community, what can we anticipate if the abolition of scarcity eliminates conflict? Further questions are raised by Sartre's discussion of anti-Semitism fourteen years earlier. There, he had used remarkably similar language to make a contrary point about groups fused in the crucible of crisis. Because the anti-Semite is "incapable of understanding modern social organization, he has a nostalgia for periods of crisis, in which the primitive community will suddenly reappear and attain its temperature of fusion. He wants his personality to melt suddenly into the group and be carried away by the collective torrent."[50]

In the *Critique,* however, Sartre discounted the potential for irrational submission in group action. Instead, he claimed that rationality was a possibility open to the individual or to the group-in-fusion, but not to any other social forms. Seriality by contrast was "anti-dialectical" and a frustration of praxis; since he identified praxis with human reason in the *Critique,* seriality also appeared "anti-rational." Alienation, pervasive in the serial collectivity, vanished in the group-in-fusion. There "alienation is only an appearance; my action is developed starting from a *common power* toward a *common objective;* the fundamental moment which characterizes the actualization of power and the objectivization of *praxis* is that of individual free practice. But it determines itself as ephemeral mediation between the common power and the common objective; through *being realized in the object,* not only does it annul itself as organic action to the profit of common objectivation in the process of accomplishment, but this annulment-towards-the-objective also lets it *discover common praxis.*"[51] In the group-in-fusion, the individual's free action contributes to the common cause desired by each member, in such a fashion that the will of each comes to coincide with the general will. No individual therefore really sacrifices any personal freedom to the social whole: this seemed to be Sartre's Rousseauean contention. The group-in-fusion here served as his utopian social vision.

But Sartre's was a utopianism fraught with tragic overtones, for the group-in-fusion represented an unstable historical moment, an evanescent social form. Born of crisis, the group was destined to decay with its passing. Just as *Being and Nothingness* held out dim prospects for the peaceful coexistence of free individuals, so the *Critique* left little hope for free groups surviving in mutual harmony. In both cases, conflict appeared as the ineliminable complement of authentic freedom.

THE PHENOMENON OF SOCIAL NECESSITY

If the group-in-fusion formed Sartre's revolutionary paradigm of collective transcendence, the series, in its role as "anti-dialectic," epitomized society as "second nature." His analysis of the series thus came to represent his primary approach to the phenomenon of social necessity. In the end, he hoped to show that all mathematically quantifiable regularity arose within social life through the free acts of individuals.[52] Indeed, he found necessity and unfreedom already inscribed in the objectifications of free praxis.

According to the *Critique,* meaningful objects came to the human world through praxis. In practice, freedom and consciousness brought "human functions" to matter: such transforming transcendence placed in a thing "its own future, its own knowledges."[53] But while objectification through practice evinced freedom, it simultaneously founded the "elementary experience" of necessity. Sartre in fact diverged from Marx in seeing objectification itself as automatically alienation and imposed necessity. The main vehicle of this "fundamental alienation" Sartre called "alterity," which denoted the alteration in meaning that occurred between an act as subjectively intended and the result as objectively interpreted by other human beings. "To the extent that, having attained our own end, we understand that we have in fact realized *something else,* outside of us, our action is altered, and we have our first dialectical experience of necessity." This form of alienation was unavoidable. Even in his tools, man was forced to mimic the inertia of material nature in order to master it: "The living body uses its inertia to overcome the inertia of things."[54] At its most extreme, the phenomenon of alterity meant that the work executed by one generation came back to haunt another, in the shape of unintended consequences that formed the inert basis for the work of a new generation.

The series, by contrast, represented a necessity imposed by the ongoing acts of a multiplicity of individuals within a collective. Serial collectivities embraced a negative unity of inertia. Rather than actively transforming the world through free praxis, individuals within serial collectivities merely endured their situation; insofar as each member of the series stood in a relationship of indifference to every other member, each faced a latent threat from every other (whereas in a group, collective concord supplied a tacit assurance that members would not work at cross-purposes). The institutions comprising a serial collectivity thus lost their original meaning for their members, becoming a ritual emcumbrance on praxis. To be sure, only the praxis of each member sustained the serial collective; yet it was a praxis bereft of teleological transcendence. Ultimately the series no longer appeared to its members as praxis at all, but rather as *exis*, or being in permanence. Where the group represented a perpetual totalizing action, meaningfully restructuring the world according to constitutive intentional acts, the series represented a reified totalization, maintained in existence by passive acts, previously constituted by tradition and habit.

Sartre at one point described necessity as "liberty's destiny in exteriority."[55] With his final discussion of the series, he took the *Critique* full circle, from the original praxis of subjectivity to the derivative *exis* of social objectivity. Although he portrayed the series as an historical sedimentation of free acts, Sartre still insisted that the continued existence of the series depended on the perpetuated perversion of praxis into *exis*. Within such an historical context, free subjectivity supported unfree objectivity. The agent within the series appeared condemned to pass freely upon himself the sentence imposed by society, which conventionally defined the framework and aspirations of most quotidian acts. Sartre's concept of the "practico-inert" attempted to demarcate this experience, its neologistic conjunction stressing the role of human action in constituting an inert *social* reality—a reality which most individuals faced passively, *as if* society were an inert *material* reality, and hence something foreign to human freedom.[56]

Through the concepts of alterity, of the series and of the practico-inert, Sartre tried to make intelligible the practical underpinnings of social necessity. He wanted to illustrate how a human dialectic, founded in practico-inert seriality, could produce its opposite, an inhuman antidialectic. On this point, Sartre had indeed modified his position since *Being and Nothingness*. Where he had earlier found only universal human freedom, he now also declared universal human slavery. Absolute ontological freedom constituted, through the mediation of serial institutions, absolute social unfreedom.[57] "For those who have read *Being and Nothingness,* I will say that the foundation of necessity is practical: it is the for-itself, as agent, discovering itself, first of all, as inert, or better, practico-inert in the milieu of the in-itself."[58] While the emphasis and language were new, the basic vision of subjectivity was not.[59]

A FORMAL MARXISM?

Apart from its specific content, Sartre's *Critique* raised a fundamental question of form. Should an *a priori* ontology or philosophical anthropology ground social theory?

At the outset of the *Critique,* Sartre asked, "On what conditions is a knowledge *of a history* possible? To what extent can the links it brings to light be necessary? What is dialectical rationality, what are its limits and fundamentals?" A little further on, he added that "it is not the real history of the human species that we want to restore, it is the *Truth of history* that we are trying to establish."[60] By insisting on individual action as "the only concrete foundation of historical dialectic," Sartre relied on ontology and anthropology to validate what he called "dialectical Reason." "We are attempting, to parody a phrase of Kant's, to lay the basis for a 'Prolegomena to any Future Anthropology.' If our critical experience, in effect, ought to yield positive results, we will have established *a priori*—and not, as the Marxists would make us believe, *a posteriori*—the heuristic value of the dialectical method when it is applied to the sciences of man."[61]

Sartre tackled his project in earnest. Like Engels, he did not avoid hypostatizing "the dialectic"; like Georg Simmel, he did not flinch from social formalism and elaborate classifications of social ensembles. Although he repudiated Engels's dialectics of nature, he took the latter's endeavor to found dialectic seriously; Sartre wanted to show that "dialectical Reason is a whole and must found itself, that is to say dialectically." While he nowhere explicitly mentioned Simmel, his use of dyads (groups of two people) and "the third" (an outsider observing a dyad) recalled that neo-Kantian thinker, just as his question, "How is history possible?" recalled Simmel's similar query, "How is society possible?" On the other hand, Sartre claimed that his own formalism consisted only "in recalling that man makes History to the same extent that History makes man."[62]

Oddly, Sartre never clarified why Marxism so obviously needed a priori support—unless he felt that Marx's image of the future could be sustained in no other fashion. To be sure, he did not undertake a logical deduction of the dialectic in the *Critique,* but he did propose an *ontological* deduction; in order for History to be possible, man must be a being of praxis, characterized by "need, transcendence and the project."[63] Since he also derived praxis from scarcity, presumably a contingent rather than necessary circumstance of human affairs, he hedged his bets. Only insofar as scarcity prevailed could there be history. Apparently, his philosophical anthropology was necessary a priori merely for *this* historical world—the only one we happen to know.

Despite such provisos, scarcity and warring Cartesian egos with insatiable needs tended to appear as immutable constants of the Sartrean social world. Thanks to the philosophical anthropology which determined both the starting point and final result of the *Critique,* Sartrean man's peculiar individuation and freedom became the tacit birthright of all historical men, rather than the historical acquisition of some men. Marx himself had abandoned philosophical anthropology in favor of a purely *historical* approach, precisely because its factual formulations were less susceptible to such questionable generalization. Ironically, the real results of Sartre's *Critique* hardly merited all the Kantian trimmings. For in the end, he simply established dialectic as a relevant heuristic device: by tracing the contours of social reality in its various permutations and contradictions, he succeeded at best in demonstrating the applicability of certain categories of something called "dialectical Reason" to certain phenomena of human life. His "critical" as opposed to "dogmatic" dialectic often boiled down to a conscientious examination of empirical evidence in context, as opposed to an arrogant disregard of inconvenient facts.

Yet Sartre's evident prejudice in favor of "dialectical Reason" compromised even this aspect of his project. It was as if he proposed to displace the a priori concepts deployed by orthodox Marxism, which were "dogmatic" because unfounded in a phenomenology of the social world, with his own set of a priori concepts, which were "critical" because founded in a description of the "complex play of *praxis* and totalisation" detailed in the *Critique.* The very formalism of his approach, however, created its own problems: for example, his phenomenological account warranted the universal applicability of key concepts without even a modicum of comparative historical research. Moreover, while this account rendered the experience of such social facts as commodity exchange intelligible, the emphasis on isolating essential social forms did not provide much guidance for uncovering the *rules* governing social relations, or for explaining how such rules informed the structure of human action. In this respect, Merleau-Ponty's concept of the institution offered a more promising point of departure, as we shall see. By contrast, Sartre generally ignored the problems of methodology raised by Marx's economic and historical works. In contending that "the certainty of the synthetic reconstruction which Marx carried out in *Capital*...defies commentary," he effectively disqualified himself from any critical discussion of the methods appropriate to empirical inquiry in the social studies.[64]

As for a "Truth" of history, Sartre, like so many other modern neo-Marxists, preserved that notion purely on faith—albeit a rather slender one. The published part of the *Critique* breaks off before his demonstration of the unity and cumulative coherence of a single history; the promised volume two has never appeared. As a result, no truth of history comes close to being established in volume one. Instead, the philosophical anthropology of the *Critique* evokes a pessimism at odds with the customary Marxist interpretation of history. To the end, Sartre basically resented other people, portrayed even in the *Critique* as encroaching on the liberty of the individual; he likewise distrusted the objectifications of men, because they exposed freedom to the pitfalls of alien interpretations and unforeseen consequences. A classless society beyond alienation had about as much plausibility in his social world as man becoming God—and in *Being and Nothingness,* he had demonstrated that *that* was impossible. As he footnoted the issue, his skepticism struck at the heart of Marx's highest hopes for history: "Must the disappearance of capitalist forms of alienation be identified with the suppression of *all* the forms of alienation?"[65] To the extent that objectification entailed alienation for Sartre, as for Hegel, alienation could as little be overcome as objectification could be dispensed with. Small wonder that communism covertly assumed the moral role of a pure utopia: less than a Truth of history and more than a wager that might be realized, communism for Sartre became a regulative *myth* —as Merleau-Ponty pointed out in 1955.[56]

THE LIMITS OF SARTREAN MARXISM

Sartre variously accomplished his purposes in the *Critique*. To a large extent, he managed to reconcile his doctrine of ontological freedom with the experience of social unfreedom. But he paid a high price for this architectonic victory. By having to accommodate his phenomenology of social forms to his idiosyncratic notions of freedom and sociability, he was encouraged to minimize or ignore contrasting phenomena of social life, such as the voluntary associations Tocqueville extolled, and the mutual aid societies esteemed by Kropotkin. Both of these paradigms, with their stress on pacific cooperation, suggest possibilities for communal freedom left unexplored by Sartre.

As descriptive analysis, on the other hand, the *Critique,* while frequently provocative in its detailed examples, lacked plausibility in its systematic structure. In part, the difficulty derived from Sartre's original sense of subjectivity. Unlike such rival "phenomenologists of the social" as Georg Simmel and Alfred Schutz, Sartre built his account on the basis of individuals largely bereft of such sociable attributes as compassion and trust. As a consequence, his description of dyads and "small group interaction," for example, rarely reach the level of compelling insight animating similar discussions by Simmel and Schutz — a damaging failure for any philosophy which grounds the cogency of its categories on the persuasiveness of its descriptions.

Further difficulties arise when an attempt is made to sort out Sartre's empirical generalizations from his a priori principles. For example, is the group-in-fusion fated to become a serial collectivity because the transience of social conflict favors such decay? Or is any group prey to instability thanks to the envy and distrust endemic to human nature under conditions of scarcity? Can the degeneration of the group be deduced from a priori principles of philosophical anthropology? The consistency of Sartre's core image of subjectivity sometimes suggests as much. Or is this development merely an observational generalization? In this last case, Sartre would have given us a set of typifications, abstracted from history, typifications presumably helpful in explaining the metamorphosis of social institutions. Unfortunately, Sartre offers not exemplary explanations of specific institutional changes but rather a confirming catalog. Although he referred to various historical events (especially those of the French and Russian revolutions), Sartre used such material illustratively. When joined to the a priori bent of his philosophical anthropology, his account of the genesis and decay of social forms thus acquired an odd taste of inevitability.

MARXISM AND THE CRITIQUE OF RATIONALISM

As we have seen, Sartre's *Critique of Dialectical Reason* supplemented rather than superseded *Being and Nothingness*. If the *Critique* laid bare the genesis of a transcendent social order, sustaining morality and stable social roles, *Being and Nothingness* equally denounced this order as a false prop for the individual's own choice of a way of life. Only the group-in-fusion, a collective incarnation of perpetual transcendence (which is what *Being and Nothingness* demanded anyhow), could accommodate the authentic individual, consciously exercising his ontological freedom.

When applied to Marxism, such concerns implied a theory of genuine individuation, linked to a critique of repressive (serial and practico-inert) social forms. Not just an image of autonomy in judgment and freedom in self-expression, authentic individuation required a person's active and ongoing self-definition, the subject's creative pursuit of possibilities. Under the conditions of advanced industrial society, however, individuation, while professed in principle, evaporated in practice, the victim of routinized patterns of thinking and acting; here human possibilities dissolved in a one-dimensional way of life, endured without any sense of alternatives.

To have confronted the attraction of such one-dimensionality is one of Sartre's great merits. In a world of routinized order, freedom may appear as a troubling source of insecurity, threatening to disrupt familiar modes of existence. Any program for social change thus finds itself beset not only by institutions of domination but also dominated individuals, fearful of the very freedom to change the world that might dispel their suffering. Sartre here disavowed Enlightenment rationalism as a tenable basis for Marxist theory. But, as he explained in *Search for a Method*, "Our intention is not to 'give the irrational its due,' but on the contrary, to reduce the part of indetermination and non-knowledge, not to reject Marxism in the name of a third path or of idealist humanism, but to reconquer man within Marxism."[67]

Ironically, Sartre's most illuminating contributions to this end came not in the *Critique* but rather in his earlier essays and his biographies. Even *Being and Nothingness* offered an effective indictment of rationalism, despite initially proceeding from rationalist premises. Through such notions as bad faith and authenticity, he attempted to grasp the individual's flight from freedom into the arms of previously established social values and roles. By reassessing the significance of passion, anxiety, and inertia in human affairs, Sartre implicitly reassessed the subjective grounds of ideological beliefs.

To be sure, these insights were not free of problems. As we have seen, Sartre's concept of authenticity lacked any discernible content, while his doctrine of absolute ontological freedom threatened to undermine critical applications of the concept. Indeed, as his philosophy progressed, the doctrine of ontological freedom increasingly became a hindrance complicating his main intention. By abandoning the notion of innate individual freedom and advocating instead something akin to Merleau-Ponty's concept of situated transcendence, he might have accomplished his primary purpose—"to give man both his autonomy and his reality among real objects"—without maintaining the Cartesian dualism haunting his outlook on human existence, "the Other," and social forms.[68]

Fortunately, since he avoided making reason an ontological given, his discussion of the struggle for individual rationality escaped the difficulties surrounding his analogous inquiry into the struggle for individual freedom. In his essay on anti-Semitism, he formulated the *problem* of rationality with unusual clarity.

How can one choose to reason falsely? It is because of a longing for impenetrability. The rational man groans as he gropes for the truth; he knows that his reasoning is no more than tentative, that other considerations may supervene to cast doubt on it. He never sees very clearly where he is going; he is "open"; he may even appear to be hesitant. But there are people who are attracted by the durability of a stone. They wish to be massive and impenetrable; they wish not to change. Where indeed would change take them?

This recognition of a subjective fright before change struck a new and pessimistic chord in radical social thought.

We have here a basic fear of oneself and of truth. What frightens them is not the content of truth, of which they have no conception, but the form itself of truth, that thing of indefinite approximation. It is as if their own existence were in continual suspension. But they wish to exist all at once and right away. They do not want any acquired opinions; they want them

to be innate. Since they are afraid of reasoning, they wish to lead the kind
of life wherein reasoning and research play only a subordinate role, wherein one seeks only what he has already found, wherein one becomes only
what he already was. This is nothing but passion.

But passion itself fueled the individual's acts; it nurtured a surrogate
strength. "Only a strong emotional bias can give a lightning-like
certainty; it alone can hold reason in leash; it alone can remain
impervious to experience and last a whole lifetime."[69]

This "arationalist" perspective illuminated much of Sartre's later
writing. Its implications for Marxism first emerged in *The Communists and Peace*. There Sartre defended a Leninist strategic position
by arguing against the inherent rationality of the proletariat. Reason was never guaranteed anyone, not even the worker; "resigna-
tion" and "revolution" equally shed light on any situation, and the
worker's response simply could not be prejudged. "Is this idealism,
irrationalism?" he asked rhetorically. "Not at all. Everything *will be*
clear, rational, everything *is* real"—but only "beginning with that
resistance" to a rational "deciphering" of the situation disclosed in
Sartre's approach. "Active experience begins in receptivity"—or
inertia.

Passion had a role to play in dissolving this inertia, as surely as
enlightened reason itself. Rejecting the sufficiency of orthodox
Marxism, and the movement it anticipated from objective class
interest to subjective class consciousness, Sartre asserted that passionate engagement comprised a crucial component in the passage
beyond objective circumstances toward revolutionary goals; passion
alone might overcome social inertia. "In short, the proletariat has
not only a relationship with its own activity, it has to deal as well
with its own inertia and, through it, with the activity of the Other
class. For it is also through our passion that we have the painful and
ambiguous experience of the real."[70]

On this account, only a frail thread of commitment sustained the
meaningful *telos* of rational Marxian practice. The revolutionary
endeavor ultimately fell back on its own human resources: an
engaged practice, more than mere "objective possibilities," sustained the revolutionary image of a better world—although this
practice was itself based on "objective possibilities." Sartre posed the
problem succinctly: subjectivity, even faced with a transcendent
image of a better social order, one that might plausibly be insti-

tuted, usually continued to equate the tried with the true. But this routinization of practical transcendence spelled its eclipse — another meaning of the practico-inert. Radical practice could ill afford such an occlusion of creative subjective initiative; after all, the future of communism resided with the rational intentions of militant proletarians. The acquisition of a committed and "passionate" rationality thus became as much an issue for social theory as the elaboration of a cogent science of political economy.

As Sartre developed his position in the *Critique,* need rather than reason became the central factor in all human action. Lack — whether of food, shelter, or implicitly also transcendental values — comprised the ineliminable motor of history; still the mere force of such needs in no way guaranteed that rationality would play a part in satisfying them. Although the *Critique* focused on the need for material necessities, *Being and Nothingness* also disclosed a metaphysical need for substantial identity. Both types could hinder as well as encourage a radical political practice; with the possible exception of material needs, neither type could be definitively met. "The dialectical totalization must include acts, passions, work, and need as well as economic categories; it must at once place the agent or the event back into the historical setting, define him in relation to the orientation of becoming, and determine exactly the meaning of the present as such."[71]

While the *Critique* hardly amplified the point, Sartre implied in *Search for a Method* that Marx's notion of an objective social struggle against exploitation had to be supplemented by an understanding of the subjective psychological struggle against inertia. The enlightened knowledge of objective exploitation could not, by itself, overcome an individual's passivity and reluctance to act decisively; dismantling routine practical responses therefore necessarily preceded any sustained commitment to a revolutionary movement. In this context, Sartre's remarks on Kierkegaard assumed an added measure of significance. "Kierkegaardian *existence* is the *work* of our inner life — resistances overcome and perpetually reborn, efforts perpetually renewed, despairs surmounted, provisional failures and precarious victories — and this work is directly opposed to intellectual knowing. . . . Ideas do not change men. Knowing the cause of a passion is not enough to overcome it; one must live it, one must oppose other passions to it, one must combat it tenaciously, in short one must 'work oneself through.' "[72]

EXISTENTIAL PSYCHOANALYSIS AND
THE AIMS OF MARXISM

Sartre's elaboration of this perspective culminated not in the derivative social theory of the *Critique* but in the "existential psychoanalysis" of his biographies, particularly his prolix tome on Flaubert's formative years, *The Idiot of the Family*. He had first announced the idea of an existential psychoanalysis in *Being and Nothingness;* there he identified such research with the recovery of a "fundamental project" that intelligibly unified any person's entire life into a coherent and meaningful whole. Flaubert figured as his example even in 1943. "*To be,* for Flaubert, as for every subject of 'biography,' means to be unified in the world. The irreducible unification which we ought to find, which is Flaubert, and which we require biographers to reveal to us—this is the unification of an *original* project, a unification which should reveal itself to us as a *non-substantial absolute.*"[73] In his early biographies (such as *Saint Genet*), Sartre attempted to reconstruct the central choice which a creative individual made of himself and his world. The existential psychoanalytic biography would reveal, concretely, how one person succeeded in making himself out of what he had been made.[74]

As he developed his own variant of Marxism, he correspondingly expanded his notion of biography to include the social and historical dimensions of a person's life. Where in *Being and Nothingness* he had described the fundamental project as "purely individual and unique," in *The Idiot of the Family* he asserted that "a man is never an individual; it would be better to call him a *singular* universal. Totalized and, by the same stroke, universalized by his epoch, he retotalizes it while reproducing it within himself as singularity."[75] But the primary focus remained the same as before: how one person, combining knowledge and passion in a fundamental project, *worked through* a situation at once unique (being his) and universal (being socially shared). From this perspective, the notions of internal struggle and external action became intertwined; a subjective "working through" always accomplished objective works, while "rational thought forges itself in action."[76] *The Idiot of the Family* reconstructed Flaubert's particular path beyond an endured, irrational childhood of "passive activity" and inertia, to his moment of fundamental choice—his decision to become a writer. Although Sartre, increasingly self-indulgent, let his biography ramble on at unconscionable length, we should not let his hermetic obtuseness obscure the rationale behind his project.

The approach of the Flaubert book was intended to complement Sartre's interpretation of dialectical reason in the *Critique*. According to the latter's social nominalism, "totalization" could only be a singular adventure. "Our critical experience represents nothing other than the fundamental identity of a singular life and human history."[77] It therefore became a critical task for existential Marxism to reconstruct the richness of history starting from the uniqueness of a single individual; as Sartre emphasized in *Search for a Method*, "Nothing can be discovered if we do not at the start proceed as far as is possible for us in the historical particularity of the object."[78] It was in this sense that Sartre called *The Idiot of the Family* the sequel to *Search for a Method*, even as he considered the latter essay an inquiry resting ultimately on the findings of the *Critique*. Dialectical nominalism would only be founded by a twofold movement: from the free individual to determining history (in a phenomenology of the social world) and from determining history to the free individual (in an exemplary and exhaustive sociopsychoanalytic existential biography). Yet while the rationale behind Sartre's biography was provocative, his choice of subject matter proved less resonant, at least from the standpoint of reorienting social thought: deciphering the enigma of the creative decisions made by an exceptional artist hardly made a compelling case for the universal applicability of a new method.[79]

His biographical notion of the individual struggling through an "oriented life" nevertheless placed Sartre's thought in principle beyond the certainties of both positivist and rationalist Marxisms. "Complexes, a style of life and the revelation of the past-surpassing as a future to be created form one and the same reality: it is the project as an *oriented life,* as man's affirmation through action, and simultaneously it is that unlocalizable mist of irrationality, which is reflected from the future in our remembrances of childhood and from our childhood in our rational choices as mature men."[80] Marxist rationalism assumed reason as much as it slighted passion; consequently Marxism, like any rationalism, tended to underestimate the importance of the individual's struggle against passivity and personal inertia.

These insights of Sartre's seem important, and, so far as they go, valid. Naturally, they have implications for radical theory. Beyond the critique of political economy and the analysis of social structure, beyond cultural criticism and the unmasking of ideologies, the individual's relation to a personal and social history merits reconsideration. Traditionally, Marxism has relied on causal assumptions to buttress its observations of correspondences between ideology and productive forces; similarly, it has anticipated a rational practice that would overcome irrational social forms. But for Sartre, after the theoretical and practical failure of both rationalism and positivism, the question of the individual's relation to history remained unsolved. How was the individual conditioned to passivity? How did he acquire rational initiative over the course of his life and the decisions he made? The complex of specific mediations between the particular individual and a universal meaning of history frustrated any easy answer to these questions.

Sartre's position also affected the shape of radical practice. As *Search for a Method* had argued, objective conditions only entered into an agent's acts insofar as they were meaningfully integrated in the project of a particular life. "If the material conditions which govern human relations are to become real conditions of *praxis,* they must be lived in the particularity of particular situations."[81] The objective diminution of buying power, for example, did not of itself lead to discontent; it only spelled revolt when an agent *felt* a need had been unfairly denied. A central aim of radical practice thus became analyzing and identifying the impact of objective factors within a person's experience. If the individual was to change prevailing circumstances, he had first to experience those circumstances as an intolerable and unnecessary imposition.

Similarly, the objective possibility for socialism had to become a vital aspiration permeating existence; if the individual was to help combat the established order, he had to experience it as alterable in the direction of a palpably better form of life. Closely related to the attainment of this transcending social outlook was his acquisition of a transcending personal outlook, a vision of himself as an autonomous subject within society, an agent with freedom and initiative. Feelings of powerlessness, inertia, and passivity had to be confronted and overcome: any truly communist revolution had to be based on rational and free action.

Although he initially espoused a rather crude variant of Leninism in *The Communists and Peace,* Sartre's later accent on subjective factors by implication argued against orthodoxy. Leninism would engineer socialism from without; a consistent Sartreanism would engender socialism from within. The individual would have to discover the social dialectic through his own decisions as a "rational transparency"; it was a discovery no party could make for the individual.[82] Indeed, Sartre's utopia of the group-in-fusion pointed toward a messianic syndicalism more than an institutionalized Leninism.[83]

He thus attempted, at the level of practice as well as of theory and history, to illuminate the relations between social circumstance and individual action. The question, How did a radical choose his project? paralleled the more general question, How did any man shape the course of his life? Both the *Critique* and the biographies represented attempts, from complementary standpoints, to grapple with such questions. "Valéry is a petit bourgeois intellectual, no doubt about it," wrote Sartre in *Search for a Method.* "But not every petit bourgeois intellectual is Valéry. The heuristic inadequacy of contemporary Marxism is contained in these two sentences. Marxism lacks any hierarchy of mediations. . . ." Existentialism by contrast "intends, without being unfaithful to Marxist principles, to find the mediations which allow the individual concrete—the particular life, the real and dated conflict, the person—to emerge from the background of the *general* contradictions of productive forces and the relations of production."[84]

His aim dictated his approach.

Contrary to the synthetic movement of the dialectic *as a method* (i.e., contrary to the movement of that Marxist thought which goes from production and the relations of production to the structure of groups, then to the internal contradictions of the group, to the environment, and, in case of need, to the individual), critical experience departs from the immediate, i.e., the individual realizing himself in his abstract [in the sense of incomplete] praxis, in order to recover, through increasingly profound conditionings, the totality of his practical links with others, the structure of diverse practical multiplicities, and through the contradictions and their conflict, the absolute concrete: historical man.[85]

It is the intransigent articulation of this aspiration, above all, that has made Sartre a central figure in contemporary Marxist philosophy. Indeed, despite the muddles of the *Critique of Dialectical Rea-*

son, his insistence on the individual's import for Marxism has raised a series of critical questions: What is the individual's ongoing role in sustaining oppressive institutions? How should a theory view such institutions: as mutable but reified human collectives, or as social "things," to be investigated and mastered by quantifiable methods of causal explanation? What are the possibilities for reasoned behavior in human beings, those creatures of habit, passion, and fear? What kinds of institutions, by cultivating the rational freedom of men, would promote "the integration of the free individual in a society conceived as the unity of the free activity of individuals?" Even if his answers to these questions have not always been satisfying, his persistence in posing them has had a salutary effect: although his elaborations may err, the philosopher has an eye for the essential.

10

Merleau-Ponty—
The Ambiguity of History

Sartre's discussion of bad faith struck a resonant chord among intellectuals in Western Europe during the postwar period. It was as if, after the shocks sustained during the war, after the nightmare of the concentration camps and the atomic bomb, after the collapse of a compromised liberalism, after the disintegration of Soviet socialism in the Stalinist state—after all this, life itself stood naked. Existence had to recapture a sense of purpose.

Existentialism spoke directly to this mood. It portrayed modern man as homeless, cast into a degrading culture that stifled the particular to encourage the average. In such circumstances, the aim of individuation was felt to require something more than a guarantee of legal rights and the advent of social planning; individuation, the professed aim of bourgeois society, appeared now as a fragile accomplishment, ravaged by mass culture, the imperatives of large-scale organization, and the totalitarian state. By addressing such problems, however, abstractly, existentialism joined one of the key issues of any genuinely radical social theory—the issue, as Marx might have put it, of the conditions of unalienated self-expression.

Without parallel in Marxism, however, was the suggestion, contained in the philosophies of Nietzsche, Heidegger, and Sartre, that man was something other than the being of potential enlightenment portrayed by rationalism. The individual, thrown back on his own resources, bereft of a transcendent order, and unable to assent, without qualifications, to any set of normative prescriptions, suddenly faced the world alone, only to find in it not the promised land of autonomy and freedom but instead an abyss of uncertain existence. Cast adrift without goals in a world apparently without aim, the individual foundered on anxiety and a fear of the very freedom classical philosophy—and Marxism—had assumed as an indubitable good.

Existentialism here afforded insight into the crisis, widely felt, in man's contemporary condition. In addition, existentialism and phenomenology professed to offer an alternative basis for philosophical insight, beyond positivism as well as rationalism. When applied to Marxism, existential phenomenology promised to direct the theory back to its premise in the interaction of real individuals, and to provide a new framework for reconsidering Marx's hopes for individuation.

The most fruitful application of existentialism to Marxism occurred in the philosophy of Maurice Merleau-Ponty. Unlike Sartre, Merleau-Ponty embraced Marxism virtually from the outset of his career. But rather than gravitating closer to the theory's orbit as he amplified his own philosophy, he eventually elaborated an independent position, skeptical of Marxism both as theory and practice. Yet his very independence facilitated a critical outlook toward the dilemmas of Marxism, which he came to consider insuperable. Simultaneously, his own philosophy, enriched by his contact with Marxism, produced the rudiments of an original phenomenology of the social world, focusing on institutions as the intersubjective nexus of meaningful existence. In contrast to Sartre's existentialism, Merleau-Ponty's phenomenology emphasized the unity of consciousness with the empirical world and man's inherent sociability.

FROM BEHAVIOR TO PERCEPTION:
THE AFFINITY OF CONSCIOUSNESS AND NATURE

In the introduction to his first book, *The Structure of Behavior,* Merleau-Ponty expressed his desire to elucidate the relations of "consciousness and nature, organic, psychological or even social."[1] By interpreting the findings of gestalt psychology within a phenomenological framework, he concluded that neither a mechanistic nor idealistic approach could adequately account for the phenomenon of behavior.

Through his study of behavior, Merleau-Ponty hoped to demarcate a primordial locus of meaning bonding consciousness, via the body, to the world. The philosophical inventory of behavior revealed meaningful action before the advent of self-conscious reflection. The truth of naturalism and realism thus turned out to be a philosophy of significant "structures."[2] It was on this basis that he approached the study of perception.

The centerpiece of Merleau-Ponty's career, and the effective foundation for much of his subsequent work, is his second book, *Phenomenology of Perception,* published in 1945. The implications and dilemmas of his brand of Marxism cannot be fully appreciated without a preliminary account of the philosophy he elaborated there.

In the *Phenomenology of Perception,* as in the *Structure of Behavior* before it, Merleau-Ponty argued that empiricism, behaviorism, and neo-Kantian rationalism all failed to account adequately for important phenomena, in this case phenomena of perception. Empiricism was wed to a stimulus-response model, taking as its fundamental unit atomic sense-data; but the holistic patterning of perception described by gestalt psychologists contradicted the atomism of the empiricist model. Rationalism, on the other hand, approached perception as if it were the lucid construct of consciousness; this account, however, also distorted our experience, which always afforded the possibility of perceptual error—perception was *not* the logical result of a series of judgments. Rationalism thus mistakenly enriched perception by elevating it to the level of self-consciousness, while empiricism falsely impoverished perception by reducing it to an empty passivity.

Merleau-Ponty felt that a new philosophy could arise from this impasse. By attempting a fresh description of the phenomenon of perception, a description unprejudiced by previous accounts, he sought to formulate a philosophical alternative to rationalism and empiricism (which in his account closely resembled the materialist epistemology endorsed by Plekhanov and Lenin). The key to this new philosophy lay in his interpretation of the close interplay in perception between the body and the *cogito,* terms which both empiricism and rationalism had tended to segregate. By linking the body and the *cogito* in his interpretations of such clinical phenomena as the perception of a "phantom limb" (the belief, for example, that an amputated leg still exists), Merleau-Ponty hoped to unravel the genesis of the "transcendental unity" of perception, a unity which idealism had placed at the foundation of consciousness. Cases like that of the phantom limb revealed the persistence of an holistic perception of the body, a perception anterior to rational judgment and emended only with difficulty (despite the evidence, say, of a missing limb).

It was this holistic perception of the body—the "phenomenal body," as subjectively experienced by the individual, in contrast with the body as objectively dissected by science—which anchored the individual in a world: "Consciousness must be faced with its own unreflective life in things and awakened to its own history, which it was forgetting."[3] The body was man's vehicle of "being in the world"; through his body, the individual became committed to a coherent structure of perceptual and behavioral dispositions.

Because these dispositions were assumed holistically, the individual's bodily perceptions could not be explained purely mechanistically. Yet the description of perception also revealed that it was the body, not consciousness by itself, which introduced coherence into perception. The foundations of the subject's contact with a world therefore lay not in external stimuli, as empiricism had it, nor in consciousness by itself, as rationalism had it, but rather in the familiarity with a world that the body itself spontaneously instituted. Such familiarity was never accomplished once and for all, as an absolute acquisition; instead, the orientation of the body evolved across time, relying on a prospective anticipation of worldly order as well as a retrospective synthesis that motivated this anticipation. Moreover, a person's bodily presence in the world at every turn suggested ambiguity rather than finality, an openness rather than the faits accomplis of rational intellection. Belief in a natural world appeared as man's original existential commitment, engendered by perception and behavior, but without any other transcendental grounds.

THE EMBODIED *COGITO* AND INTERSUBJECTIVITY

Although Merleau-Ponty retained the notion of the *cogito,* he radically reinterpreted this Cartesian (and Husserlian) concept. For him, the true subject of perception was not consciousness as such, but "existence, or being in the world through a body."[4] Consciousness, implicated in the world by its corporeal incarnation, comprised "nothing but a network of intentions," enmeshed in a past and future, a physical, ideological, and moral situation. Thrust by behavior and perception into a "pre-objective presence" to the world, the *cogito* possessed a world prior to self-conscious judgment. The incarnate *cogito* could be distinguished, not by the "I think" of Descartes and Husserl, but rather by an "I can." "This new cogito, because it is anterior to revealed truth and error, makes both possible."[5]

The embodied *cogito* described in the *Phenomenology of Perception* did not subsist like an inanimate thing; its environment did not consist of a static collection of objects. Instead, as existentially reinterpreted, it actively oriented itself. The new *cogito,* like the phenomenal body, was thus distinguished by its involvement in a task and situation, rather than by any formal, a priori predicates. Because this incarnate *cogito* existed through action, it could never coincide with itself; it always remained suspended between what it had and what it tried to have, between what it was and what it intended to be. The existential subject authentically discovered itself not through an identity posited in reflection but rather through acting. But the act was never pure, and always remained grounded in an antecedent world: consciousness was thus inextricably involved in circumstances.

Indeed, Merleau-Ponty's emphasis on the body set him apart from Sartre, who in *Being and Nothingness* had focused on the for-itself of consciousness. Merleau-Ponty in fact argued that Sartre's fateful dualism between the in-itself and for-itself did not rend the subject's original insertion in a world, before the advent of explicit conceptual judgment.

"The thing presents itself to the person who perceives it as a thing in itself, and thus poses the problem of a genuine *in-itself-for-us*."[6] This initial identification of the subject with a world signaled the individual as a "captive or natural spirit," anchored in the world by his sentient incarnation. For the body, the natural world did not appear a threatening and massive objectivity; rather, the natural world became the "horizon of all horizons, the style of all possible styles, which guarantees for my experience a given, not a willed, unity underlying all the disruptions of my personal and historical life. Its counterpart within me is the given, general and pre-personal existence of my sensory functions in which we have discovered the definition of the body."[7]

If man's body opened him to a world, then the *cogito* could no longer be radically divorced from the body; it confronted the world only via the body. The unity of mind and body worked both ways. Just as consciousness encountered a world through the body, so a world—and other people—encountered consciousness through the body: "That expressive instrument called a face can carry an existence, as my own existence is carried by my body...."[8] Another person's body appeared not as a mute object, but rather as a "manifestation of behavior." In contrast to Sartre, Merleau-Ponty refused to treat the existence of other people as problematic, let alone threatening. To be sure, "I am necessarily destined never to experience the presence of another person to himself. Yet each other person does exist for me as an unchallengeable style or setting of coexistence, and my life has a social atmosphere."[9]

Merleau-Ponty's philosophy of subjectivity flowed from his comprehension of the body and *cogito*. "Insofar as, when I reflect on the essence of subjectivity, I find it bound up with that of the body and that of the world, this is because my existence as subjectivity is merely one with my existence as a body and with the existence of the world, and because the subject that I am, when taken concretely, is inseparable from this body and this world."[10] Although he installed subjectivity at the heart of his philosophy, that subjectivity always implied, and was implicated in, objectivity. The individual, through his body, formed part of the objective world, just as consciousness, through bodily action, transformed that objective world. Similarly, through his body and acts, the individual was open to an intersubjective world of shared understanding. While objective perceptions arose at the level of private experience, the subject for the most part valued and evaluated his perceptions in terms of the world shared perceptually with other subjects. Moreover, the individual, through his body and acts, necessarily exposed himself to the perception of others: their interpretation of his behavior and validation of his perceptions in turn helped found the individual's sense of self, as well as his understanding of the world. "Solipsism," argued Merleau-Ponty, "would be strictly true only of someone who managed to be tacitly aware of his existence without being or doing anything."[11]

The social realm consequently assumed a central position within his thought. "We must . . . rediscover, after the natural world, the social world, not as an object or sum of objects, but as a permanent field or dimension of existence: I may well turn away from it, but not cease to be situated relatively to it. Our relationship to the social is, like our relationship to the world, deeper than any express perception or judgement."[12]

Merleau-Ponty's investigations of perception thus ended by charting a philosophical alternative to empiricism and rationalism, a philosophy of intersubjectivity tracing the affinity of consciousness and nature, mind and body, self and society. By returning to the existence each individual lived, and describing it with a minimum of presuppositions, his existential phenomenology attempted to mediate the antinomies of the philosophical tradition.

SITUATED VS. ABSOLUTE FREEDOM

Despite a common background in existential phenomenology, Merleau-Ponty and Sartre derived fundamentally different outlooks on man from their early investigations. These differences were most firmly drawn by Merleau-Ponty in his discussion of freedom at the close of the *Phenomenology of Perception.*

Sartre, it will be recalled, had asserted a kind of absolute freedom for the conscious human being. It was this claim that Merleau-Ponty disputed. To be sure, he never doubted man's experience of freedom: freedom indeed appeared to him as a phenomenologically verified certainty. The phenomenal subject always maintained a "power of placing in abeyance" the determinants of its existence, and "this suffices to insure our freedom from determinism."[13] But such a freedom could never be divorced from the individual's insertion in a world; instead, the concept of freedom only made sense in conjunction with this insertion. If freedom were everywhere, as seemed to be the case in Sartre's *Being and Nothingness,* then freedom in effect would be nowhere: as an omnipresent endowment, freedom lost its field of application, and thus its traditional significance and critical import. "Free action, in order to be discernible, has to stand out from a background of life from which it is entirely, or almost entirely, absent."[14]

While Sartre properly emphasized the subject's freedom, he distorted the scope of this freedom by rendering it absolute. The subject, argued Merleau-Ponty, always faced a previously established situation, an environment and world not of its own making. Its life, as intersubjectively open, acquired a social atmosphere which it did not itself constitute. Social roles pressed upon the individual as plausible courses for his life to take. Certain modes of behavior became habitual. *Probably*, this world, these habits, a familiar comportment: probably these would not change overnight. It was unlikely that an individual would suddenly choose to be something radically other than what he had already become. The Sartre of *Being and Nothingness* underestimated the weight of this realm of relative constraint and habitual inertial. Here as elsewhere, charged Merleau-Ponty, Sartre remained beholden to rationalist dualisms. "The rationalist's dilemma: either the free act is possible, or it is not — either the event originates in me or is imposed on me from outside — does not apply to our relations with the world and with our past. Our freedom does not destory our situation, but gears itself to it: as long as we are alive, our situation is open, which implies both that it calls up specially favored modes of resolution, and also that it is powerless to bring one into being by itself."[15]

The individual sustained a psychological and historical structure, endowed with a certain style of existence, which had to be granted a certain persistence. To be sure, the individual's existence, like his perceptions, received meaning from his projects, from the goals he assigned himself. Yet although the subject gave direction and significance to his life, such projects generally remained merely lived, rather than explicitly thought. The individual thus existed within an inarticulate momentum, establishing probabilities and patterns of behavior. He always exercised his freedom within this temporal framework; antecedent circumstance as well as prospective ends suggested decisions and prompted acts. "The situation thus comes to the aid of decision, and in this exchange between the situation and the person who takes it up, it is impossible to determine precisely the 'share contributed by the situation' and the 'share contributed by freedom.'"[16]

In Merleau-Ponty's philosophy, men faced a previously constituted world that nevertheless accommodated free action. This world acted upon the individual as surely as he acted upon it, in a perpetual exchange. For Merleau-Ponty, there was "never determinism and never absolute choice," by the very nature of man's being in the world.

Through this account of freedom, the *Phenomenology of Perception* offered nothing less than a new *empirical* anthropology—and a much more compelling picture of being human than that provided by Sartre's philosophical anthropology. Merleau-Ponty's insistence on the life-world as the foundation of phenomenology went further than anything suggested by Husserl and gave his philosophy a strongly empirical bent; it also placed his thought beyond any a priori categorizations, such as Sartre's bifurcation of being into an in-itself and for-itself. His interpretation of phenomenology indeed spared his philosophy the idealist and rationalist overtones still present in the phenomenologies of Husserl as well as Sartre. While his thought here converged with Heidegger's, Merleau-Ponty avoided the ontological emphasis that characterized *Being and Time*. Rooted in experimental science, yet maintaining a poetic regard for the virtually ineffable primacy of subjective experience, his philosophy occupied a unique position within the phenomenological movement.

THE SOURCES OF MERLEAU-PONTY'S MARXISM

Merleau-Ponty's interest in Marxism developed early. References to philosophical issues in historical materialism occur in the *Phenomenology of Perception* as well as his first postwar writings on politics. Indeed, his phenomenology, with its accent on intersubjectivity and the natural world, was, superficially at least, more compatible with the Marxian theory than other brands of phenomenology, Sartre's included.

Ironically, Merleau-Ponty developed his Marxism along lines that could not always be reconciled with his phenomenology. In fact, the two principal sources of his interpretation of Marxism—Lukács's neo-Hegelian Marxism (as elaborated in *History and Class Consciousness*) and Merleau-Ponty's own phenomenology of perception—were implicitly in conflict on a number of points.

On the one hand, his phenomenology of perception prompted him to view history as ambiguous and to approach man's insertion in the social order as problematic. From this perspective, he raised doubts about the assumptions Marxism made about the rationality of human action; as a consequence, he was inclined to view the historical program of Marxism as a gamble rather than a forgone conclusion. He was finally led to reconsider the process of politicization, and to redescribe, in the *Phenomenology of Perception,* the acquisition of a critical "class consciousness."

On the other hand, though, Merleau-Ponty elaborated a form of Marxism derived from Lukács, Hegel, the Husserl of the *Crisis,* and the young Marx—the Marx who, in his "Toward the Critique of Hegel's Philosophy of Right: Introduction," portrayed the proletariat as a material force for "the total redemption of humanity." From Lukács he added an understanding of the proletariat as the potentially unified subject-object of history, the demiurge of Absolute Knowledge appearing within human prehistory and transcending the fractured conditions of capitalism toward the future of communism; from Hegel, he borrowed the dialectic of mutual recognition, and placed its resolution at the end of history. When wed to Husserl's idea of an historical *telos* immanent to subjectivity, and to Marx's original depiction of the proletariat as the heart of human emancipation, these convergent strands in Merleau-Ponty's thought encouraged him to identify the proletariat with man's alienated essence, and to seek in proletarian politics a virtually apocalyptic class consciousness aiming at a more humane society, where men might treat each other as ends rather than means.

Such an essentialist vision of the proletariat and its historical mission contradicted the chief import of Merleau-Ponty's phenomennology of perception, with its emphasis on the contingency and open-ended nature of meaning: it also placed a burden of true consciousness upon the proletariat that his tentative recasting of the process of politicization in the final section of the *Phenomenology of Perception* should have warned him against.

While he eventually abandoned the essentialist concept of the proletariat, he did so not so much because he found the notion at odds with his own philosophy, as because he felt that the essentialist notion had been empirically discredited by the events of the postwar period. Such a result entailed a critique of Marxian politics as unrealistic; yet he provided few clues to what form a new political understanding might take. Merleau-Ponty's interpretation of Marxism therefore remained suspended between two fundamentally different ways of portraying society, history, and the possibilities for rational action they afforded. On one level, his overt Marxism can be identified with his fluctuating estimation of the proletariat and its ability to fulfill its rational humanistic mission; what, in *Humanism and Terror,* he had provisionally affirmed—the possibility of an authentically proletarian politics according to the essentialist model —he would eventually come to disavow in *Adventures of the Dialectic.*

But on another level, his early Marxism should be seen as promising a radical theory revised on the basis of his phenomenology of perception. This promise found its issue, not in Merleau-Ponty's overt Marxism, but rather in his mature discussions of language and the being of social institutions.

Where the "Hegelian" Merleau-Ponty portrayed the proletariat as the potential vessel of an Absolute human meaning, the "phenomenological" Merleau-Ponty described the proletariat as an inchoate yet coherent conjunction of individuals, each helping, however tacitly, to sustain a shared sense of community and purpose, the significance of which always remained open to new interpretations. The "Hegelian" Merleau-Ponty posited a rational end of history as a condition of moral coherence. The "phenomenological" Merleau-Ponty by contrast localized the ultimate rationale of history in individual action.

These particular agents of history were rarely creatures of explicit judgment, but they were rarely unreflective prisoners of fate either. What the Hegelian presumed, albeit with doubts—a conceivably univocal coherence governing all of human history—the phenomenologist undermined by anchoring history and meaning in the ineluctable amphibolies of human existence—equivocations and ambiguities perpetually clarified, but never surmounted.

FROM PERCEPTION TO HISTORY

By tacitly according a paradigmatic status to his theory of perception, Merleau-Ponty minimized the distance between perception and history. In both areas, similar issues arose, such as the relation of consciousness to the objective world; such similarities enabled him to draw analogies between problems of historical understanding and the structure of human perception in general.

History, like perception, suggested a logic in contingency, a reason in unreason; historical forces, like perceptual figures, only came actively into focus through a human endeavor that, by actualizing them, defined them.[17] Like perception, history could never be construed accurately as a mechanical play of mute factors, whether economic or geographic. History, as surely as perceptual objects, existed only in relation to the individuals that assumed it, with a more or less clear consciousness. More than a struggle of powers, history represented a play of meanings: both history and perception were irreducibly significant activities which established a meaningful world.

Merleau-Ponty depicted history as a field of transindividual meanings, a symbolic system — a vast repository of frequently contradictory significations. These generalized meanings, which comprised traditions of discourse, defined our situation as human beings; although we conferred significance upon a personal history, our historical environment itself embodied a significance of its own, represented in customs, habits, and explicit moral prescriptions. The interplay of particular and general meanings marked the individual's engagement in a social world. Where Sartre had remarked that man was condemned to freedom, Merleau-Ponty argued that man was condemned to meaning.[18]

His emphasis on history as a symbolic system naturally aligned him with the antireductionist trend in Marxism. Repudiating a reduction of cultural to economic phenomena, or a reduction of history to a conflict of class interests, he found the essence of Marxism in its treatment of economic and cultural history as two indivisible moments of a single process. Similarly, labor, the central concept of Marxism, had to be viewed not merely as the production of riches, but also as "the activity by which man projects a human environment around himself and goes beyond the natural data of his life."[19] The real subject of history was not man considered simply as a factor in production, but the whole man, man engaged in symbolic activities as well as manual labor, "man as creativity . . . trying to endow his life with form."[20] Merleau-Ponty encountered such subjects during World War II in the French Resistance, which "offered the rare phenomenon of an historical action which remained personal."[21] It was precisely this intersection of history with the personal that Merleau-Ponty fought to preserve within Marxism.

SOCIAL BEING: THE INSTITUTION

Like Sartre, Merleau-Ponty approached the social world from an ontological standpoint: What was the being of the social world? How did the individual participate in common tasks and relations, and how did the particular take shape through shared meanings and behavior? How did social structures inform individual behavior? Merleau-Ponty felt that the problem of the specific "existential modality" of the social world was "at one" with all other problems of transcendence: whether discussing the impingement of the natural world on perception, or the influence of the economic world on consciousness, the question remained: "How can I be open to phenomena which transcend me and which nevertheless exist only to the extent that I take them up and live them?"[22]

Merleau-Ponty founded his original social philosophy on an interpretation of man as a "being in the world." This being was a creature of significant structures; the world man inhabited was meaningfully formed, not only by language and symbols, but also by perception and behavior. He used this image of man, in large part derived from Heidegger, to criticize rationalist accounts of consciousness as "constituting." More than a perpetually renewed constitutive act, the "me" of personhood had to be viewed as a relatively durable institution, "the field of my becoming" with a history of its own.

Although his work, larded with metaphors, remained characteristically oblique on this point—his thought is often more suggestive than substantial—he clearly hoped that his notion of the institution would surmount the difficulties surrounding the idealist concept of the constituting ego, particularly in its application to the social realm. Where the constituted objectivity of idealism, as a pure reflection of the ego's acts, rendered the existence of other transcendental egos suspect, "instituted objectivity," claimed Merleau-Ponty, arose precisely as a "hinge" between self and others, since its being qua institution resided in a mutuality of recognition.

This notion of "institution" had applications beyond the description of consciousness. In Merleau-Ponty's hands, the concept of the institution became a critical pivot for interpreting social reality. His definition of the term was broad. "Each institution is a symbolic system that the subject takes over and incorporates as a style of functioning, as a global configuration, without having any need to conceive it at all. . . . One understands here by institution those events of an experience which endow it with durable dimensions, in relation to which a sequence of other experiences will have meaning, forming a comprehensible connection or history—in other words, those events which deposit a meaning in me, not by an appeal to survival and residue, but as an appeal to coherence, the requirement of a future."[23]

Institutions, in short, provided contexts for coherent action. As meaningful structures, they prompted behavior not by external causation but rather by internal determination, by embodying norms and rules, by proffering roles. Neither thing nor ego, the institution represented a mixed milieu. While the norms of an institution afforded more or less compelling grounds for behavior, they in most cases did not necessitate behavior.

Merleau-Ponty took this notion of the institution to be central to a phenomenologically clarified social theory. It also pointed the way to a defensible interpretation of Marxism.

Both the Marxism of the young Marx and "Western Marxism" in 1923 lacked the means of expressing the inertia of the infrastructure. . . . In order to understand simultaneously the logic of history and its detours, its meaning and what opposes it, they had to understand its specific domain: the institution. The institution develops, not according to causal laws like those governing nature, but always in relation to what it signifies; not according to eternal ideas, but always by subsuming under its laws more or less fortuitous events and letting itself be changed by what they suggest. Torn by all these contingencies, repaired by the involuntary acts of men who are caught up in it but must live, this web can be called neither spirit nor matter, but only history. This order of "things" indicating "relations among persons," susceptible to all those weighty conditions that link it to the order of nature, yet open to all that personal life can invent, is, in modern language, the domain of symbolism. Marx's thought should have found its way out in it.[24]

By implication at least, Merleau-Ponty here posited a sense of necessity tied to mutable norms rather than nature. While norms applied to an agent conventionally, and thus in a sense contingently, institutional norms nonetheless represented de facto compulsions, and thus embodied a certain necessity, a necessity effectuated by the continued observance of convention. If history always remained open to transformation, if institutions could be modified, it was equally true that history carried the conventional weight of custom and habit—the inertia of institutions. It was this inertia that founded the social domain of what Marx had called "second nature."

Language assumed a paradigmatic position in Merleau-Ponty's account. In contrast to Sartre, who approached the phenomenon of sociability through the alienating gaze of other people, Merleau-Ponty portrayed language as the social institution par excellence; language comprised an open field of communication which accommodated self-expression. Equipped with its own rules and structure, language to be sure presented an institutional compulsion that the speaking subject of necessity submitted to; yet language also existed as individual speech, speech which could speak the as yet unspoken, speech that could sustain, re-create, and, in the case of poetry, overturn conventions as well as conform to them.

He drew a parallel between language and other social institutions. He even hinted that such parallels were relevant to Marxism: "The reciprocal relations between the will to express and the means of expression correspond to those between the productive forces and the forms of production."[25] But usually he contented himself with remarking that "history is no more external to us than language."[26] Like language, history comprised a more or less confining field of possibilities for expression, a field nevertheless open, within limits, to creative intervention.

A picture of society as a network of meaningful, rule-governed institutions emerged from Merleau-Ponty's account. The proper task of sociology and economics lay in disclosing the rules informing social and economic action and in tracing the implications and consequences of these rules.

This portrayal of society and the tasks of a social science augmented his views on human behavior. As social action, the individual's behavior proceeded in reference to institutionalized rules, norms, and principles; such rules supplied reasons for, and warranted interpretations of, behavior. But the institutional grounds of social action could not be treated, mechanistically, as natural causes of action: the individual's assumption (whether coerced or voluntary) of an institutional framework alone endowed institutional norms with any force in a person's life. Although such social inquiries as sociology and economics might have as their object rule-governed social action, they did not face an object distinguishable by inherent regularities. The regularities of social action were instead bound to time and place: institutional phenomena were never necessary in the sense of Newtonian physics or analytic logic.

At the same time, Merleau-Ponty used his concept of the institution to argue against the idealist view of consciousness as purifiable or somehow extractable from its contingent relationships. If existence could be described as a "permanent act" by which a person assumed empirical conditions for his own ends, then an individual's thoughts and actions always remained implicated in circumstances, both institutional and natural.

Merleau-Ponty called this perpetual involvement in a world the individual's "situation." A field of contact between agent and objects, a person's situation was articulated via a constant interchange of motives and decisions. "Motives," as Merleau-Ponty defined the term, denoted "the situation as fact," circumstances as they constrained and shaped action; "decision," on the other hand, denoted "the situation as undertaken," circumstances as mastered and transformed by action. As situated, the individual's free acts arose within the context of a unitary world. Neither a juxtaposed assortment of things, nor the intrusion of materiality on an ineffable spirit, a person's situation had to be interpreted as a coherent whole, encompassing social institutions and a personal history as well as nature.

Such a view approximated Marx's 1844 description of man as a sentient, suffering being, "a being," as Merleau-Ponty reinterpreted Marx, "with a natural and social situation, but one who is also open, active and able to establish his autonomy on the very ground of his dependence."[27] The concepts of situation, motive, and decision thus complemented Merleau-Ponty's social philosophy of the institution: through such notions, he attempted to comprehend the individual's open-ended dependency, the hallmark of man's finitude, and the meaning of being in a world.

ON BECOMING A PROLETARIAN

Merleau-Ponty's most provocative application of his phenomenology of social institutions occurred not in any of his avowedly political texts but rather in the final pages of the *Phenomenology of Perception*. Here he hinted at what shape a phenomenologically revised neo-Marxian theory might assume. His account centered on a non-deterministic, nonessentialist understanding of social class—an understanding implicitly at variance with the neo-Hegelian notion of class Merleau-Ponty himself would deploy, almost contemporaneously, in *Humanism and Terror*.

In the *Phenomenology,* he argued that "one phenomenon releases another, not by means of some objective efficient cause, like those which link together natural events, but by the meaning which it holds out."[28] The proper avenue for approaching human behavior was therefore meaningful interpretation rather than causal explanation. But "in order to understand an action, its horizon must be restored—not merely the perspective of the actor, but the 'objective' context."[29] While he consistently denied any purely economic causality, Merleau-Ponty also denied that economic factors were irrelevant to interpreting historical acts. Economics simply did not comprise some independent realm of activity, carried on apart from a wider historical context of human existence. Indeed, precisely because economic acts opened onto a broader social horizon, and the individual, as existing in a social world, was already engaged in this realm, economic institutions helped articulate the subject's situation as surely as political, cultural, and personal institutions. "An existential conception of history does not deprive economic situations of their power of *motivation*."[30]

The *Phenomenology of Perception* elaborated the implications of "the existential modality of the social" for interpreting social relations. "What makes me a proletarian is not the economic system or society considered as systems of impersonal forces, but these institutions as I carry them within me and experience them; nor is it an intellectual operation devoid of motive, but my way of being in the world within this institutional framework."[31] Where classical Marxism had spoken of objective interests, Merleau-Ponty talked of a shared situation. An individual's social situation was not constituted through a series of more or less explicit choices; nor was it thrust upon the individual as an inexorable fate. Rather, from the outset, subjects coexisted within a social setting, a coexistence traced out in cooperative tasks and familiar gestures as well as in shared concerns. The individual's existence "as a proletarian" was in the first instance lived through as a common style and content of existence, not necessarily an explicit convergence of interests. Although the individual's existence was informed by tacit social projects, for the most part his social environment remained preconscious and unreflected.

Yet on the day an individual declared himself "a worker," this decision did not appear fortuitous, a radical upsurge of pure volition; on the contrary, "It is prepared by some molecular process, it matures in co-existence before bursting forth into words and being related to objective ends."[32] An individual's social situation formed an ineluctable element in his meaningful comportment toward a world long before he explicitly assumed that situation. His free decision could affirm or repudiate his proletarian situation, but it could never annul it: the subject could never instantaneously become other. Similarly, to be a worker or a bourgeois was not only to be aware of being one or the other; more crucially, "it was to *identify* oneself as worker or bourgeois through an implicit or existential project which merges into our way of patterning the world and co-existing with other people."[33] The privileged status of revolutionary situations resided in their ability to compel men to articulate decisions that would otherwise remain unspoken. "A revolutionary situation, or one of national danger, transforms those preconscious relationships with class and nation, hitherto merely lived through, into the definite taking of a stand; the tacit commitment becomes explicit."[34]

The proletariat here appeared as a social collectivity bonded together through shared aspirations and fears as much as a common relation to the means of producing economic wealth. A commonality of existential situation characterized individuals from the same class; as a consequence, a social class appeared generally as a quasi-conscious, amorphous yet hardly arbitrary conjunction of subjects. Their common hopes, fears, desires, and interests only became fully realized when shared situations were articulated by an explicitly sociopolitical awareness and action.

On this account, an individual who called himself a proletarian might take up a humanistic meaning of history as his own goal; still there were no factors compelling him to embrace such a universal meaning. The proletariat as a class lacked any necessary reason for embodying the essentialist claims made on its behalf by the Marx of 1843, the Lukács of 1923, and the Merleau-Ponty of 1947. Subjects and their history did not come packaged with an inherent rationalist interest, nor did they reflexively accede to a determinism of objective events. Stripped of such supports, social theory could merely invite each individual to make historical reason triumph over barbaric contingency. In this endeavor there could be no empirical certainties, just as there could be no metaphysical charter. The vision of the rational end of history in a communist society where each individual respected every other became one perspective among several. Its plausibility was directly linked with the prospects for its realization.

TERRORISM AND THE LOGIC OF HISTORY

However pregnant Merleau-Ponty's social philosophy might seem, the fact remains that his Marxism by and large elaborated different concerns. To grasp the difficulties in his position, we must return to the immediate postwar period, when he was struggling to develop an independent perspective as the political editor of *Les Temps modernes,* a journal he had helped found with Sartre. Although his postwar essays on politics acclaimed Marxism — at least the Marxism of Marx — as the core social philosophy of the twentieth century, Merleau-Ponty maintained a studied distance from the French Communist Party. The philosophical dilemmas in his Marxism first became clear in 1947, with the publication of *Humanism and Terror.* In this muddled little tract, he mixed elements of his phenomenology with a portrait of the proletariat as the vessel for a truth of history — a truth which, once established, might give us an absolute yardstick for judging historical acts.

As its title indicates, *Humanism and Terror* addressed itself to the problem of political violence; by what standards could violence and terrorism be judged? From the outset, Merleau-Ponty rejected any neo-Kantian moral philosophy that would evaluate acts on the basis of intentions rather than consequences. Moreover, he felt strongly that any absolute condemnation of violence was unrealistic; violence has ruled all societies to date, and violence in some circumstances might even form a necessary precondition of justice. The question was therefore not the condemnation or approval of violence, but rather a discrimination between "progressive" and "regressive" violence. According to Merleau-Ponty, progressive violence tended to cancel itself out, by aiming at a more human social order, while the regressive type sustained an exploitative regime in power. Throughout the book, he called revolutionary and "Marxist" violence progressive, because it putatively had a "future of humanism."

The argument of *Humanism and Terror* concerned the Moscow Trials and Arthur Koestler's fictional account of them in *Darkness at Noon*. But the more general problematic of the book involved the evaluation of historical acts as just or unjust, progressive or regressive. Merleau-Ponty's position on these matters proved paradoxical, and was fraught with problems.

Basically, he argued that although the meaning of history necessarily remains ambiguous to its immediate participants, we must nevertheless judge acts on the presumption of a rational historical end, namely, communism. He derived this position by a kind of backward deduction. Accepting the view that any historical act can be meaningful only if history in the large exhibits a coherent meaning, Merleau-Ponty suggested that the justice or injustice of a political act had to be measured against its world-historical consequences, rather than in terms of a subjectively universal ethic or natural law. He further asserted that Marxism comprised the only valid philosophy of history for the twentieth century. The notion of communism as the coherent end of human prehistory, filtered through Husserl's concept of a rationally regulative historical *telos,* was thus erected as the ultimate standard for judging historical acts. This variant of Marxism "deciphers events, discovers in them a common meaning and thereby grasps a leading thread which, without dispensing us from fresh analysis at every stage, allows us to orient ourselves toward events. . . . It seeks . . . to offer men a *perception of history* which would continuously clarify the lines of force and vectors of the present."[35]

But a Marxism clear as to the basic drift of history would hardly imply a philosophy of ambiguity. Here Merleau-Ponty's philosophical arguments in the *Phenomenology of Perception* came into play. As he succinctly put it in *Humanism and Terror,* "There is no science of the future."[36] The meaning of history deciphered by Marxism remained provisional and uncertain. No univocal meaning could be guaranteed history, because (as the *Phenomenology* had already argued at some length) determinism in any predictive sense was incompatible with the essence of human existence, the eventual object of history. Merleau-Ponty therefore affirmed that chaos remained as likely an historical outcome as humane relations among men (i.e., communism), and it was this doubt about the eventual outcome of history that rendered its contemporary meaning ambiguous. Marxism, stripped of a rationalist theology or deterministic support, became Merleau-Ponty's philosophy of ambiguity.

Another problem now arose. If no historical act could be definitively judged unless history evinced a coherent meaning, then the ambiguity of history might plausibly be taken as a signal that historical acts could not in fact be meaningfully judged, at least in any irrevocable sense.

But Merleau-Ponty argued nothing of the sort. Instead, he contended that a modified Marxism supplied a more adequate provisional meaning of history than any other available standpoint. Because Marxism embraced the only "universal and human politics," its truth had to be avowed, even though this truth could not be proven. In this fashion, Merleau-Ponty provisionally justified revolutionary violence, since such violence aimed at creating a humanistic society where each man would recognize every other as a peer: a progressive end of history provided a rational standpoint for judging existent societies and historical acts.

The application to the Moscow Trials of this rather complicated train of argument resulted in a convoluted defense of terrorism, and specifically of the trials. Unfortunately, Merleau-Ponty's treatment of the trials as a paradigm of revolutionary violence relied on several problematic empirical premises: that Bukharin and his cohorts in fact formed a political opposition, intentionally or unintentionally, to the policies of the Soviet Union; that this "opposition" represented a genuine threat to the survival of the Soviet Union; and finally that the Soviet Union sustained the hope of socialism. This chain of contentions allowed Merleau-Ponty to argue that Bukharin's continuing political independence could reasonably be construed a threat to socialism, the progressive end of history.

He would eventually change his mind about several of these points, but they remained the backbone of his empirical argument in *Humanism and Terror*. Much confusion surrounded his cavalier attitude toward questions of fact. He at one point defended himself by pleading that "we have not examined whether in fact Bukharin led an organizational opposition nor whether the execution of the old Bolsheviks was really indispensable to the order and the national defense of the U.S.S.R." — as if such empirical considerations were too mundane for his philosophical investigation.[37]

Throughout his discussion of the trials, Merleau-Ponty remained committed to his own interpretation of Marxism. He defended progressive violence, not because it was objectively necessary or somehow inescapable, but rather because the eventual meaning history assumed might in the long run show that such violence helped build a better society. He asserted that only his brand of Marxism, devoted to understanding "concrete subjectivity and concrete action" within an historical situation, could comprehend the real significance of the Moscow Trials:

Revolutionaries dominate the present the same way historians dominate the past. That is certainly the case with the Moscow Trials: the prosecutor and the accused speak in the name of universal history, as yet unfinished, because they believe they can reach it through the Marxist absolute of action which is indivisibly objective and subjective. The Moscow Trials only make sense between revolutionaries, that is to say between men who are convinced that they are *making history* and who consequently already see the present as past and see those who hesitate as traitors.[38]

Yet his argument, for all its involution, remained equivocal and inconsistent. Although he depicted a logic of history-in-process, he simultaneously defended, albeit with qualifications, the totalitarian arbitration of the Communist Party, and the desirability of a univocal interpretation of history. His discussion of the Moscow Trials only muddied the argument further. By the end, Merleau-Ponty had posed the question, not of the justice or necessity of the trials, but instead the more dubious question of whether their victims could be construed as dying for a revolution that might potentially realize a new humanity. In a backhanded way, he was in effect asserting that a liquidation of putative opposition elements (which he bizarrely styled a country's "unhappy consciousness") could be justified by a progressive future outcome of history. It was a position that Merleau-Ponty, as an intellectual "way above the crowd," could afford to take; yet it was a position that could hardly afford much solace for anyone actively trying to institute communism without abandoning elementary standards of justice and proof—standards defensible in the here and now, without any reference to a possible moral utopia.[39]

As he became disillusioned with Marxism and communist politics, Merleau-Ponty came to abandon or revise many of the philosophical and empirical propositions he had defended in 1947. Despite his sympathetic interpretation of the Moscow Trials, the French Communist Party did not roll out the welcome mat. Not only did he still offer a heretical version of Marxism in their eyes, he also raised critical reservations about the fate of contemporary communism. His doubts centered on the role of the proletariat—and these doubts would only deepen, not dissolve.

ADVENTURES OF THE PROLETARIAT

Merleau-Ponty's declining estimation of Marxism as a philosophy paralleled his declining estimation of Marxism as a movement. He came to question the proletariat's potential as an empirical force dedicated to radical social change. Yet the proletariat was the linchpin of his Marxism. It was the proletariat that unified subject and object, theory and practice, the ideal and real; it was the proletariat that embodied a universal meaning of history *in potentia*.

What seemed surprising, given Merleau-Ponty's characteristic skepticism toward idealist claims, was his continuing maintenance, with few philosophical qualms, of such an essentialist view of the proletariat, modeled on elements extracted from Lukács, Hegel, and Marx. Indeed, he came to doubt whether the empirical proletariat would ever uphold the lofty claims made in its name, as the presumptive bearer of humanity's rational future. In the period between his two major treatments of Marxist political problems, *Humanism and Terror* in 1947 and *Adventure of the Dialectic* in 1955, Merleau-Ponty revised his estimate of the empirical proletariat; ultimately, he felt that events had refuted the essentialist view.

Adventures of the Dialectic chronicled this disenchantment. Where in 1947 he had advocated a kind of critical adhesion to the Communist Party, in 1955 he denounced the obsolescence of Communist practice. The apparent cause for this newfound skepticism lay in the Korean War. But his turnabout had significant implications for his broader understanding of Marxism. Increasingly, he refused to take Marxian philosophical categories at face value.

While *Humanism and Terror* had insisted that only some form of Marxism could properly comprehend revolutionary action, Merleau-Ponty now stated that materialist philosophy was incapable of analyzing the Soviet Union without reference to "occult qualities."[40] By tracing the decline of Marxian philosophical thought during the twentieth century, from its highwater mark in 1923 (in Lukács's *History and Class Consciousness*) to its degeneration in Sartre's hands (in *The Communists and Peace*), *Adventures of the Dialectic* attempted to confront squarely some of the difficulties facing Marxism.

Although he had always denied Marxism the crutch of empirical determinism or rationalist necessity, in the immediate postwar period he had still believed that the proletariat might possibly fill the lofty role assigned it by the theory. By 1955, this hope had been replaced by distrust. It was not only the absence of militance among contemporary workers that bothered him; it was also the seemingly unavoidable degeneration of revolutionary fervor into bureaucratic torpor.

Merleau-Ponty felt that classical Marxism had rested on the "ferment of negation" being "materially" incarnated in an actual historical force. According to him, Marxism could only maintain its ultimate verity on this real historical basis, the proletariat conceived as *Selbstaufhebung,* a self-transcending being and the agent of universal history through meaningful negation. But he now argued that the party and proletariat necessarily navigated within the plenitude of a positive world; the proletariat could therefore never exist as pure philosophical negativity, but only as one positive institution among others. This circumstance in turn encouraged a set of fateful identifications: "The proletariat *is* the revolution, the Party *is* the proletariat, the heads *are* the Party . . . as being is being."[41] Even if a militant proletariat did exist, the chances for success at the task of negative transcendence toward a better society seemed dim; its negativity would surely be corrupted by bureaucratic institutionalization.

Merleau-Ponty thus came to hold that negativity only descended into history at privileged moments: for the most part, even revolutionary policies were represented by mere functionaries, who could not help but corrupt the aims of the movement. What had once appeared to him as a process that might create humane relations among men now seemed more a vicious cycle of unsuccessful attempts to seize institutional power. While allowing that revolutions might remain true as movements, he now entertained no doubts that they were "false as regimes."[42]

It was a melancholy conclusion. From start to finish, *Adventures of the Dialectic* represented the work of a disappointed man — perhaps because Merleau-Ponty could never quite escape his nostalgia for the Hegelio-Marxist Absolute. As he wrote at the outset of *Adventures* in regard to Max Weber, "Demystification is also depoetization and disenchantment. We must keep the capitalistic refusal of the sacred as external, but renew within it the demands of the absolute that it has abolished. We have no grounds for affirming that this recovery will be made."[43]

Merleau-Ponty nevertheless continued to identify with what he called the *Stimmung* or mood of Marxism, its conviction of being on the threshhold of Absolute Truth. Yet he recognized that such a Marxian philosophy of history, which would grant history an ultimate tendency and coherent meaning, could no longer be realistically reconciled with empirical events. "There is less a sense of history than an elimination of nonsense."[44] In reaction, he moved away from Hegel, toward Machiavelli, the spokesman for politics as the creative mastery of fate. If history had no univocal sense or direction, then politics should be judged, not by some chimerical reference to ultimate historical meaning, but rather by the manifold immanent meanings traced by the political actors themselves.[45]

The tendency of Merleau-Ponty's argument obviously cast doubt on the substance of Marx's original enterprise. But he nonetheless upheld a chastened dialectic at the end of its "adventures." "Is the conclusion of these adventures then that the dialectic was a myth? But the illusion was only to precipitate in an historical fact — the birth and growth of the proletariat — the total signification of history, to think that history itself organized its own recovery, that proletarian power would be its own supression, negation of the negation. . . . What then is obsolete is not the dialectic, but the pretension of terminating it in an end of history or in a permanent revolution. . . ."[46]

A MARXISM WITHOUT GUARANTEES?

The rejection of determinism as a tool of the human sciences lay at the heart of all of Merleau-Ponty's social thought, be it Marxian or phenomenological. In discussing culture, causal thinking remained insufficient, for it could never on principle account for creative meaning. Similarly, politics could not be construed as a chapter in some preordained history any more than it could be regarded as an exercise in pure morality; instead, Merleau-Ponty found in politics "an action which invents itself." A philosophically coherent Marxism would have to admit the absence of determinism and the importance of creative meaning, as well as the centrality of subjective factors — even though such a reformed Marxism might become a philosophy that "Marx undoubtedly would not have wished to recognize as his own."[47]

During the immediate postwar period, Merleau-Ponty had attempted to accommodate Marxism to his own thought, in the process producing several rather disingenuous restatements of the deterministic prejudices of orthodox Marxism. "For Marxism . . . the historical determination of effects by causes passes through human consciousness, with the result that men make their own history, although their doing so is neither disinterested nor lacking in motives. . . . Since human decision is motivated by the course of events, it will therefore seem — at least in retrospect — to be called forth by these events, so that no rupture or hiatus between effects and causes will ever be discernible in completed history."[48] Such a line of reasoning obviously blunted the cutting edge of his critique of determinism in the social sciences.

By 1955, he was taking a different tack. In *Adventures of the Dialectic,* he detected a fatal equivocation in Marx's own theory between determinism and a genuine dialectic steering clear of abstract alternatives such as idealism and materialism. Marx's concept of society as "second nature" most strikingly crystallized this equivocation by analogically justifying the treatment of social relations as natural data. Merleau-Ponty felt the practical consequences of such an objectivistic understanding could only prove onerous. If society was literally a second nature, men would be justified in governing it as they governed first nature: through technical domination. Technical action would replace meaningful comprehension; in Marxist practice, the professional revolutionary would displace the self-conscious proletariat, and guiding historical development would become the prerogative of a party elite. The "milieu of the revolution" would less and less be "relations between men, and more and more 'things' with their immanent necessity."[49] Orthodox Marxism had already taken this turn.

It would be a mistake to pretend that Marx himself could emerge unscathed from an historical development clearly implicating his own theory. Merleau-Ponty therefore criticized Marx (somewhat inaccurately) for positing a dialectic of history executed behind humanity's back. This formulation illicitly attributed dialectic to things—relations of production, means of production—rather than men.

If the revolution is in things, how could one hesitate to brush aside by any means resistances which are only apparent? If the revolutionary function of the proletariat is engraved in the infrastructure of capital, the political action which expresses it is justified just as the Inquisition was justified by Providence. In presenting itself as the reflex of that-which-is, the historical process in itself, scientific socialism . . . grants itself the basis of an absolute knowledge at the same time as it authorizes itself to extract from history by violence a meaning which resides there, yet profoundly hidden. The melange of objectivism and extreme subjectivism, the one constantly sustaining the other, which defines Bolshevism already exists in Marx when he admits that the revolution is present before being recognized.[50]

Such an indictment called into question the very point of remaining a Marxist, of whatever persuasion. "There is not a great deal of sense in making a fresh start from Marx if his philosophy is implicated in this failure, as if this philosophy remained intact throughout the affair, by right bounding the interrogation and self-criticism of humanity."[51]

Nonetheless, Merleau-Ponty himself, in his description of "becoming a proletarian" in the *Phenomenology of Perception,* had hinted at the viability of a modest Marxism, freed from a deterministic dialectic of history. The elimination from Marxism of guarantees, whether factual or metaphysical, left the ultimate significance of history open. Such a Marxism could not claim before the fact to embody the essential meaning of history. Its prognostications would instead assume the status of negative propositions: "The world economy cannot be organized and its internal contradictions cannot be overcome . . . as long as socialistic ownership of the instruments of production is not everywhere established. . . . Marxism would remain a politics which is as justified as any other. It would even be the only universal and human politics. But it would not be able to take advantage of a pre-established harmony with the course of events."[52]

Philosophically, historical materialism would then become one heuristic scheme among others — the most potentially fruitful perhaps, but one that still had perpetually to prove its utility in actual contact with events. Far from reducing history to one of its sectors, which would determine in advance the path to be followed, a chastened historical materialism would merely claim that "there is a close connection between the person and his external world, between the subject and the object which determines the alienation of the subject in the object, and, if the movement can be reversed, will determine the reintegration of the world with man."[53]

A modest Marxism, suggested Merleau-Ponty, held out the hope, although it could not guarantee it, that truth, reason, and logic would prevail in the course of history. But if contemporary conditions contained scant (if any) indicators that actually pointed in this rational direction, if the proletariat seemed unable to fulfill the mission prescribed for it by the Marxian theory — then Marxism was reduced to a gamble, a vow, a wager. Such a philosophy of history could no longer assume a rationality immanent in history. Instead, history became an "adventure" in which reason could hardly be counted an inevitable component.[54]

Unfortunately, such a modest version did not accord with Marx's own Marxism: Marx had preserved the premise of immanent historical rationality precisely in his expectations for the proletariat; and orthodox Marxism had transformed this optimistic prognosis of the meaning of history into an absolute political criterion, now interpreted purely objectively. What the later Marx wanted from Hegel was "no longer dialectical inspiration but a rationalism to be used for the benefit of 'matter,' i.e., 'relations of production,' considered as an external self-given order and a totally positive force. . . . It becomes a question of annexing Hegel's logic to economics. . . . Action that will change the world is no longer undivided philosophical and technical *praxis,* an infrastructural movement and at the same time an appeal to a total critique of the subject, but rather a purely technical action comparable to that of the engineer who constructs a bridge."[55] In his last political writings, Merleau-Ponty thus referred to Marxism as just another name for a "rationalistic politics." A Marxism stripped of rationalist as well as deterministic guarantees could not, he came to feel, justify the designation "Marxism" any longer.

While it might retain a relative heuristic value, Marxism could not therefore be considered true — "certainly no longer true in the sense it was believed to be true."[56] The options in Merleau-Ponty's eyes were simple. One either remained a dogmatic Marxist, owing allegiance to Communism as a movement, or one opted for a powerless, skeptical radicalism, without immediate political efficacy, but also without intellectual compromises. "It is clear that a revolutionary politics cannot be maintained without its pivot, that is, proletarian power. If there is no 'universal class' and exercise of power by that class, the revolutionary spirit becomes pure morality or moral radicalism again. Revolutionary politics was a doing, a realism, the birth of a force. The non-Communist left often retains only its negations. This phenomenon is a chapter in the great decline of the revolutionary idea. . . . Its principal hypothesis, that of a revolutionary class, is not confirmed by the actual course of events."[57]

At its inception, Merleau-Ponty's adherence to Marxism had depended on an essentialist view of history and the proletariat: the latter provisionally incarnated the teleological meaning of history. He came to criticize Marxism harshly because he felt that history could no longer sustain such a conception. Despite his attempts to formulate a Marxism without guarantees, his idiosyncratic fusion of Lukács's 1923 view of class and Husserl's later notion of the *telos* of history thus ultimately fueled a despair at ever realizing a rational historical philosophy. Disheartened and politically exhausted, Merleau-Ponty failed to entertain the possibility that the proletariat — and history — had been misunderstood in the essentialist conception from the outset.

Out of this impasse nonetheless emerged a call for a new left. Beyond disillusioned revolt, he proposed a revival of Machiavellian *virtù*, a "real spiritual strength" that might forge "a way between the will to please and defiance, between self-satisfied goodness and cruelty," in the name of "an historical undertaking all may adhere to."[58] The judgment of historical action could no longer classify "men and societies according to their approximation to the canon of the classless society," for although such a canon is "what our social criticism demands, there is no force in history which is destined to produce it."

Merleau-Ponty now viewed history as a far more tentative venture, "not so much a movement toward an homogeneous or a classless society as the quest, through always atypical cultural devices, for a life which is not unliveable for the greatest number."[59] Such a course would hardly satisfy whoever still believed in secular salvation; still "unremitting *virtù*" might conquer whatever prospects for a better world remained open. "History never confesses, not even her lost illusions, but neither does she dream of them again."[60]

THE LESSONS OF MERLEAU-PONTY'S MARXISM

In its evasions as well as its accomplishments, Merleau-Ponty's Marxism remains instructive. To take the negative side first, the tortured logic of *Humanism and Terror* reveals the illogic of any philosophy of history founded on criteria gleaned from an harmonious end of history, an end somehow deciphered before the event. Truth might well be on the horizon, but if we have not yet encountered it, how can it shed light on the mundane world of the here and now? The kind of absolute criteria such truth yields, seems, upon reflection, to invite the application of arbitrary criteria. Indeed, Merleau-Ponty's commitment to a supratemporal Absolute—the classless society of communism—vitiated this critique of Soviet Communism and compromised his handling of the Moscow Trials. Because he strained to interpret Stalin's policies as harboring the seeds of a rational future, he neglected to scrutinize sufficiently the Soviet theory and practice of socialism; similarly, because he averred that Marxism was correct in its belief that truth—the classless society of communism—will win out, he proved eager, in effect, to justify the Stalinist state on the grounds that it pointed the way toward this truth.

Fortunately, Merleau-Ponty's social thought does not begin and end with *Humanism and Terror*. In fact, his philosophy of the human subject implicitly contradicted his vision of an Absolute end of history. For the human subject depicted in the *Phenomenology of Perception* always maintained an openness toward the world, always elaborated a range of meanings, drawing freely from a fund of available significations. It is one of Merleau-Ponty's great merits to have elaborated this vision of subjectivity; in so doing, he left to his readers a legacy that can even be fruitfully applied to the critique of his essentialist philosophy of history in *Humanism and Terror*.

For Merleau-Ponty, who departed from the Cartesian (and Husserlian) tradition on this point,

The "subject" is no longer just the epistemological subject, but also the human subject, who, by means of a continual dialectic, thinks in terms of its situation, forms its categories in contact with its experience, and modifies this situation and this experience by the meaning it discovers in them. In particular, this subject is no longer alone, is no longer consciousness in general or pure being for itself. It is in the midst of other consciousnesses which likewise have a situation; it is for others, and because of this, it undergoes an objectification and becomes generic subject. *For the first time since Hegel, militant philosophy is reflecting not on subjectivity, but on intersubjectivity.* [61]

This image of (inter)subjectivity represented an historical result. For Merleau-Ponty as for Marx, "The history which produced capitalism symbolizes the emergence of subjectivity." [62]

Consciousness, while in no way the constitutive support of the social world, did on this view become an ineliminable vessel of meaning; in this capacity, its importance for any social theory could scarcely be belittled. Similarly, as Merleau-Ponty's sketch of belonging to a social class in his *Phenomenology* suggested, the human subject, in its passions as well as conscious disposition, comprised a critical element in any radical strategy. His social philosophy implied a practical focus on the individual and his everyday concerns as the ultimate existential basis for any authentically emancipatory movement. Otherwise, the individual might find himself sacrificed to party directives, the victim of an ostensibly objective meaning of history escaping his grasp.

Thus Merleau-Ponty, despite his advocacy of an essentialist notion of the proletariat in *Humanism and Terror*, held out the hope, in his philosphy of the human subject, of a new form of radical theory founded on an existential notion of class. According to the existential conception, a class was viewed as an institution comprised of concrete subjects who were only contingently related to the claims of a reasonable history, through the ongoing practical accomplishments of individuals within the class committed to social change. Here he provided a basis for restoring to radical theory a dimension it had been in danger of losing, even in his own Marxism —the dimension of real individuals as the premise of theory and practice, a dimension Marx himself had constantly reiterated.

On this point, Merleau-Ponty's intentions rejoined those of Marx. Nevertheless, the image of subjectivity he proposed differed significantly from that offered by Marx. Although both considered subjectivity as intersubjectivity; although both grasped subjectivity as objective and, through action, objectifying; although both spoke of the individual's dependency in regard to social situations—despite all such similarities, Merleau-Ponty broke sharply with Marx's necessitarian formulations, his focus on interest and labor as paradigms of human action, and his optimistic hopes for a rational outcome of history.

Marx himself, thanks to his tacit expectations of the rationality and purposiveness of human action, both individual and collective, was able to merge that concrete conjunction of individuals called the proletariat with the image of a social force aiming rationally at the coherent outcome of history, the classless society of communism. In contrast, Merleau-Ponty, by consistently depriving Marxism of any guarantees, either rationalistic or deterministic, illuminated this relation between the concrete and rational, empirical and universal, "is" and "ought" as profoundly problematic. It seemed questionable whether the real subjects of history could ever embody the universal negativity—the proletariat in and for itself—required by the Marxist theory.

When he pursued this line of thought, Merleau-Ponty suggested that the locus of political change had to become the individual, not conceived merely abstractly, as a potential participant in a universal history, but also concretely, as a person haunted by habitual concerns, inarticulate needs, and fears as well as hopes. The cultivation of *these* fallible subjects, 'involved [*entrainées*] but not manipulated," alone could bring to radical politics "the mark of truth."[63] If the vaunted dialectic of Marxism was to retain any liberating significance, it could only be through such contact with real individuals, only through the attempt, perpetually renewed, to elucidate a significance of history which enabled each individual to *care* enough about his common world to want to risk *changing* it with others: only on this condition could dialectic clarify historical processes. Otherwise, dialectic became an empty formal husk, invoked but unsubstantiated, an absolute without a human anchor.

Merleau-Ponty also fruitfully differed from Marx in his depiction of society as an order of symbolic structures, and his understanding of institutional rules as normative rather than causal. Within institutions, tradition and explicit norms prescribe a form of life: that is, a coherent nexus of meaningful behaviors, intentional acts, and tacit gestures. While the individual may assume a previously "legislated" network of norms, the prescriptive power of such instituionalized norms depends on a community of individuals "fulfilling" the prescribed intentions in practice. Without this ongoing fulfillment, a normative order has no foundation beyond force and mere coercion. Consent through communication and action sustains institutions in existence: social conventions, unlike natural objects, must maintain their objective meaning on no grounds but those human beings supply. But since such grounds are institutionally codified in rules governing behavior and belief, and since such codes are used by human beings to articulate their intentions without any one of them necessarily comprehending what is entailed by entering into a specific institutional practice and communicating in terms of its code, the individual can never be considered absolutely free: for the intelligible articulation of his intentions rests on his previous initiation into institutions and their practices, beginning with that most conservative of institutions, language.

Despite the restricted application of their special methods, disciplines in search of general rules, such as linguistics and economics, have provided an increasingly rigorous access to such institutional rules. The most authoritative of these disciplines investigate generally stable social relations and institutions, such as language, economic exchange, and kinship systems; they seek to uncover, through procedures open to critical inspection, the rule-governed context of individual behavior, even beyond the explicit intentions of individuals. Institutional rules may form, even where they do not consciously inform, the meaningful behavior of social agents; such rules articulate that nebulous region Marx called "second nature," the unreflective arena of habit, custom, convention, and style.

To stress that the social studies uncover prescriptive *rules* rather than framing natural laws hardly corrects a long-standing misunderstanding; it does, however, suggest that previous inquiries have sometimes mistaken prescriptive force for natural fact. The substitution of "rules" for the notion of "laws" helps to underline the open-ended and malleable applicability of most rules, which are tied to context and concrete instance. For this reason, the knowledge of rules, while it may supply foresight, does not confer the power to predict.

The very meaning of "following a rule" remains in dispute among contemporary philosophers. And yet to point up this ambiguity, to argue the context-bound nature of meaning, only amplifies the primary point: such ambiguity and context-bound applicability, the open-endedness of meanings-in-use — such is the practical significance of being governed by a rule. As Merleau-Ponty remarked, institutions at best motivate or warrant, rather than simply "cause," behavior. By supplying tacit grounds where they do not explicitly prescribe behavior, rules map out the style of an institution: yet institutional styles, like social relations, collapse, develop, alter. Meanings-in-use, by their mere being-in-usage, remain open to the novel.

Here was a compelling, albeit fragmentary, interpretation that illuminated the metaphorical notion of society as a "second nature," an interpretation that might conceivably clarify and overcome the dilemmas in Marx's original understanding of social and historical laws. Merleau-Ponty thus anticipated the terms for a new debate over the methods of social inquiry.

These terms supported a vision of man as creatively engaged in shaping a history, and yet enmeshed in conventional constraints. it was a vision that afforded the prospect of a social theory beyond the antinomies of the Marxian tradition, although Merleau-Ponty himself only hinted at the shape such a theory might assume; it was a vision that offered radical thought a novel interpretation of subjectivity as an instituting self beyond either positivist determinism or rationalist necessity. The hard price paid for such insights was the abandonment of Marxism as Merleau-Ponty understood it.

Epilogue

In a sense, the appropriate ending of this essay is contained in its beginning: for the greatest accomplishment of "existential Marxism" may well be the standpoint it has provided for rereading Marx himself, and for uncovering the visionary theorist of individual emancipation behind the critic of classical political economy. Thanks to the special emphases of Sartre and Merleau-Ponty, as well as to the numerous Marx manuscripts published only within the past fifty years, it has become possible to restore the integrity of Marx's thinking, and to demonstrate the importance he assigned to subjective agency, as well as to individuation: a true communist society would transfigure human existence.

Of coure, this rereading of Marx has not supported all of the polemical points of interpretation associated with Sartre and Merleau-Ponty; but it has cast Marx's characteristic doctrine of historical necessity in a new light that forecloses any purely objectivistic interpretation (such as that currently associated with Louis Althusser), or any cant denigrating claims for individuation as "the old liberal rhetoric" (to quote Lucio Colletti's epithet).[1]

As has been shown in detail, Marx himself consistently lauded individuation as a paramount progressive tendency of history. Similarly, while he advanced a deterministic theory of economics and history, he did so only on the basis provided by rational human agency: because he assumed that men calculated shrewdly in pursuing their material affairs, he could construct a science of political economy; because proletarians could perceive their common interest in a social revolution which would extend the scope of freedom, a practical sense of progress and the meaning of history seemed possible as well.

At the same time, Sartre and Merleau-Ponty have contributed, not merely to the rediscovery but also to the redefinition of the Marxist understanding of subjectivity. Merleau-Ponty has elaborated the valid core of Marx's understanding: his view of humans as sentient, embodied beings, sociable creatures who define themselves through an endless variety of tasks and roles, through the creation of durable works that can be shared with others. But while Merleau-Ponty's phenomenology enlarged Marx's image of the individuality liberated through communism, Sartre's philosophy of existence illuminated the inertia and fear of freedom jeopardizing Marx's project. Both Merleau-Ponty and Sartre denied not only the determinism of evolutionary positivism but also the native rationality of the human subject. Their redefinition of subjectivity thus went to the heart of Marx's original understanding by questioning the primacy of purposeful labor and enlightened interest among the modes of being human. Yet as Sartre insisted, their intention was never "to give the irrational its due" but instead to reduce the "indetermination and non-knowledge" eroding the subjective foundations of Marx's theory. Together, Sartre and Merleau-Ponty have helped clarify a number of vital issues affecting the sense of subjectivity and individuation in Marxism.

They have shown the significant freedom of human beings and the impossibility of a predictive science of society; they have also described the subjective as well as historical grounds of human institutions, and thus the necessity of interpreting conventional social relations as intrinsically open-ended and mutable, however fixed they may appear. They have examined the role of habitual, unthinking action in sustaining such inert institutions and the importance of cultivating freedom and rationality as well as individuality, with an awareness that these are problematic acquisitions of fallible human beings, rather than increasingly universal values fostered by historical development and exhibiting the "fixity of popular prejudice." Finally, they have indicated, if only indirectly, the urgency of creating new situations and conceiving new institutions that will encourage men to emancipate themselves—institutions that ultimately will enable men to become free individuals rather than the powerless subjects of the prevailing socialist and capitalist systems.

To be sure, these accomplishments have not been without problems, especially severe ones in the case of Sartre's dualistic ontology, as has been noted. But one particularly troubling problem common to both Sartre and Merleau-Ponty is worth stressing: despite their incisive criticism of Marx's rationalism and determinism, both were reluctant to extend their phenomenological philosophy to Marx's theory of history. Indeed, Merleau-Ponty's own phenomenology, consistently elaborated, discredited any univocal interpretation of history and raised instead the prospect of unsynchronized multiple histories. Similarly, Sartre's description of the fear of truth, which he once called "that thing of indefinite approximation," should have warned him of the dangers in attempting to establish a "Truth" of history, or in trying to validate a "dialectical Reason" a priori. In addition to enriching their understanding of subjectivity and individuation, Marxism for Merleau-Ponty and Sartre too often functioned as a secular faith that blunted their doubt and blurred their distinctive vision. As a result, their "existential Marxism" did not always adequately meet the challenge to a rationalist theory of history contained in the thought of Nietzsche and Heidegger. Nor did it consistently amplify the most promising, if difficult, implications of their own existential phenomenology—such as the uncertainties inherent in a theory of history grounded in human existence. But then, a Truth of History is more reassuring than an existence whose meaning may be suspended by an unanticipated turn of events, a failure of *virtù*, a lack of care and commitment.

This observation, as well as the trajectory of Merleau-Ponty's career, inevitably raises the difficult question of the value of Marxism today. This question cannot be resolved on a purely philosophical basis: Marx's sociology of classes is involved, as are his characteristic economic categories and hypotheses. Moreover, the present essay has by no means examined all of the relevant contemporary proposals for the renewal of Marxist philosophy; these range from the phenomenological accounts of the Italian philosopher Enzo Paci and the Czech theoretician Karel Kosík to the critical theory of Jürgen Habermas.

But if I may nevertheless hazard a personal opinion, it would be that Marxism has indeed not turned out to be true in most of the ways Marx had anticipated: the rate of profit has not declined in the fashion foreseen by Marx, the lot of the worker has not steadily deteriorated, industrial society has not polarized into two self-consciously hostile camps, and class conflict has not proven to be the school for enlightened interest Marx expected. As a result, a proletarian revolution has yet to occur in any advanced industrial country. Instead, Marx's concept of the proletariat as the harbinger of true humanity has become the ideological property of mass parties in the parliamentary political arena, while in avowedly "communist" one-party states, the proletariat as universal class has become a myth cloaking universal domination. In defiance of Marx's hope, communism has come to mean "labor camps, plus electrification." Merleau-Ponty's conclusions thus seem warranted: it is doubtful whether a Marxism stripped of rationalist assumptions, its allegiance with the proletariat, and most of its economic prognoses, any longer merits the name Marxism.

On the other hand, a project like the one Marx originally undertook, of supplying insight into the practical possibilities for extending the range of human freedom, seems to me central to any social theory that does not simply assume fatalistically the given social conditions. Merleau-Ponty himself eloquently made the case for retaining, even in the face of adversity, this kind of transcending outlook on history: such a philosophy "awakens us to the importance of daily events and action. For it is a philosophy which arouses in us a love for our times which are not the simple repetition of human eternity nor merely the conclusion to premises already postulated. It is a view which like the most fragile object of perception—a soap bubble, or a wave—or like the most simple dialogue, embraces indivisibly all the order and all the disorder of the world."[2] The problem, as Merleau-Ponty's own work illustrates, is to maintain such a transcending outlook without succumbing to the chimera that history climaxes teleologically in a "final goal," or the illusion that Marxism provides a necessary and sufficient standpoint for interpreting this ambiguous and inherently heterogeneous process. For the central categories of Marxism are as subject to decay as the capitalist society they were intended to help dissolve. Such problems, however, bear witness not merely to the limitations of a particular thinker, or even to the inadequacies of a particular theory, but also, and more fundamentally, to the difficulties in formulating a thoroughgoing critique of contemporary society that is actively oriented toward the possibilities for a better form of life without being arbitrary.

Theodor Adorno expressed these difficulties well.

The only philosophy which can be responsibly practiced in face of despair is the attempt to contemplate all things as they would present themselves from the standpoint of redemption.... Perspectives must be fashioned that displace and estrange the world, reveal it to be, with its rifts and crevices, as indigent and distorted as it will appear one day in the messianic light. To gain such perspective...is the simplest of things...but it is also the utterly impossible thing.... Even its own impossibility it must at last comprehend for the sake of the possible. But beside the demand thus placed on thought, the question of the reality or unreality of redemption itself hardly matters.[3]

As the present essay has endeavored to show, the perceptions generated by such a philosophy applied to the issue of individuation are not insignificant: from the perspectives this philosophy affords, individuation appears a frail accomplishment, threatened from without by economic as well as political forms of domination and from within by the fear of being different. But the idea of the authentically free individual is kept alive in the philosophy's commitment to exploring alternative social forms capable of cultivating the expressive and rational capabilities of human beings, as well as satisfying their material needs. That Marxism has not yet created or even always adequately conceived the appropriate social forms is true enough; yet the challenge remains, with the dignity and freedom of being human at stake.

Individuation, a question of autonomy, self-expression, and a personal commitment to freedom, as well as a matter of material well-being, is then seen as the endowment, not of a monadically self-reliant agent, but rather of a person open to, and realizing his aims through, the institutions he inhabits. Without the tools and knowledge to objectify himself, without the respect that would dignify these personal powers, without the opportunity to participate actively in the life of society, without the confidence and real possibility to shape effectively his own existence — without these, the individual may appear as an actor endowed with a formal liberty, and even with a certain inherent particularity, but he remains in fact a prisoner of circumstance, enmeshed in a web of events which manifest a contrary logic. The sense of subjectivity is thus bound up in a world that must become the individual's own. For, as Hegel remarked, "The concrete self-feeling of even the strongest natures requires a certain range of external relationships, an adequate portion, so to speak, of the universe; for without such an individual world the human soul . . . would have no individuality at all, and would not attain to a specifically distinct individuality."[4] A philosophy committed to realizing this vision of individuation will, on principle, pursue its aims with practical intentions, through an understanding of oppressive social relations and the possibilities for freedom they conceal: that is the authentic legacy of Marxism.

Notes

ABBREVIATIONS USED IN NOTES

A = Friedrich Engels, *Anti-Dühring* [*Herr Eugen Dühring's Revolution in Science*], trans. Burns (New York, 1939).

AD = Maurice Merleau-Ponty, *Adventures of the Dialectic,* trans. Bien (Evanston, Ill., 1973).

C = Karl Marx, *Capital.* Vol. I, trans. Moore and Aveling (Chicago, 1906). Vol. III (Moscow, 1966).

CDR = Jean-Paul Sartre, *Critique of Dialectical Reason,* trans. Sheridan-Smith (London, 1976).

CPE = Karl Marx, *Critique of Political Economy,* trans. Stone (Chicago, 1904).

CW = Karl Marx and Friedrich Engels, *Collected Works* (New York, 1975 ff.). First number indicates volume.

DN = Friedrich Engels, *Dialectics of Nature,* trans. Dutt (New York, 1940).

G = Karl Marx, *Grundrisse,* trans. Nicolaus (New York, 1973).

GK = Karl Marx, *Grundrisse der Kritik der politischen Ökonomie* (*Rohentwurf*) (Berlin, 1953).

MEGA = Karl Marx and Friedrich Engels, *Historisch-kritische Gesamtausgabe,* ed. Rjazanov and Adoratskij (Berlin and Moscow, 1927 ff.). In three parts; roman numeral indicates part, succeeding number indicates volume, and final numeral, after slash, when present, gives half-volume number.

MEW = Karl Marx and Friedrich Engels, *Werke* (Berlin, 1956 ff.). First number indicates volume.

SC = Karl Marx and Friedrich Engels, *Selected Correspondence,* trans. Lasker (Moscow, 1965).

SM = Jean-Paul Sartre, *Search for a Method,* trans. Barnes (New York, 1967).

SW = Karl Marx and Friedrich Engels, *Selected Works,* in three volumes (Moscow, 1969).

For the German text of Marx's works prior to *The Communist Manifesto,* the MEGA is used; for all other works, except the *Grundrisse,* the MEW is used. Whenever possible, citations in English refer to the CW currently being published.

INTRODUCTION: MARXISM AND THE SENSE OF SUBJECTIVITY

1. Quoted in Alain Schapp and Pierre Vidal-Naquet, *The French Student Uprising,* trans. Jolas (Boston, 1971), p. 442.

2. Louis Althusser, *Lenin and Philosophy and Other Essays,* trans. Brewster (London, 1971), p. 160.

3. Karel Kosík, *Dialectics of the Concrete,* trans. Kovanda and Schmidt (Boston, 1976), p. 70.

4. Max Horkheimer, "Materialism and Metaphysics," in Horkheimer, *Critical Theory,* trans. O'Connell (New York, 1972), p. 29.

5. Alexis de Tocqueville, *Democracy in America,* ed. Bradley (New York, 1945), II, 104, 106.

6. Karl Marx, "Draft of an Article on Friedrich List's Book *Das Nationale System der Politischen Oekonomie,*" CW 4, p. 276.

7. Georg Simmel, "Group Expansion and the Development of Individuality," in Simmel, *On Individuality and Social Forms,* ed. Levine (Chicago, 1971), p. 272.

8. For example, David McLellan, *Karl Marx: His Life and Thought* (New York, 1975); Carl Schorske, *German Social Democracy, 1905-1917* (New York, 1955); George Lichtheim, *Marxism in Modern France* (New York, 1966); Mark Poster, *Existential Marxism in Postwar France* (Princeton, N.J., 1975). For more titles, see the bibliography following.

1: MARX'S HOPES FOR INDIVIDUATION

1. Marx, *The Difference Between the Democritean and Epicurean Philosophy of Nature,* MEGA I, 1/1, p. 65; CW 1, p. 86. The dissertation proper contains some paradoxical insights into Marx's later materialism. Somewhat surprisingly, an "in spite of the insufficiency and weakness of his physical explanations," to quote Auguste Cornu, "Marx preferred the philosophy of Nature of Epicurus to that of Democritus, because, rejecting the determinism of Democritus, he [Epicurus] had shown the possibility for man to act freely." See Cornu, *Karl Marx et Friedrich Engels: leur vie et leur oeuvre* (Paris, 1955 ff.), I, 200.

2. For a full discussion, see Heinz Lubasz, "Marx's Initial Problematic:

The Problem of Poverty," *Political Studies,* 24 (March, 1976), 24-42.

3. Marx, "Comments on the Latest Prussian Censorship Instruction," MEGA I, 1/1, pp. 162-163; CW 1, p. 120.

4. Marx, "The Leading Article in No. 179 of the *Kölnische Zeitung:* Religion, Free Press and Philosophy," MEGA I, 1/1, p. 241; CW 1, p. 193.

5. Ludwig Feuerbach, "Preliminary Theses on the Reform of Philosophy," in *The Fiery Brook: Selected Writings of Ludwig Feuerbach,* trans. Hanfi (Garden City, N.Y., 1972), p. 154.

6. Marx, *Critique of Hegel's "Philosophy of Right,"* MEGA I, 1/1, pp. 426-427; CW 3, p. 23.

7. Ibid., p. 406; CW 3, p. 8.

8. Ibid., p. 426; CW 3, p. 23.

9. Ibid., p. 432; CW 3, p. 28.

10. G. W. F. Hegel, *Philosophy of Right,* trans. Knox (London, 1952), p. 198 (§303).

11. Marx, *Critique of "Philosophy,"* MEGA I, 1/1, pp. 435-437, 499; CW 3, pp. 31-33, 81.

12. Ibid., p. 435; CW 3, p. 30.

13. Ibid., pp. 542-544; CW 3, pp. 119-121.

14. Marx, "Toward the Critique of Hegel's Philosophy of Right: Introduction," MEGA I, 1/1, pp. 616, 620; CW 3, pp. 183, 187.

15. Marx, "Critical Marginal Notes on the Article 'The King of Prussia and Social Reform. By a Prussian,'" MEGA I, 3, p. 22; CW 3, p. 205.

16. Marx, *Economic and Philosophic Manuscripts of 1844,* MEGA I, 3, p. 110; CW 3, p. 293.

17. Ibid., pp. 85-89; CW 3, pp. 274-278.

18. See Feuerbach, *The Essence of Christianity,* trans. Eliot (New York, 1957), pp. 1-2.

19. Marx, *Economic and Philosophic,* MEGA I, 3, pp. 160-161; CW 3, p. 336.

20. Ibid., p. 89; CW 3, p. 277.

21. Ibid., pp. 158, 166-168; CW 3, pp. 334, 341-342. Cf. Marx's note on "Hegel's Construction of the Phenomenology," MEGA I, 5, p. 531; CW 4, p. 665.

22. Marx, *Economic and Philosophic,* MEGA I, 3, pp. 91, 115, 161; CW 3, pp. 279, 297, 336-337. Cf. Hegel, *Phenomenology of Mind,* trans. Baillie (New York, 1967), pp. 229-240.

23. Marx, "Excerpt-Notes of 1844," MEGA I, 3, p. 536; CW 3, p. 217.

24. Marx, *Economic and Philosophic,* MEGA I, 3, p. 116; CW 3, p. 298.

25. Ibid., p. 117; CW 3, p. 299.

26. Ibid.

27. Ibid., pp. 83-84, 86, 136; CW 3, pp. 272, 275, 314.

28. Marx, "Excerpt-Notes," MEGA I, 3, pp. 532, 535; CW 3, pp. 213, 227.

29. Marx, *Economic and Philosophic,* MEGA I, 3, p. 149; CW 3, p. 326.

30. Ibid., pp. 111-113, 120-121; CW 3, pp. 293-299, 301-302.

31. Ibid., p. 121; CW 3, p. 296.

32. Marx, "Excerpt-Notes," MEGA I, 3, p. 547; CW 3, pp. 227-228.

33. Marx, *Economic and Philosophic,* MEGA I, 3, p. 126; CW 3, p. 306.

34. Marx, "Excerpt-Notes," MEGA I, 3, p. 547; CW 3, p. 228.

35. Cf. Marx, "Letter to His Father: on a Turning-Point in Life," MEGA I, 1/2, pp. 215, 218; CW 1, pp. 12, 18.

36. Marx, *Critique of Political Economy,* MEW 13, p. 10; CPE, p. 13.

37. See Marx and Friedrich Engels, *The German Ideology,* MEGA I, 5, p. 215; CW 5, p. 236: "Owing to the fact that Feuerbach showed the religious world as an illusion of the earthly world . . . German theory too was confronted with the question which he left unanswered: how was it that people 'got into their heads' these illusions? Even for the German theoreticians, this question paved the way to the materialistic outlook on the world. . . . This path was already indicated in the *Deutsch-Französische Jahrbücher* — in the *Einleitung zur Kritik der Hegelschen Rechtsphilosophie* and *Zur Judenfrage.* But since at the time this was done in philosophical phraseology, the traditionally occurring philosophical expressions such as 'human essence,' 'genus,' etc., gave the German theoreticians the desired excuse for misunderstanding the real trend of thought and believing that here again it was a question merely of giving a new turn to their worn-out theoretical garments."

38. Ibid., pp. 10-11; CW 5, pp. 31-32.

39. Ibid., pp. 32-32, 37-38, 58-59; CW 5, pp. 58, 61-62, 88-89.

40. Ibid., p. 410; CW 5, p. 432.

41. Ibid., p. 16; CW 5, p. 37.

42. Ibid., p. 25; CW 5, p. 49.

43. Ibid., pp. 460-461; CW 5, p. 476.

44. Ibid., pp. 57-58; CW 5, p. 88.

45. Ibid., p. 60; CW 5, p. 81.

46. Ibid., p. 22; CW 5, p. 47.

47. Ibid., pp. 417-418; CW 5, pp. 439-440.

48. Max Stirner, *The Ego and His Own,* trans. Byington (New York, 1973), p. 55.

49. Ibid., pp. 167, 169.

50. Ibid., p. 366.

51. See Engels to Marx, 11-19-44, MEGA III, 1, pp. 6-7.

52. Marx and Engels, *German Ideology,* MEGA I, 5, pp. 227-228, 232; CW 5, pp. 247, 252.

53. Ibid., MEGA I, 5, pp. 108, 193, 242, 270; CW 5, pp. 129, 214, 262, 291-292.

54. See Marx and Engels, *Manifesto of the Communist Party,* MEW 4, p. 467; CW 6, p. 489.

55. Marx, "Speech at the Anniversary of the *People's Paper,*" SW I, p. 500.

56. Marx, *Political Economy,* MEW 13, p. 7; CPE, p. 9. Marx mentions his six-part plan in a letter to Engels, 4-2-58, MEW 29, p. 312; SC, p. 104.

57. Marx, *Grundrisse,* GK, p. 203, G, p. 296.

58. Ibid., pp. 205-207, 211-212, 268-270; G, pp. 297-300, 304-305, 363-364.

59. Ibid., pp. 65, 213-214; G, pp. 146-147, 305-307.

60. Ibid., p. 359; G, p. 455.

61. Ibid., pp. 358, 361; G, pp. 454, 457.

62. Ibid., pp. 215, 584-585, 716; G, pp. 308, 698-699, 831-832.

63. Ibid., pp. 154, 156; G, pp. 242-243, 245. Cf. Marx, *Economic and Philosophic,* MEGA I, 3, p. 148; CW 3, p. 325: "Money is the alienated ability of mankind."

64. Marx, *Grundrisse,* GK, p. 395; G, p. 496.

65. Ibid., pp. 74-75, 79-80, 204, 313-314, 545; G, pp. 156-157, 161-162, 296, 409-410, 651-652.

66. Ibid., pp. 75-76; G, p. 158.

67. Marx, *Political Economy,* MEW 13, pp. 32-33; CPE, pp. 46-47. Cf. Marx, *Grundrisse,* GK, p. 440; G, pp. 541-542.

68. Marx, *Grundrisse,* GK, p. 6; G, p. 84 (emphasis added).

69. Marx, *Capital,* MEW 23, p. 52; C I, p. 534.

70. Ibid., p. 349; C I, p. 361.

71. Ibid., pp. 93, 618, 791; C I, pp. 91, 649, 837.

72. Marx, "Marginal Notes to the Program of the German Workers' Party," MEW 19, p. 21; SW III, p. 19.

73. Theodor Adorno, *Minima Moralia,* trans. Jephcott (London, 1974), p. 103 (§66).

74. Marx, *Grundrisse,* GK, p. 599; G, p. 712.

75. Ibid., pp. 231, 426; G, pp. 324-325, 527-528.

76. Ibid., pp. 387-388; G, p. 488.

2: THE "REAL INDIVIDUAL" AND MARX'S METHOD

1. Feuerbach, "Principles of the Philosophy of the Future," in *The Fiery Brook,* p. 175.

2. Feuerbach, "Preliminary Theses," in ibid., p. 161.

3. See Feuerbach, "Principles," in ibid., pp. 225-226 (§33); also Feuerbach, "Towards a Critique of Hegel's Philosophy," in ibid., pp. 76 ff.

4. Marx, *Critique of "Philosophy,"* MEGA I, 1/1, p. 424; CW 3, pp. 21-22; see also Marx, *Economic and Philosophic,* MEGA I, 3, pp. 117, 149; CW 3, pp. 298-299, 326.

5. Marx and Engels, *The Holy Family,* MEGA I, 3, pp. 227-232, 304; CW 4, pp. 57-61, 127.

6. Ibid., p. 179; CW 4, p. 7.

7. Ibid., p. 265; CW 4, p. 93.

8. Marx and Engels, *German Ideology,* MEGA I, 5, p. 10; CW 5, p. 31.

9. Ibid., pp. 65-66; CW 5, pp. 78-79.

10. Ibid., p. 416; CW 5, p. 437.

11. See Marx, *Grundrisse,* GK, p. 176; G, pp. 264-265.

12. Marx, *The Poverty of Philosophy,* MEGA I, 6, p. 173; CW 6, p. 159.

13. Marx, *Grundrisse,* GK, p. 111; G, p. 197.

14. Marx, *Political Economy,* MEW 13, p. 76; CPE, p. 120.

15. Marx, *The Eighteenth Brumaire of Louis Bonaparte,* MEW 8, p. 115; SW I, p. 398.

16. Marx, *Grundrisse,* GK, p. 21; G, p. 100.

17. Marx, *Capital* (Hamburg, 1867), p. 27. My thanks to Cyril Levitt for pointing out this passage from the first edition of *Capital;* it does not appear in later editions.

18. Marx, *Grundrisse,* GK, pp. 22, 945; G, p. 101.

19. Ibid., pp. 24-25; G, p. 104.

20. Ibid., pp. 5-6; G, pp. 83-84.

21. Ibid., p. 9; G, p. 85.

22. Marx, *Capital,* MEW 23, p. 27; C I, p. 25.

23. Ibid., p. 16; C I, p. 15.

24. Marx, *Grundrisse,* GK, p. 176; G, pp. 264-265.

25. Marx and Engels, *German Ideology,* MEGA I, 5, p. 60; CW 5, p. 81.

26. Marx, *Grundrisse,* GK, p. 111; G, pp. 196-197.

27. Ibid., pp. 22, 599; G, pp. 101, 712.

28. Marx and Engels, *German Ideology,* MEGA I, 5, p. 60; CW 5, p. 81.

3: MARX'S CONCEPT OF LABOR

1. Marx, *Political Economy,* MEW 13, pp. 8-9; CPE, pp. 11-12; cf. Marx and Engels, *German Ideology,* MEGA I, 5, p. 16; CW 5, p. 37.

2. Ernst Bloch, *On Karl Marx,* trans. Maxwell (New York, 1971), p. 86.

3. See Cornu, *Karl Marx et Friedrich Engels,* IV, 133-134.

4. Marx, *Economic and Philosophic,* MEGA I, 3, pp. 125, 152-153, 156; CW 3, pp. 305, 329, 332-333.

5. Marx and Engels, *German Ideology,* MEGA I, 5, p. 10; CW 5, p. 31.

6. Marx, *Economic and Philosophic,* MEGA I, 3, p. 88; CW 3, pp. 276-277.

7. Ibid., p. 88; CW 3, pp. 276-277.

8. Ibid., p. 114; CW 3, p. 297.

9. Ibid., where Marx criticizes "immature communism" (e.g., Cabet) for seeking a proof of the communist essence in the existent historical process. "By so doing it [immature communism] simply makes clear that by far the greater part of this process contradicts its own claim, and that, if it has ever existed, precisely its being in the *past* refutes its pretension to being *essential being.*"

10. Marx, "Theses on Feuerbach," MEGA I, 5, p. 533; CW 5, p. 6 (§1).

11. Ibid., p. 534; CW 5, p. 7 (§3).

12. Ibid.; CW 5, p. 6 (§2).

13. Lucien Goldmann, *The Human Sciences and Philosophy,* trans. White and Anchor (London, 1969), p. 28.

14. See Marx, "Theses," MEGA I, 5, pp. 534-535; CW 5, pp. 7-8 (§6 and §9).

15. Ibid., p. 535; CW 5, p. 8 (§10).

16. Ibid. (§11).

17 Marx and Engels, *German Ideology,* MEGA I, 5, p. 31, CW 5, p. 58.

18. Hegel, *Phenomenology,* p. 422.

19. Ibid., pp. 420-421.

20. Ibid., p. 429.

21. Ibid., p. 428.

22. Jean Hyppolite, *Genèse et structure de la Phénoménologie de l'Esprit de Hegel* (Paris, 1946), p. 286.

23. Hegel, *Science of Logic,* trans. Johnston and Struthers (London, 1929), II, 348.

24. Ibid., p. 381.

25. Ibid., p. 383.

26. Ibid., pp. 386-388.

27. Hegel, *The Logic,* trans. Wallace (London, 1892), p. 88 (§42).

28. See Marx, *Political Economy,* MEW 13, pp. 23-24; CPE, p. 33; and Marx, *Capital,* MEW 23, pp. 57-58; C I, pp. 49-50.

29. Marx, *Capital,* MEW 23, p. 193; C I, p. 198.

30. Ibid., pp. 193, 198-199; C I, pp. 198, 204-205.

31. Ibid., p. 194; C I, p. 199.

32. Marx, *Grundrisse,* GK, pp. 206, 208; C, pp. 298-299, 301.

33. Ibid., p. 265; G, p. 360.

34. Ibid., pp. 265-266; G, p. 361. Cf. Marx, *Capital,* MEW 23, pp. 195, 198; C I, pp. 198, 204-205.

35. Marx, *Capital,* MEW 23, p. 345; C I, pp. 357-358.

36. Ibid., p. 351; C I, p. 364.

37. Marx and Engels, *Manifesto,* MEW 4, p. 476; CW 6, p. 499.

38. Georg Lukács, "The Dialectics of Labor: Beyond Causality and Teleology," trans. Gucinski, *Telos,* 6 (Fall, 1970), 174.

4: REASON, INTEREST, AND THE NECESSITY OF HISTORY — THE AMBIGUITIES OF MARX'S LEGACY

1. Marx, *Capital,* MEW 25, pp. 260, 274-275, 276-277; C III, pp. 250, 264, 266.

2. Ibid., MEW 23, p. 16; C I, p. 15.

3. Ibid., p. 26; C I, p. 23.

4. Ibid., MEW 25, p. 32; C III, p. 25.

5. Ibid., p. 184; C III, p. 175: "Such a general rate of surplus value — viewed as a tendency like all other economic laws...."

6. Marx, *Poverty,* MEGA I, 6, p. 191; CW 6, p. 177.

7. Ibid., p. 227; CW 6, p. 211.

8. See Marx and Engels, *Manifesto,* MEW 4, pp. 470-471; CW 6, pp. 492-493.

9. Marx and Engels, *Holy Family,* MEGA I, 3, p. 206; CW 4, p. 36.

10. Marx and Engels, *German Ideology,* MEGA I, 5, p. 60; CW 5, pp. 52-53.

11. Marx and Engels to Bebel, Liebknecht, Bracke, and others, 9-17-79, MEW 19, p. 165; SC, p. 327.

12. Marx, "An Exchange of Letters," MEGA I, 1/1, p. 561; CW 3, p. 137.

13. Marx, "Toward the Critique," MEGA I, 1/1, p. 615; CW 3, p. 182.

14. Marx to Schweitzer, 10-13-68, MEW 32, p. 570; SC, p. 215.

15. See Marx, *Grundrisse,* GK, p. 716; G, p. 832.

16. Ibid., pp. 366-367; G, p. 463.

17. Albert O. Hirschman, *The Passions and the Interests* (Princeton, 1977), pp. 43-44; in this context, Hirschman cites the Helvétius passage quoted above.

18. Hegel, *Philosophy of Right,* p. 124 (§187).

19. Adam Ferguson, *An Essay on the History of Civil Society* (Edinburgh, 1966), pp. 11, 15.

20. Hegel, *Philosophy of Right,* p. 189 (§288).

21. See, e.g., Marx, "Proceedings of the Sixth Rhine Province Assembly.

Third Article Debates on the Law on Thefts of Wood," MEGA I, 1/1, pp. 266-304; CW I, pp. 224-263; "The Supplement to Nos. 335 and 336 of the Augsburg *Allgemeine Zeitung* on the Commissions of the Estates in Prussia," MEGA I, 1/1, pp. 321-335; CW 1, pp. 292-306; "Justification of the Correspondent from the Mosel," MEGA I, 1/1, pp. 355-383; CW 1, pp. 332-358.

22. Marx, *Political Economy,* MEW 13, pp. 7-8; CPE, p. 10.

23. Marx, *Economic and Philosophic,* MEGA I, 3, p. 144; CW 3, p. 321; Marx, *Critique of "Philosophy,"* MEGA I, 1/1, p. 547; CW 3, p. 123.

24. Marx, "Justification," MEGA I, 1/1, p. 373; CW 1, p. 349.

25. Tocqueville, *Democracy,* I, 252; Marx cites Tocqueville in "On the Jewish Question."

26. Marx, "Justification," MEGA I, 1/1, p. 368; CW 1, p. 343.

27. Ibid., p. 373; CW 1, p. 349.

28. Marx, "Proceedings," MEGA I, 1/1, p. 298; CW 1, p. 256.

29. Marx, "Toward the Critique," MEGA I, 1/1, p. 619; CW 3, p. 186.

30. Adam Smith, *The Wealth of Nations* (New York, 1937), p. 249. For Marx's comments in 1844, see his *Economic and Philosophic,* MEGA I, 3, pp. 44-45; CW 3, pp. 240-241; and MEGA I, 3, pp. 72-73; CW 3, pp. 263-264, where he disputes Smith's other important claim, that the landlords as well as the workers have an interest identical with society's. Marx copied out the relevant passages: see MEGA I, 3, p. 472 ("Aus den Exzerptheften: Adam Smith, Recherches sur la nature et les causes de la richesse des nations"). Some years later, Marx returned to the same passage: see MEW, 26.2, pp. 373-374; see also Marx, *Theories of Surplus Value,* II, trans. Ryazanskaya (Moscow, 1968), p. 372.

31. Marx and Engels, *Holy Family,* MEGA I, 3, p. 299; CW 4, p. 123; idem, *German Ideology,* MEGA I, 5, p. 22; CW 5, p. 47; idem, *Manifesto,* MEW 4, p. 464; CW 6, p. 487.

32. Marx, *Manifesto,* MEW 4, p. 472; CW 6, pp. 494-495.

33. Marx and Engels, *Holy Family,* MEGA I, 3, p. 296; CW 4, p. 120.

34. Ibid., MEGA I, 3, p. 307; CW 4, pp. 130-131.

35. Marx, "On Poland," MEW 4, p. 416; CW 6, p. 388; Marx and Engels, *German Ideology,* MEGA I, 5, p. 65; CW 5, p. 77.

36. Marx and Engels, *German Ideology,* MEGA I, 5, p. 228; CW 5, p. 247; Marx and Engels, *Holy Family,* MEGA I, 3, p. 310; CW 4, p. 134.

37. Cf. Marx and Engels, *German Ideology,* MEGA I, 5, pp. 64, 192; CW 5, pp. 80, 213.

38. Marx, *The Ethnological Notebooks of Karl Marx,* ed. Krader (Assen, Netherlands, 1972), p. 329. My thanks to Cyril Levitt for pointing out this important passage.

39. In *The German Ideology* interest was also historically situated as a

defining aspect of classes in contradistinction to feudal estates. See Marx and Engels, *The German Ideology*, MEGA I, 5, p. 52; CW 5, p. 90: "By the mere fact that it is a *class* and no longer an *estate*, the bourgeoisie is forced to organize itself no longer locally, but nationally, and to give a general form to its average interests."

40. Ibid., p. 177; CW 5, p. 195.

41. See Marx, "Proceedings," MEGA I, 1/1, pp. 283, 291; CW 1, pp. 241, 249; see also ibid., p. 303; CW 1, p. 261: "Interest by its very nature is blind, immoderate, one-sided; in short, it is lawless natural instinct. . . ."

42. Ibid., pp. 289-290; CW 1, p. 247.

43. Marx and Engels, *Manifesto*, MEW 4, p. 493; CW 6, p. 519; Marx, *Capital*, MEW 25, pp. 204, 208; C III, pp. 194, 198; Marx, *Economic and Philosophic*, MEGA I, 3, p. 135; CW 3, p. 313; Marx, *Grundrisse*, GK, p. 155; G, p. 244.

44. Marx, *Capital*, MEW 23, pp. 421-422; C I, p. 436.

45. Smith, *Wealth*, p. 249; see also p. 734, where Smith describes the modern worker "as stupid and ignorant as it is possible for a human creature to become"—a section of Smith's book cited by Marx in *Capital*, MEW 23, pp. 383-384; C I, pp. 397-398.

46. See Hirschman, *Passions*, pp. 110-111, for a development of this point.

47. See Marx and Engels, *Holy Family*, MEGA I, 3, pp. 252-253; CW 4, pp. 81-82: "The *interest* of the bourgeoisie in the 1789 Revolution . . . *'won'* everything. . . . The Revolution was a 'failure' only for the mass which did not have in the *political* 'idea' the idea of its real *'interest.'* . . . If the Revolution was a failure, it was not because the mass was *'enthusiastic'* over it and *'interested'* in it, but because the most numerous part of the mass, the part distinct from the bourgeoisie, did not have a revolutionary principle of its *own*, but *only* an *'idea,'* and hence only an object of momentary enthusiasm and only seeming uplift." By contrast, the interest of the bourgeoisie—a class which knew its "real interest"—was a powerful historical factor: "That *interest* was so powerful that it was victorious over the pen of Marat, the guillotine of the Terror and the sword of Napoleon."

48. Ibid., p. 309; CW 4, p. 133.

49. Hegel, *Philosophy of Right*, pp. 124-125 (§187).

50. But cf. the acid remarks on Hegel's philosophy of education in Marx, *Capital*, MEW 23, p. 385n; C I, p. 399n.

51. Marx, "Critical Marginal Notes," MEGA I, 3, pp. 17-19; CW 3, pp. 201-202; Engels, *The Condition of the Working Class in England*, MEGA I, 4, p. 112; CW 4, p. 410.

52. Marx and Engels, *German Ideology*, MEGA I, 5, pp. 67-68; CW 5, p. 79.

53. Marx, *Poverty*, MEGA I, 6, p. 226; CW 6, p. 211; Marx and Engels, *Manifesto*, MEW 4, p. 471; CW 6, pp. 493-494.

54. Marx, *Eighteenth Brumaire*, MEW 8, p. 198; CW I, p. 479.

55. Cf. Marx, "Leading Article," MEGA I, 1/1, p. 241; CW 1, p. 193.

56. Marx and Engels, "Address of the Central Committee to the Communist League," MEW 7, p. 254; SW I, p. 185; cf. Marx, *Poverty*, MEGA I, 6, p. 191; CW 6, pp. 177-178.

57. See Marx and Engels, *Manifesto*, MEW 4, pp. 471-472; CW 6, pp. 493-494.

58. Marx, *Poverty*, MEGA I, 6, p. 225; CW 6, p. 210.

59. Marx, "Instructions for the Delegates of the Provisional General Council. The Different Questions," SW II, p. 81.

60. Ibid., p. 83. Marx also warned against a preoccupation with purely economic issues here: "Too exclusively bent upon the local and immediate struggle with capital, the Trades' Unions have not yet fully understood the power of acting against the system of wages slavery itself."

61. Marx and Engels, *Manifesto*, MEW 4, p. 472; CW 6, p. 495.

62. Hegel, *Logic*, p. 147 (§81).

63. See Hegel, *Die Vernunft in der Geschichte*, ed. Hoffmeister (Hamburg, 1955), p. 29 (L).

64. Hegel, *Science*, II, 185.

65. Ibid., p. 213.

66. Hegel, *Philosophy of History*, trans. Sibree (New York, 1956), p. 54.

67. Smith, *Wealth*, p. 13.

68. See Helmut Fleischer, *Marxism and History*, trans. Mosbacher (New York, 1973), pp. 119-121.

69. Marx, "An Exchange," MEGA I, 1/1, p. 574; CW 3, p. 143.

70. Smith, *Wealth*, p. 324.

71. See Hirschman, *Passions*, pp. 48-56, on "Assets of an Interest-Governed World: Predictability and Constancy."

72. Hegel, *Logic*, p. 350 (§206). Marx footnoted the first part of this passage in his discussion of the labor process: see Marx, *Capital*, MEW 23, p. 194n; C I, p. 199n.

73. Marx, "Speech," SW I, p. 501. Karl Löwith identified Marx's "shrewd spirit" with Hegel's "cunning of Reason" in Löwith, *Meaning in History* (Chicago, 1949), p. 36.

74. Elie Halévy, *The Growth of Philosophic Radicalism*, trans. Morris (Boston, 1955), pp. 52-53; cf. Leonard Krieger, *Kings and Philosophers, 1689-1789* (New York, 1970), pp. 210-215, on "The New Rationalism."

75. See Jean-Jacques Rousseau, *The Social Contract*, Book II, chap. 1.

76. See ibid., chap. 7; in "On the Jewish Question," Marx cites this chapter, although his understanding of the text is questionable.

77. Marx, *Capital*, MEW 23, p. 74; C I, p. 69; and "An Exchange," MEGA I, 1/1, p. 574; CW 3, p. 143. A different impression is left by Marx's rhetoric on other occasions: see Marx and Engels, *Manifesto*, MEW 4, p. 465; CW 6, p. 487: "Constant revolutionizing of production ... distinguish[es] the bourgeois epoch from all earlier ones. All fixed, fast-frozen relations, with their train of ancient and venerable prejudices and opinions, are swept away, all new-formed ones become antiquated before they can ossify. All that is solid melts into air, all that is holy is profaned...."

78. Marx, "Speech," SW I, p. 501.

79. Marx and Engels, *Holy Family*, MEGA I, 3, p. 207; CW 4, p. 37.

5: ENGELS AND THE DIALECTICS OF NATURE

1. Engels to Bloch, 9-21-90, SC, p. 417.

2. Engels, *Ludwig Feuerbach and the End of Classical German Philosophy*, MEW 21, p. 298; SW III, pp. 365-366.

3. Engels, *Herr Eugen Dühring's Revolution in Science [Anti-Dühring]*, MEW 20, p. 265; A, p. 310.

4. Ibid., MEW 20, pp. 12, 22, 129; A, pp. 17, 29, 152.

5. Engels, *Anti-Dühring*, MEW 20, pp. 55, 131-132; A, pp. 68, 155.

6. Engels, *Dialectics of Nature*, MEW 20, p. 475; DN, p. 153.

7. Engels, *Ludwig Feuerbach*, MEW 21, p. 270; SW III, p. 339.

8. See Engels, "Speech at the Graveside of Karl Marx," SW III, p. 162.

9. See, e.g., Engels, *The Origin of the Family, Private Property and the State*, SW III, p. 201.

10. See Engels, *Dialectics*, MEW 20, p. 500; DN, pp. 234-235.

11. Ibid., p. 466; DN, p. 187.

12. Ibid., p. 469.

13. Ibid., p. 325.

14. Marx, *Economic and Philosophic*, MEGA I, 3, p. 123; CW 3, p. 304. See also ibid., p. 170; CW 3, p. 345: "Nature fixed in isolation from man—is *nothing* for man."

15. Marx and Engels, *German Ideology*, MEGA I, 5, p. 554; CW 5, p. 28.

16. Engels, *Ludwig Feuerbach*, MEW 21, p. 300; SW III, pp. 369-370.

17. Engels, *Dialectics*, MEW 20, p. 466; DN, p. 187.

18. See Marx, *Economic and Philosophic*, MEGA I, 3, pp. 122-123; CW 3, pp. 302-303; and Marx and Engels, *German Ideology*, MEGA I, 5, pp. 32-33; CW 5, pp. 38-39. Marx did say in the 1844 manuscripts that sense perception must be the basis of all science; but he later revised this view, in coming to hold the position that no accurate science could be attained

without reference to human practice—the point at which Marx conceded to classical idealism its moment of truth.

19. Engels, "Special Introduction to the English Edition of 1892 of *Socialism: Scientific and Utopian*," SW III, p. 101.

20. Engels, *Dialectics,* MEW 20, p. 497; DN, p. 230. Marx, *Grundrisse,* GK, p. 505; G, p. 611.

21. Engels, *Ludwig Feuerbach,* MEW 21, p. 276; SW III, p. 347.

22. Engels, *Anti-Dühring,* MEW 20, pp. 260, 262; A, pp. 304-305, 307.

23. Engels, *Dialectics,* MEW 20, p. 324; DN, pp. 19-20.

24. Engels, *Anti-Dühring,* MEW 20, p. 106; A, p. 125, where Engels also claims that "freedom of the will therefore means nothing but the capacity to make decisions with real knowledge of the subject."

25. Marx, *Capital,* MEW 25, p. 828; C III, p. 820.

26. Engels, *Anti-Duhring,* MEW 20, p. 250; A, p. 293.

27. Ibid., p. 249; A, p. 292.

28. Ibid., p. 250; A, p. 293; and Engels, *Socialism: Scientific and Utopian,* SW III, p. 151.

29. Engels to Zasulich, 4-23-85, SC, p. 384.

30. Engels, *Ludwig Feuerbach,* MEW 21, p. 307; SW III, p. 376.

6: THE RISE OF ORTHODOX MARXISM

1. George V. Plekhanov, *Fundamental Problems of Marxism* (New York, 1969), p. 48.

2. Ibid., p. 46; on his debt to Engels, see p. 23; for a typical example of Plekhanov validating dialectics through natural science, see p. 47.

3. Plekhanov, *The Development of the Monist View of History,* trans. Rothstein (Moscow, 1956), p. 14.

4. Plekhanov, *Fundamental,* p. 32.

5. Antonio Labriola, *Essays on the Materialistic Conception of History,* trans. Kerr (New York, 1966), p. 113. On psychology, see pp. 111-113.

6. Plekhanov, *Development,* p. 330. Cf. Engels, *Dialectics,* MEW 20, p. 325; DN, p. 21: "The motion of matter is not merely crude mechanical motion. . . ."

7. Plekhanov, *Development,* p. 206 (italics dropped).

8. Ibid., p. 153.

9. Labriola, *Essays,* p. 18.

10. Ibid., p. 17.

11. Ibid., p. 63.

12. Plekhanov, *Development,* p. 277.

13. Karl Kautsky, in *Neue Zeit,* 1901-1902, xx, 1, no. 3, quoted (enthu-

siastically) by Lenin in *What Is to Be Done?*, in *Essential Works of Lenin,* ed. Christman (New York, 1966), p. 81.

14. See Marx, "Theses," MEGA I, 5, p. 534; CW 5, p. 4 (§3).

15. Kautsky, *The Road to Power,* trans. Simons (Chicago, 1909), p. 50. Also see Carl Schorske, *German Social Democracy, 1905-1917* (New York, 1955), pp. 111-115.

16. Plekhanov, *Development,* p. 292. On the elimination of teleology, see Plekhanov, "The Materialist Conception of History," in *Fundamental,* p. 112: "By entirely eliminating teleology from social science and explaining the activity of social man by his needs and by the means and methods of satisfying them, prevailing at the given time, dialectical materialism for the first time imparts to this science the 'strictness' of which her sister — the science of nature — would often boast over her."

17. Max Adler, *Marx als Denker* (Vienna, 1921), p. 80 (originally published in 1908).

18. V. I. Lenin, *Materialism and Empirio-Criticism* (New York, 1927), p. 44.

19. Ibid., p. 106.

20. Marx, *Capital,* MEW 23, pp. 93-94; C I, pp. 91-92.

21. Lenin, *Materialism,* p. 357.

22. Lenin, "The Three Sources and Three Component Parts of Marxism," in Lenin, *Selected Works* (Moscow, 1968), p. 21. See also Lenin, *Materialism,* p. 319.

23. Ibid., pp. 138-139.

24. Ibid., p. 337.

25. See, e.g., Lenin, *Two Tactics of Social Democracy in the Democratic Revolution,* in *Selected Works,* p. 60.

26. See Lenin, "On Cooperation," in *Selected Works,* p. 695.

27. Lenin, "A Talk With Defenders of Economism," in *Selected Works,* p. 46.

28. Lenin, *What Is to Be Done?*, in *Essential Works,* p. 91.

29. Ibid., pp. 80-83, 112.

30. Ibid., pp. 160-161.

31. Lenin, "Conspectus of Hegel's *Science of Logic,*" in Lenin, *Collected Works* (Moscow, 1963), 38; 201, 212.

32. Ibid., p. 195.

33. Kautsky, *The Class Struggle,* trans. Bohm (New York, 1971), p. 158.

34. Althusser, *Lenin and Philosophy,* pp. 115, 117. (Althusser in the same essay attributes the "discovery" of history as a subjectless process to Marx.)

35. Plekhanov, *Development,* pp. 248-249.

36. For a brief analysis of contemporary Soviet philosophy and its atti-

tude toward "subjective" factors, see Helmut Fleischer, "The Acting Subject in Historical Materialism," in *Philosophy in the Soviet Union,* ed. Laszlo (New York, 1967), pp. 13-29.

7: REVOLUTIONARY RATIONALISM —
LUXEMBURG, LUKÁCS, AND GRAMSCI

1. Rosa Luxemburg, "Reform or Revolution," in *Rosa Luxemburg Speaks,* ed. Waters (New York, 1970), p. 59.

2. Luxemburg, "What Does the Spartacus League Want?" in *Selected Political Writings,* ed. Howard (New York, 1971), p. 369.

3. Luxemburg, "What Is Economics?" in *Luxemburg Speaks,* p. 236.

4. Luxemburg, "The Junius Pamphlet: the Crisis in the German Social Democracy," in ibid., p. 269.

5. Ibid., p. 331.

6. Luxemburg, "Speech," in ibid., pp. 419-420 (emphasis added).

7. Luxemburg, "The Junius Pamphlet," in ibid., p. 325.

8. Luxemburg, "Spartacus League," in *Selected Political Writings,* p. 371.

9. Luxemburg, "Speech," in *Luxemburg Speaks,* p. 412.

10. In his 1967 preface to *History and Class Consciousness;* see Georg Lukacs, *History and Class Consciousness,* trans. Livingstone (Cambridge, Mass., 1971), p. xiii.

11. Lukács, *The Theory of the Novel,* trans. Bostock (Cambridge, Mass., 1971), p. 56.

12. Lukács, *Political Writings 1919-1929,* trans. McColgan, pp. 15, 24-25, 26.

13. Ibid., pp. 26, 36.

14. Lukács, *History,* p. 6.

15. Ibid., p. 185.

16. Ibid., p. 28. This curious comment seems also to contradict Hegel's *Phenomenology,* which may be read precisely as a development from the particular to the universal.

17. Ibid., p. 80.

18. Ibid., p. 41.

19. Ibid., p. 335.

20. Lukács, *History,* p. 209; cf. p. 4: "Fatalism and voluntarism are only mutually contradictory to an undialectical and unhistorical mind."

21. Antonio Gramsci, *Selections from Political Writings 1910-1920,* trans. Mathews (London, 1977), p. 34. See also Anton Pannekoek, *Workers Councils* (Cambridge, Mass., n.d.), p. 29: "Minds submissive to the

doctrines of the masters cannot hope to win freedom. They must overcome the spiritual sway of capitalism over their minds before they can actually throw off its yoke."

22. Gramsci, *Selections from the Prison Notebooks,* ed. and trans. Hoare and Smith (New York, 1971), p. 265.

23. Ibid., pp. 352-354.

24. See Georges Sorel, "The Decomposition of Marxism," in Irving Louis Horowitz, *Radicalism and the Revolt Against Reason* (Carbondale, Ill., 1968), p. 252; and Sorel, *The Illusions of Progress,* trans. Stanley (Berkeley and Los Angeles, 1969), pp. 207-214.

25. Gramsci, *Prison Notebooks,* p. 412.

26. Ibid., p. 127n.

27. Ibid., p. 445.

28. Ibid., p. 430.

29. Ibid., p. 171.

30. Ibid., p. 438. Sorel's influence is apparent here.

31. Ibid., p. 412.

32. Ibid., p. 178.

33. Ibid., p. 172.

8: THE PROSPECTS FOR INDIVIDUATION RECONSIDERED

1. Quoted from a letter written "near the end" of Weber's life, by Arthur Mitzman, in *The Iron Cage* (New York, 1969), p. 182.

2. Friedrich Nietzsche, *The Gay Science,* trans. Kaufmann (New York, 1974), p. 266 (§335); Nietzsche, *The Will to Power,* trans. Kaufmann and Hollingdale (New York, 1968), p. 307 (§569).

3. Ibid., p. 267 (§481); Nietzsche, *On the Genealogy of Morals,* trans. Kaufmann (New York, 1969), p. 59 (II, §2).

4. Nietzsche, *Will to Power,* pp. 9, 40, 150 (§3, §57, §260).

5. Nietzsche, *Gay Science,* p. 175 (§117).

6. See, e.g., Nietzsche, *Will to Power,* pp. 267, 269-270, 271-272 (§481, §488, §492); also Nietzsche, *Beyond Good and Evil,* trans. Kaufmann (New York, 1966), pp. 25-27 (§19).

7. Nietzsche, *Gay Science,* p. 280 (§343).

8. Nietzsche, *Thus Spake Zarathustra,* trans. Kaufmann, in Kaufmann, ed., *The Portable Nietzsche* (New York, 1954), p. 129.

9. Nietzsche, *Will to Power,* p. 198 (§363).

10. Nietzsche, *Beyond Good and Evil,* pp. 111-112 (§200).

11. Nietzsche, *Will to Power,* pp. 17, 463 (§20, §866).

12. Edmund Husserl, *Cartesian Meditations,* trans. Cairns (The Hague, 1960), p. 86: "This idealism . . . is *sense-explication* achieved *by actual* [phenomenological] work, an explication carried out as regards every type of existent ever conceivable by me. . . . But that signifies: systematic uncovering of the constituting intentionality itself. *The proof of this idealism is therefore phenomenology itself."*

13. Husserl, *The Crisis of European Science and Transcendental Phenomenology,* trans. Carr (Evanston, Ill., 1970), p. 6 (§2).

14. See ibid., p. 299: "The reason for the failure of a rational culture . . . lies not in the essence of rationalism itself, but solely in its being rendered superficial, in its entanglement in 'naturalism' and 'objectivism.'"

15. Husserl to Lévy-Bruehl, 3-11-1935, quoted in Herbert Spiegelberg, *The Phenomenological Movement* (The Hague, 1969), p. 84.

16. Martin Heidegger, *Being and Time,* trans. Macquarrie and Robinson (New York, 1962), p. 165 (I, 4, §27).

17. Ibid., p. 436 (II, 5, §74): "Once one has grasped the finitude of one's existence, it snatches one back from the endless multiplicity of possibilities which offer themselves as closest to one — those of comfortableness, shirking, and taking things lightly — and brings Dasein into the simplicity of its *fate* [*Schicksal*]. This is how we designate Dasein's primordial historizing, which lies in authentic resoluteness and in which Dasein *hands* itself *down* to itself, free for death, in a possibility which it has inherited and yet has chosen. . . . If Dasein, by anticipation, lets death become powerful in itself, then, as free for death, Dasein understands itself in its own *superior power,* the power of its finite freedom, which 'is' only in its having chosen to make such a choice, it can take over the *powerlessness* of abandonment to its having done so, and can thus come to have a clear vision for the accidents of the Situation that has been disclosed. But if fateful Dasein, as Being-in-the-world, exists essentially in Being-with Others, its historizing is a cohistorizing and is determinative for it as *destiny* [*Geschick*]. . . . Only in communicating and in struggling does the power of destiny become free. Dasein's fateful destiny in and with its 'generation' goes to make up the full authentic historizing of Dasein." Cf. Heidegger, *The Essence of Reasons,* trans. Malick (Evanston, 1969), p. 131: "For only in its Dasein with others can Dasein surrender its individuality in order to win itself as an authentic self."

18. Ibid., p. 127: *"Freedom is the reason for reasons."*

19. See Goldmann, *Lukács et Heidegger* (Paris, 1973), esp. pp. 91 ff. Goldmann speculates that the term "reification" (*Verdinglichung*) in *Being and Time* alludes to Lukács; the term appears twice in the book: see Heidegger, *Being,* pp. 72, 487 (I, 1, §10; II, 6, §83).

20. Ibid., p. 224 (I, 5, §38), where everyday existence in the social world is characterized by "falling, with temptation, tranquilization, alienation and entanglement as its essential characteristics."

21. Max Weber, *The Protestant Ethic and the Spirit of Capitalism,* trans. Parsons (New York, 1958), p. 182.

22. On the irrational aspects of action, see Weber, "Critical Studies in the Logic of the Cultural Sciences," in Weber, *The Methodology of the Social Sciences,"* trans. Shils and Finch (New York, 1949), p. 125. On the category of interest, see Weber's introduction to the *Wirtschaftsethik der Weltreligionen,* cited by Wolfgang J. Mommsen in *The Age of Bureaucracy* (New York, 1977), p. 106.

23. Weber, "Science as a Vocation," in Gerth and Mills, eds., *From Max Weber* (New York, 1946), pp. 137, 148, 149.

24. Horkheimer, "Materialism and Metaphysics," in Horkheimer, *Critical Theory,* p. 12.

25. Horkheimer, "The Latest Attack on Metaphysics," ibid., p. 138; "Notes on Science and the Crisis," ibid., p. 7.

26. Adorno, *Minima,* p. 154 (§99).

27. Adorno, "Sociology and Psychology," trans. Wohlfarth, *New Left Review,* 46 (November-December, 1967), 71; Adorno, *Negative Dialectics,* trans. Ashton (New York, 1973), p. 123; Horkheimer, "The Latest Attack," *Critical Theory,* p. 146n; Adorno, *Minima,* p. 154 (§99).

28. Adorno, *Minima,* pp. 38, 148-150 (§97, §17).

29. Horkheimer and Adorno, *Dialectic of Enlightenment,* trans. Cumming (New York, 1972), p. 204.

30. Herbert Marcuse, "Philosophy and Critical Theory," in Marcuse, *Negations,* trans. Shapiro (Boston, 1968), pp. 135, 142.

31. Horkheimer, "Traditional and Critical Theory," *Critical Theory,* pp. 211, 214-215.

32. Horkehimer, "Postscript," *Critical Theory,* p. 251; "Latest Attack," ibid., p. 162.

33. Horkheimer, "Preface," ibid., p. viii.

34. Marcuse, *An Essay on Liberation* (Boston, 1969), pp. 18-19.

35. Adorno, *Negative Dialectics,* pp. 4, 207, 231, 360.

36. The influence of Kojève, whose lectures depicted Hegel as the forerunner of both Heidegger and Marx, was critical; see Alexandre Kojève, *Introduction to the Reading of Hegel,* trans. Nichols (New York, 1969). Kojève placed the master-slave relation at the heart of Hegel's phenomenology, a move echoed in Sartre's phenomenology, when the latter interprets human relations along a sadomasochistic axis of subjective domination (I look at you) and objective submission (I am looked at).

9: SARTRE—THE FEAR OF FREEDOM

1. Jean-Paul Sartre, *The Psychology of Imagination,* trans. Frechtman (New York, 1966), p. 243; cf. Descartes, *Principles of Philosophy,* I, 6.

2. Sartre, "Cartesian Freedom," in *Literary and Philosophical Essays,* trans. Michelson (New York, 1962), p. 184; cf. Sartre, *Being and Nothingness,* trans. Barnes (New York, 1956), p. 483: "Success is not important to freedom."

3. Heidegger, *The Essence of Reasons,* p. 127; also see Sartre, "Cartesian Freedom," in *Literary and Philosophical Essays,* pp. 196-197.

4. Sartre, *Being,* pp. 34, 440.

5. Ibid., p. 435.

6. Ibid., p. 478.

7. Hegel, *Philosophy of History,* p. 19.

8. Sartre, *Being,* p. 40.

9. Ibid., p. 93; cf. p. 620: "Consciousness is *in fact* a project of founding itself; that is, of attaining to the dignity of the in-itself-for-itself, or in-itself-as-self-cause."

10. Ibid., p. 90.

11. Ibid., p. 70n. For comments on Heidegger's concept of authenticity, see pp. 545, 564.

12. Ibid., p. 529.

13. Sartre, *Anti-Semite and Jew,* trans. Becker (New York, 1965), p. 90.

14. Ibid., p. 141.

15. Sartre, *Being,* p. 83.

16. Sartre, *Anti-Semite,* pp. 59-60.

17. Sartre, David Rousset, and Gérard Rosenthal, *Entretiens sur la politique* (Paris, 1949), p. 40. Sartre has traced his own political trajectory in a fine essay on Merleau-Ponty in idem, *Situations,* trans. Eisler (New York, 1966), pp. 156-226.

18. Sartre, "Materialism and Revolution," in *Literary and Philosophical Essays,* p. 236.

19. Ibid., pp. 234-235.

20. Ibid., pp. 241-242.

21. Sartre, "Materialism," in *Literary and Philosophical Essays,* p. 225; cf. *Being,* p. 436.

22. See, e.g., Sartre, "Materialism," p. 237.

23. Sartre, *The Communists and Peace,* trans. Fletcher and Berk (New York, 1968), pp. 98, 226.

24. Maurice Merleau-Ponty, *Les Aventures de la dialectique* (Paris, 1955), p. 135; AD, p. 99.

25. Sartre, *Communists,* pp. 80-81, 107.

26. Sartre, *Communists,* p. 80.

27. Ibid., p. 193.

28. Ibid., p. 207.

29. Ibid., p. 222.

30. Ibid., p. 272.

31. Ibid., p. 253.

32. Ibid., p. 246.

33. Sartre, *Critique de la raison dialectique* (Paris, 1960), pp. 18-21; SM, pp. 8-14.

34. In several spots, Sartre mistakenly attributes Engels's quip that materialism is the study of nature, "just as it is, without foreign admixture," to Marx; see, e.g., ibid., p. 30n; SM, p. 32n.

35. See ibid., pp. 30-31n, 109; SM, pp. 32-33n, 178.

36. Ibid., p. 64; SM, p. 92.

37. By "totalizing" Sartre intends to describe those ongoing human processes which bring meaning and coherence to a world, praxis foremost among them.

38. Sartre, *Critique,* p. 548; CDR, p. 557.

39. Ibid., p. 361; CDR, p. 322.

40. Sartre, *Being,* p. 244; cf. idem, *Critique,* p. 142; CDR, p. 51: "The epistemological point of departure must always be *consciousness* as apodictic certainty of itself. . . ."

41. Ibid., p. 142; CDR, p. 51.

42. Sartre, *Being,* pp. 267, 271, 364.

43. Sartre, *Communists,* p. 250.

44. Alfred Schutz, *The Problem of Social Reality* (The Hague, 1967), p. 203.

45. Sartre, *Critique,* p. 205; CDR, p. 129.

46. Sartre, *Being,* pp. 420-421.

47. Sartre, *Critique,* p. 643; CDR, p. 679.

48. Ibid., p. 394; CDR, p. 361. Cf. *Communists,* pp. 222-223n: "The [collective] subject is the group *brought together* by the situation, *structured* by its very action, *differentiated* by the objective requirements of the *praxis* and by the division of labor, at first random, then systematic, which the *praxis* introduces, *organized* by the leaders which it chooses for itself or which it discovers for itself, finding *in their person* its own unity."

49. See Georges Lefebvre, *The French Revolution, From its Origins to 1793,* trans. Evanson (New York, 1962), e.g., p. 237, where Lefebvre describes the insurrection of August 10, 1792, as a "defensive reaction"; or p. 122, where the revolutionary mentality is defined by three components:

"fear, defensive reaction, and punitive will." Cf. Sartre on the "pledged group" and terror.

50. Sartre, *Anti-Semite*, p. 30; idem, *Critique*, p. 425; CDR, p. 401.

51. Ibid., p. 470; CDR, p. 458.

52. See esp. Sartre's discussion of Lévi-Strauss in this regard: Sartre, *Critique*, pp. 490 ff.; CDR, pp. 479 ff.

53. Ibid., pp. 248-249; CDR, pp. 181-182.

54. Ibid., pp. 167, 281-282; CDR, pp. 82, 222.

55. Ibid., p. 285; CDR, p. 227.

56. Ibid., pp. 157-158; CDR, p. 71.

57. Ibid., p. 369; CDR, p. 331: "All men are slaves inasmuch as their vital experience unfolds in the practico-inert field, originally conditioned by scarcity."

58. Ibid., p. 286n; CDR, p. 227n.

59. In a 1969 interview, Sartre described his current view of subjectivity as "the small margin in an operation whereby an interiorization re-exteriorizes itself in an act." He failed to add that this "small margin" still carried the entire burden of freedom and transcendence; in other words, subjectivity remains for Sartre the meaningful hinge of history, the source of creativity, the reason history progresses rather than merely repeats itself. See Sartre, "Itinerary of a Thought," in *Between Existentialism and Marxism*, trans. Matthews (London, 1974), p. 35.

60. Sartre, *Critique*, pp. 135, 142; CDR, pp. 40, 51-52.

61. Ibid., p. 153; CDR, p. 66.

62. Ibid., p. 180 (on formalism), 194 (on the dyad and third), 130 (on dialectical Reason); CDR, pp. 33-34, 97, 115. Cf. Simmel's introduction to *Soziologie*, "How Is Society Possible?" in his *On Individuality and Social Forms*, ed. Levine (Chicago, 1971), pp. 6-22.

63. See Sartre, *Critique*, p. 106; SM, p. 171.

64. Ibid., p. 276; CDR, p. 216.

65. Ibid., p. 349n; CDR, p. 307n.

66. See Merleau-Ponty, *Les Aventures*, esp. pp. 181-182; AD, pp. 134-135. Cf. Sartre, *Communists*, p. 127: "An action of some importance requires unity of direction; and he [the worker], precisely, needs to believe that there is a truth.... He must be able to trust his class leaders profoundly enough to believe he is getting the truth from them.... Doubt and uncertainty: these seem to be intellectual virtues. But he must struggle to change his conditions, and these virtues of the mind can only paralyze action...."

67. Sartre, *Critique*, p. 59; SM, p. 83.

68. Sartre, "Itinerary," in *Between Existentialism and Marxism*, p. 37.

69. Sartre, *Anti-Semite,* pp. 18-19.

70. Sartre, *Communists,* pp. 253, 270.

71. Sartre, *Critique,* p. 86; SM, p. 133.

72. Ibid., p. 20; SM, p. 12.

73. Sartre, *Being,* p. 561.

74. Sartre, *Critique,* p. 63; SM, p. 91: "For us man is characterized above all by his going beyond a situation, and by what he succeeds in making of what he has been made—even if he never recognizes himself in his objectification."

75. Sartre, *L'Idiot de la famille* (Paris, 1971), p. 7; *Being,* p. 563.

76. Sartre, *L'Idiot,* p. 1372.

77. Sartre, *Critique,* p. 156; CDR, p. 70; see also ibid., p. 140, CDR, p. 49.

78. Ibid., p. 89; SM, p. 140.

79. Sartre, *L'Idiot,* p. 7, and *Critique,* p. 9; CDR, pp. 821-822. Sartre's obsession with the individual imports an idiosyncratic reductionism into his work. The individual becomes a molecular universal history, with his own coherent *telos* and in-itself-for-itself (identity). Perhaps this is the impulse behind his insistence that biography reduce the role of contingency and chance to an absolute minimum: "What we intend to show is that *this* Napoleon was necessary." (Ibid., p. 58; SM, p. 83.) No wonder *L'Idiot* runs over 3,000 pages!

80. Sartre, *Critique,* p. 72; SM, p. 108.

81. Ibid., p. 66; SM, p. 97.

82. Ibid., p. 133; CDR, p. 38: "The dialectic is only discovered in an observer situated in interiority, i.e., an inquirer who lives his inquiry simultaneously as a possible contribution to the ideology of the epoch and as a particular *praxis* of an individual defined by his personal and historical adventure in the midst of a more ample history which conditions it."

83. André Gorz has consistently applied Sartre's philosophy to elaborate a sober—and attractive—version of syndicalism. See idem, *Strategy for Labor,* trans. Nicolaus and Ortiz (Boston, 1967), and idem, *Le Socialisme difficile* (Paris, 1967).

84. Sartre, *Critique,* pp. 44-45; SM, p. 56.

85. Ibid., p. 143; CDR, p. 52.

10: MERLEAU-PONTY — THE AMBIGUITY OF HISTORY

1. Maurice Merleau-Ponty, *The Structure of Behavior,* trans. Fisher (Boston, 1963), p. 3.

2. Ibid., p. 224.

3. Merleau-Ponty, *Phenomenology of Perception,* trans. Smith (London, 1962), p. 31.

4. Merleau-Ponty, *Phenomenology,* p. 309n.

5. Ibid., p. 296. Cf. idem, *Sense and Non-Sense,* trans. Dreyfus (Evanston, 1964), p. 52: "We must rediscover a commerce with the world and a presence to the world which is older than intelligence."

6. Merleau-Ponty, *Phenomenology,* p. 322. Cf. p. 455: "The synthesis of *in itself* and *for itself* which brings Hegelian freedom has, however, its truth. In a sense, it is the very definition of existence, since it is effected at every moment before our eyes in the phenomenon of presence, only to be quickly re-enacted, since it does not conjure away our finitude."

7. Ibid., pp. 254, 333.

8. Ibid., p. 351. Cf. idem, *The Primacy of Perception,* ed. Edie (Evanston, 1964), pp. 116-117: "My consciousness is turned primarily toward the world, turned toward things; it is above all a relation to the world. The other's consciousness as well is chiefly a certain way of comporting himself toward the world. Thus it is in his conduct, in the manner in which the other deals with the world, that I will be able to discover his consciousness."

9. Merleau-Ponty, *Phenomenology,* p. 364.

10. Ibid., p. 408.

11. Ibid., p. 361.

12. Ibid., p. 362.

13. Ibid., p. 395.

14. Ibid., p. 437.

15. Ibid., p. 442.

16. Ibid., p. 453.

17. See Merleau-Ponty, *Résumés de cours* (Paris, 1968), p. 46: "There is history if there is a logic *in* contingency, a reason *in* unreason, if there is a historic perception that, like the other, leaves in the background what does not come to the foreground grasps the lines of force at their inception, and through achieving them actively, traces them. This comparison should not be understood as an organicism or timid finalism, but rather as a reference to the fact that all symbolic systems—perception, language and history— only become what they are when they need to become what they are, in order to be taken up in the human endeavor."

18. Merleau-Ponty, *Phenomenology,* p. xix.

19. Merleau-Ponty, *Sense,* pp. 107-108.

20. Ibid., p. 171n.

21. Ibid., p. 151.

22. Merleau-Ponty, *Phenomenology,* p. 363.

23. Merleau-Ponty, *In Praise of Philosophy,* trans. Wild and Edie

(Evanston, 1963), pp. 55-56; and idem, *Résumés de cours,* p. 61.

24. Merleau-Ponty, *Les Aventures,* p. 88; AD, pp. 64-65.

25. Merleau-Ponty, *In Praise,* p. 55.

26. Merleau-Ponty, *Primacy,* p. 9.

27. Merleau-Ponty, *Sense,* p. 130.

28. Merleau-Ponty, *Phenomenology,* p. 50.

29. Merleau-Ponty, *Les Aventures,* pp. 17-18; AD, p. 11.

30. Merleau-Ponty, *Phenomenology,* p. 172n.

31. Ibid., p. 443.

32. Ibid., p. 446.

33. Ibid., p. 447 (emphasis added).

34. Ibid., p. 363.

35. Merleau-Ponty, *Humanism and Terror,* trans. O'Neill (Boston, 1969), p. 98.

36. Ibid., p. xxxiii.

37. Ibid., p. xv.

38. Ibid., pp. 22, 29.

39. See ibid., pp. xxxiv, 185.

40. Merleau-Ponty, *Les Aventures,* p. 115; AD, p. 84.

41. Ibid., pp. 121-122; AD, p. 89.

42. Ibid., p. 279; AD, p. 207.

43. Ibid., p. 34; AD, p. 23. See also Sartre, *Situations,* p. 57, on Merleau-Ponty's nostalgia for the Golden Age of childhood, and his persistent quest for this "absolute."

44. Merleau-Ponty, *Les Aventures,* pp. 55, 73-74; AD, pp. 39, 53.

45. See ibid., p. 41; AD, p. 28: "If history does not have a direction like a river, but only a meaning, not a truth but only errors to be avoided, if practice is not deduced from a dogmatic philosophy of history, it is not superficial to base a politics on the analysis of the political man." Cf. the essay on Machiavelli in *Signs,* trans. McCleary (Evanston, 1964), pp. 211-223.

46. Merleau-Ponty, *Les Aventures,* pp. 276-277; AD, pp. 205-206.

47. Merleau-Ponty, *Signs,* p. 275; *Les Aventures,* p. 8; AD, p. 4.

48. Merleau-Ponty, *Sense,* p. 106.

49. Merleau-Ponty, *Les Aventures,* pp. 89, 114, 131-132; AD, pp. 65, 84, 95-96. This line of argument anticipates Albrecht Wellmer's use of Jürgen Habermas; see Wellmer, *Critical Theory of Society,* trans. Cumming (New York, 1971).

50. Merleau-Ponty, *Les Aventures,* pp. 116-117; AD, pp. 85-86.

51. Ibid., p. 124; AD, p. 91.

52. Merleau-Ponty, *Sense,* pp. 121-122.

53. Merleau-Ponty, *Les Aventures,* p. 47; AD, p. 33.

54. Cf. Goldmann, *The Hidden God*, trans. Thody (London, 1964), pp. 298-302.

55. Merleau-Ponty, *Les Aventures de la dialectique*, p. 86; AD, p. 63.

56. Merleau-Ponty, *Signs*, pp. 9, 13. In his last lecture course, Merleau-Ponty, implicitly opposing Sartre's claims for Marxism as "the unsurpassable framework of knowledge" for our time, pointedly remarked, that "one could even say Hegel maintains more of a sense of negativity and tension." See "Philosophy and Non-Philosophy Since Hegel," trans. Silverman, *Telos*, 29 (Fall, 1976), 46, 105.

57. Merleau-Ponty, *Signs*, p. 329.

58. Ibid., p. 217.

59. Ibid., pp. 130-131.

60. Ibid., p. 35.

61. Merleau-Ponty, *Sense*, p. 134.

62. Merleau-Ponty, *Les Aventures*, p. 53; AD, p. 38.

63. Ibid., p. 72; AD, p. 52.

EPILOGUE

1. On Althusser's animus toward subjectivity, see esp. *Lenin and Philosophy*. For Colletti's quote, see his *From Rousseau to Lenin*, trans. Merrington and White (London, 1972), p. 140. "Marcuse acclaims 'the interior space of the private sphere'; he invokes 'that isolation in which the individual, left to himself, can think and demand and find'; he acclaims the 'private sphere' as the only one which 'can give significance to freedom and independence of thought.' How can we fail to recognize in this the old liberal rhetoric?"

2. Merleau-Ponty, *Humanism*, pp. 188-189.

3. Adorno, *Minima*, p. 247 (§153).

4. Hegel, *Philosophy of Mind*, trans. Wallace and Miller (Oxford, 1971), p. 91 (§402).

Bibliography

MARX AND ENGELS

Engels, Friedrich. *Anti-Dühring* [*Herr Eugen Dühring's Revolution in Science*]. Trans. Burns. New York, 1939.

Marx, Karl. *Capital,* Vol. I. Trans. Fowkes. London, 1976.

———. *Capital,* Vol. I. Trans. Moore and Aveling. Chicago, 1906.

———. *Capital,* Vol. II. Trans. Lasker. Moscow, 1956.

———. *Capital,* Vol. III. Moscow, 1966.

———. *Critique of Hegel's "Philosophy of Right."* Trans. Jolin and O'Malley. Cambridge, 1970.

———. *Critique of Political Economy.* Trans. Stone. Chicago, 1904.

———. *Economic and Philosophic Manuscripts of 1844.* Trans. Milligan. New York, 1964.

———. *The Ethnological Notebooks of Karl Marx.* Ed. Krader. Assen, Netherlands, 1972.

———. *Grundrisse.* Trans. Nicolaus. New York, 1973.

———. *Grundrisse der Kritik der politischen Ökonomie (Rohentwurf).* Berlin, 1953.

———. *Das Kapital.* Hamburg, 1867.

———. *The Poverty of Philosophy.* Trans. Quelch. Chicago, n.d.

———. *Theories of Surplus Value.* Trans. Burns, Ryazanskaya, and Cohen. 3 vols. Moscow, 1963-71.

———. *Writings of the Young Marx on Philosophy and Society.* Trans. Easton and Guddat. Garden City, N.Y., 1967.

Marx, Karl, and Friedrich Engels. *The American Journalism of Marx and Engels.* Ed. Christman. New York, 1966.

———. *Collected Works.* New York, 1975 ff.

———. *The German Ideology.* Trans. Ryazanskaya. Moscow, 1968.

———. *Historisch-kritische Gesamtausgabe.* Ed. Rjazanov and Adoratskij. Berlin and Moscow, 1927 ff.

———. *The Holy Family.* Trans. Dixon. Moscow, 1956.

———. *Selected Correspondence.* Trans. Lasker. Moscow, 1965.

————. *Selected Works.* 3 vols. Moscow, 1969.
————. *Werke.* Berlin, 1956 ff.

Works on Marx and Engels

Althusser, Louis. *For Marx.* Trans. Brewster. London, 1970.
Althusser, Louis, and Etienne Balibar. *Reading Capital.* Trans. Brewster. New York, 1970.
Avineri, Shlomo. *The Social and Political Thought of Karl Marx.* Cambridge, 1968.
Axelos, Kostas. *Marx, penseur de la technique: de l'alienation de l'homme à la conquête du monde.* Paris, 1961.
Bloch, Ernst. *On Karl Marx.* Trans. Maxwell. New York, 1971.
Blumenberg, Werner. *Karl Marx.* Trans. Scott. London, 1972.
Cornu, Auguste. *Karl Marx et Friedrich Engels: leur vie et leur oeuvre.* 4 vols. Paris, 1955 ff.
Fetscher, Iring. *Marx and Marxism.* New York, 1971.
Fleischer, Helmut. *Marxism and History.* Trans. Mosbacher. New York, 1973.
Garaudy, Roger. *Karl Marx: the Evolution of His Thought.* Trans. Apotheker. New York, 1967.
Godelier, Maurice. "System, Structure and Contradiction in Capital." In Milliband and Saville, eds., *The Socialist Register 1967.* London, 1967.
Heller, Agnes. *The Theory of Need in Marx.* London, 1976.
Hook, Sidney. *From Hegel to Marx.* Ann Arbor, Mich., 1962.
Kolakowski, Leszek. *Toward a Marxist Humanism.* Trans. Peel. New York, 1969.
Korsch, Karl. *Karl Marx.* New York, 1938.
Kosík, Karel. *Dialectics of the Concrete.* Trans. Kovanda and Schmidt. Boston, 1976.
Lefebvre, Henri. *Dialectical Materialism.* Trans. Sturrock. London, 1968.
Lindsay, A. D. *Karl Marx's Capital.* London, 1925.
Lubasz, Heinz. "Marx's Initial Problematic: the Problem of Poverty," *Political Studies,* 24 (March, 1976), 24-42.
Lukács, Georg. "The Dialectics of Labor: Beyond Causality and Teleology," trans. Gucinski, *Telos,* 6 (Fall, 1970), 162-174.
Mandel, Ernest. *The Formation of the Economic Thought of Karl Marx.* Trans. Pearce. New York, 1971.
McLellan, David. *Karl Marx: His Life and Thought.* New York, 1974.
————. *Marx before Marxism.* New York, 1970.
Meek, Ronald. *Economics and Ideology and Other Essays.* London, 1967.
Mehring, Franz. *Karl Marx.* Trans. Fitzgerald. Ann Arbor, 1962.

Mészáros, István. *Marx's Theory of Alienation*. London, 1970.

Nicolaus, Martin. "Proletariat and Middle Class in Marx: Hegelian Choreography and the Capitalist Dialectic," in Weinstein and Eakins, eds., *For a New America*. New York, 1970.

———. "The Unknown Marx," *New Left Review*, 48 (March-April, 1968), 41-61.

Ollman, Bertell. *Alienation*. Cambridge, 1971.

O'Malley, Joseph. "Marx's 'Economics' and Hegel's *Philosophy of Right:* An Essay on Marx's Hegelianism," *Political Studies*, 24 (March, 1976), 43-56.

Petrović, Gajo. *Marx in the Mid-Twentieth Century*. Garden City, 1967.

Rubel, Maximilien. *Karl Marx: Essai de biographie intellectuelle*. Paris, 1971.

Schaff, Adam. *Marxism and the Human Individual*. Trans. Wojtasiewicz. New York, 1970.

Schmidt, Alfred. *The Concept of Nature in Marx*. Trans. Fowkes. London, 1971.

Thomas, Pat. "Marx and Science," *Political Studies*, 24 (March, 1976), 1-23.

MARXISM, FROM ORTHODOXY TO CRITICAL THEORY

Adler, Max. *Marx als Denker*. Vienna, 1921.

Adorno, Theodor. "The Actuality of Philosophy," *Telos*, 31 (Spring, 1977), 120-133.

———. *The Jargon of Authenticity*. Trans. Tarnowski and Will. Evanston, Ill., 1973.

———. *Minima Moralia*. Trans. Jephcott. London, 1974.

———. *Negative Dialectics*. Trans. Ashton. New York, 1973.

———. *Prisms*. Trans. Weber. London, 1967.

———. "Society." Trans. Jameson, *Salmagundi*, nos. 10-11 (1969-70), 144-153.

———. "Sociology and Psychology." Trans. Wohlfarth, *New Left Review*, 46 (November-December, 1967), 67-80; 47 (January-February, 1968), 79-97.

Bernstein, Eduard. *Evolutionary Socialism*. Trans. Harvey. New York, 1961.

Frankfurt Institute for Social Research. *Aspects of Sociology*. Trans. Viertel. Boston, 1972.

Gramsci, Antonio. *History, Philosophy and Culture in the Young Gramsci*. Trans. Piccone. St. Louis, 1975.

———. *Letters from Prison*. Trans. Lawner. New York, 1973.

––––––. *Selections from Political Writings 1910-1920*. Trans. Mathews. London, 1977.

––––––. *Selections from the Prison Notebooks*. Trans. Hoare and Smith. New York, 1973.

––––––. "Soviets in Italy," *New Left Review,* 51 (September-October, 1968), 28-58.

Horkheimer, Max. *Critical Theory*. Trans. O'Connell. New York, 1972.

––––––. *Eclipse of Reason*. New York, 1974.

Horkheimer, Max, and Theodor Adorno. *Dialectic of Enlightenment.* Trans. Cumming. New York, 1972.

Kautsky, Karl. *The Class Struggle*. Trans. Bohm. New York, 1971.

––––––. *The Dictatorship of the Proletariat*. Trans. Stenning. Ann Arbor, 1964.

––––––. *The Road to Power*. Trans. Simons. Chicago, 1909.

Korsch, Karl. *Marxism and Philosophy*. Trans. Halliday. London, 1970.

Labriola, Antonio. *Essays on the Materialistic Conception of History.* Trans. Kerr. New York, 1966.

––––––. *Socialism and Philosophy*. Trans. Unterman. Chicago, 1934.

Lenin, V. I. *Collected Works*. Vol. 38. Moscow, 1963.

––––––. *Essential Works of Lenin*. Ed. Christman. New York, 1966.

––––––. *Materialism and Empirio-Criticism*. New York, 1966.

––––––. *Selected Works*. Moscow, 1968.

Lukács, Georg. *History and Class Consciousness*. Trans. Livingstone. Cambridge, Mass., 1971.

––––––. *Lenin*. Trans. Jacobs. London, 1970.

––––––. "The Old Culture and the New Culture." Trans. Breines, *Telos,* 5 (Spring, 1970), 21-30.

––––––. *Political Writings 1919-1929*. Trans. McColgan. London, 1972.

––––––. *Soul and Form*. Trans. Bostock. London, 1974.

––––––. *Theory of the Novel*. Trans. Bostock. Cambridge, Mass., 1971.

Luxemburg, Rosa. *The Accumulation of Capital*. Trans. Child. New York, 1951.

––––––. *Rosa Luxemburg Speaks*. Ed. Waters. New York, 1970.

––––––. *Selected Political Writings*. Ed. Howard. New York, 1971.

Marcuse, Herbert. *Counterrevolution and Revolt*. Boston, 1972.

––––––. *Eros and Civilization*. New York, 1955.

––––––. *An Essay on Liberation*. Boston, 1969.

––––––. *Negations*. Trans. Shapiro. Boston, 1968.

––––––. *One-Dimensional Man*. Boston, 1964.

––––––. *Reason and Revolution*. Boston, 1960.

––––––. *Soviet Marxism*. New York, 1961.

––––––. *Studies in Critical Philosophy*. Trans. de Bres. London, 1972.

Pannekoek, Anton. *Workers Councils.* Cambridge, Mass., n.d.
Plekhanov, George V. *The Development of the Monist View of History.* Trans. Rothstein. Moscow, 1956.
————. *Fundamental Problems of Marxism.* New York, 1969.

Works on Marxism, from Orthodoxy to Critical Theory

Althusser, Louis. *Lenin and Philosophy and Other Essays.* Trans. Brewster. London, 1971.
Arato, Andrew, "Reexamining the Second International," *Telos,* 18 (Winter, 1973-74), 2-52.
Breines, Paul. "Praxis and Its Theorists: the Impact of Lukács and Korsch in the 1920s," *Telos,* 11 (Spring, 1972), 67-103.
Cammett, John M. *Antonio Gramsci and the Origins of Italian Communism.* Stanford, Calif., 1967.
Davidson, Alastair. *Antonio Gramsci: Towards an Intellectual Biography.* London, 1977.
Fiori, Giuseppi. *Antonio Gramsci, Life of a Revolutionary.* Trans. Nairn. London, 1970.
Fischer, Louis. *The Life of Lenin.* New York, 1965.
Gay, Peter. *The Dilemma of Democratic Socialism.* New York, 1962.
Geras, Norman. *The Legacy of Rosa Luxemburg.* London, 1976.
Howard, Dick, and Karl Klare, eds. *The Unknown Dimension: European Marxism Since Lenin.* New York, 1972.
Jacoby, Russell. "Toward a Critique of Automatic Marxism: the Politics of Philosophy from Lukács to the Frankfurt School," *Telos,* 10 (Winter, 1971), 119-146.
Jay, Martin. *The Dialectical Imagination.* Boston, 1973.
Joll, James. *The Second International 1889-1914.* New York, 1966.
Jordan, Z. A. *The Evolution of Dialectical Materialism.* London, 1967.
Lewin, Mosche. *Lenin's Last Struggle.* Trans. Smith. New York, 1968.
Lichtheim, George. *From Marx to Hegel.* New York, 1974.
————. *Marxism: An Historical and Critical Study.* New York, 1965.
Mészáros, István. *Lukács' Concept of Dialectic.* London, 1972.
Nettl, Peter. *Rosa Luxemburg.* London, 1969.
Pannekoek, Anton. *Lenin as Philosopher.* London, 1975.
Piccone, Paul, "From Spaventa to Gramsci," *Telos,* 31 (Spring, 1977), 35-65.
Rose, Gillian. "How Is Critical Theory Possible? Theodor W. Adorno and Concept Formation in Sociology," *Political Studies,* 24 (March, 1976), 69-85.

Schmidt, James. "Lukács' Concept of Proletarian *Bildung*," *Telos*, 24 (Summer, 1975), 2-40.

Schorske, Carl. *German Social Democracy, 1905-1917*. New York, 1955.

Wellmer, Albrecht. *Critical Theory of Society*. Trans. Cumming. New York, 1971.

PHENOMENOLOGY AND EXISTENTIAL MARXISM

Heidegger, Martin. *Being and Time*. Trans. Macquerrie and Robinson. New York, 1962.

―――. *The Essence of Reasons*. Trans. Malick. Evanston, Ill., 1969.

―――. *Existence and Being*. Chicago, 1965.

―――. *Hegel's Concept of Experience*. New York, 1970.

―――. *Introduction to Metaphysics*. Trans. Mannheim. Garden City, 1961.

―――. *Kant and the Problem of Metaphysics*. Trans. Churchill. Bloomington, Ind., 1962.

―――. "Letter on Humanism," trans. Lohner. In Barrett and Aiken, eds., *Philosophy in the Twentieth Century*. New York, 1962.

Husserl, Edmund. *Cartesian Meditations*. Trans. Cairns. The Hague, 1960.

―――. *The Crisis of European Science and Transcendental Phenomenology*. Trans. Carr. Evanston, 1970.

―――. *Formal and Transcendental Logic*. Trans. Cairns. The Hague, 1969.

―――. *The Idea of Phenomenology*. Trans. Alston. The Hague, 1964.

―――. *Ideas*, trans. Gibson. New York, 1962.

―――. *Logical Investigations*. Trans. Findlay. London, 1970.

―――. *Phenomenology and the Crisis of Philosophy*. Trans. Lauer. New York, 1965.

―――. *The Phenomenology of Internal Time Consciousness*. Trans. Churchill. Bloomington, Ind., 1964.

Merleau-Ponty, Maurice. *Adventures of the Dialectic*. Trans. Bien. Evanston, Ill., 1973.

―――. *Les Aventures de la dialectique*. Paris, 1955.

―――. *Humanism and Terror*. Trans. O'Neill. Boston, 1969.

―――. *In Praise of Philosophy*. Trans. Wild and Edie. Evanston, 1963.

―――. *Phenomenology of Perception*. Trans. Smith. London, 1962.

―――. "Philosophy and Non-Philosophy Since Hegel," trans. Silverman, *Telos*, 29 (Fall, 1976), 43-105.

―――. *The Primacy of Perception*. Ed. Edie. Evanston, 1964.

―――. *The Prose of the World*. Trans. O'Neill. Evanston, 1973.

———. *Résumés de cours*. Paris, 1968.

———. *Sense and Non-Sense*. Trans. Dreyfus. Evanston, 1964.

———. *Signs*. Trans. McCleary. Evanston, 1964.

———. *The Structure of Behavior*. Trans. Fisher. Boston, 1963.

———. *The Visible and the Invisible*. Trans. Lingis. Evanston, 1968.

Nietzsche, Friedrich. *Beyond Good and Evil*. Trans. Kaufmann. New York, 1966.

———. *The Gay Science*. Trans. Kaufmann. New York, 1974.

———. *On the Genealogy of Morals/Ecce Homo*. Trans. Kaufmann. New York, 1967.

———. *The Portable Nietzsche*. Ed. and trans. Kaufmann. New York, 1954.

———. *The Use and Abuse of History*. Trans. Collins. Indianapolis, Ind., 1957.

———. *The Will to Power*. Trans. Kaufmann and Hollingdale. New York, 1968.

Sartre, Jean-Paul. *Anti-Semite and Jew*. Trans. Becker. New York, 1965.

———. *Being and Nothingness*. Trans. Barnes. New York, 1956.

———. *Between Existentialism and Marxism*. Trans. Matthews. London, 1974.

———. *The Communists and Peace*. Trans. Fletcher and Berk. New York, 1968.

———. *Critique de la raison dialectique*. Paris, 1960.

———. *Critique of Dialectical Reason*. Trans. Sheridan-Smith. London, 1976.

———. *The Ghost of Stalin*. Trans. Fletcher. New York, 1968.

———. *L'Idiot de la famille*. Paris, 1971.

———. *Literary and Philosophical Essays*. Trans. Michelson. New York, 1962.

———. *Psychology of Imagination*. Trans. Frechtman. New York, 1966.

———. *Saint Genet*. Trans. Frechtman. New York, 1963.

———. *Search for a Method*. Trans. Barnes. New York, 1967.

———. *Situations*. Trans. Eisler. New York, 1966.

———. *The Transcendence of the Ego*. Trans. Williams and Kirkpatrick. New York, 1957.

Sartre, Jean-Paul, David Rousset, and Gérard Rosenthal, *Entretiens sur la politique*. Paris, 1949.

Works on Phenomenology and Existential Marxism

Aron, Raymond. *History and the Dialectic of Violence*. Trans. Cooper. New York, 1975.

————. *Marxism and the Existentialistis.* New York, 1970.

Aronson, Ronald. *"L'Idiot de la famille:* The Ultimate Sartre?" *Telos,* 20 (Summer, 1974), 90-107.

Biemel, Walter. *Martin Heidegger: an Illustrated Study.* Trans. Mehta. New York, 1976.

Danto, Arthur. *Nietzsche as Philosopher.* New York, 1965.

Desan, Wilfrid. *The Marxism of Jean-Paul Sartre.* Garden City, 1966.

Goldmann, Lucien. *Lukács et Heidegger.* Paris, 1973.

Jaspers, Karl. *Nietzsche.* Trans. Walraff and Schmitz. Chicago, 1965.

Laing, R. D., and D. G. Cooper. *Reason and Violence: A Decade of Sartre's Philosophy 1950-1960.* New York, 1971.

Lukács, Georg. *Existentialisme ou Marxisme?* Paris, 1961.

Manser, Anthony. *Sartre: a Philosophic Study.* New York, 1966.

Odajnyk, Walter. *Marxism and Existentialism.* Garden City, 1965.

O'Neill, John. *Expression, Perception and History: The Social Phenomenology of Maurice Merleau-Ponty.* Evanston, 1970.

Paci, Enzo. *The Function of the Sciences and the Meaning of Man.* Trans. Piccone and Hansen. Evanston, 1972.

Piccone, Paul. "Phenomenological Marxism," *Telos,* 9 (Fall, 1971), 3-31.

Poster, Mark. *Existential Marxism in Postwar France.* Princeton, 1975.

Rabil, Albert. *Merleau-Ponty: Existentialist of the Social World.* New York, 1967.

Ricoeur, Paul. *Husserl: An Analysis of his Phenomenology.* Trans. Ballard and Embree. Evanston, 1967.

Schaff, Adam. *A Philosophy of Man.* New York, 1963.

Spiegelberg, Herbert. *The Phenomenological Movement.* The Hague, 1969.

Thody, Philip. *Sartre.* New York, 1971.

Trân-Dúc-Tháo. *Phénoménologie et matérialisme dialectique.* Paris, 1951.

Waelhens, A. De. *La Philosophie de Martin Heidegger.* Louvain, 1971.

Warnock, Mary, ed. *Sartre.* Garden City, 1971.

OTHER WORKS CONSULTED

Adorno, Theodor et al. *The Positivist Dispute in German Sociology.* Trans. Adey and Frisby. London, 1976.

Arato, Andrew. "The Neo-Idealist Defense of Subjectivity," *Telos,* 21 (Fall, 1974), 108-161.

Arendt, Hannah. *Between Past and Future.* New York, 1968.

————. *The Human Condition.* Garden City, 1959.

————. *On Revolution.* New York, 1965.

Benjamin, Walter. *Charles Baudelaire: A Lyric Poet in the Era of High Capitalism.* Trans. Zohn. London, 1973.
————. *Illuminations.* Trans. Zohn. New York, 1969.
Bernstein, Richard J. *Praxis and Action.* Philadelphia, 1971.
Borkenau, Franz. *World Communism.* Ann Arbor, 1962.
Buber, Martin. *Between Man and Man.* Trans. Smith. New York, 1965.
Burrow, J. W. *Evolution and Society.* Cambridge, 1970.
Cassirer, Ernst. *The Philosophy of the Enlightenment.* Trans. Koelln and Pettegrove. Princeton, 1951.
Cavell, Stanley. *Must We Mean What We Say?* New York, 1969.
Cole, G. D. H. *A History of Socialist Thought.* 5 vols. London, 1953-1960.
Colletti, Lucio. *From Rousseau to Lenin.* Trans. Merrington and White. London, 1972.
————. *Marxism and Hegel.* Trans. Garner. London, 1973.
Collingwood, R. G. *The Idea of History.* London, 1956.
Comte, Auguste. *Auguste Comte and Positivism.* Ed. Lenzer. New York, 1975.
————. *Introduction to Positive Philosophy.* Ed. Ferre. Indianapolis, 1970.
Descartes, René. *Philosophical Essays.* Trans. Lafleur. Indianapolis, 1964.
Dilthey, Wilhelm. *Dilthey's Philosophy of Existence.* Trans. Kluback and Weinbaum. London, 1960.
————. *Pattern and Meaning in History.* Trans. Rickman. New York, 1962.
d'Entrèves, A. P. *Natural Law.* London, 1970.
Enzensberger, Hans Magnus. *The Consciousness Industry.* Trans. Roloff. New York, 1974.
Ferguson, Adam. *An Essay on the History of Civil Society.* Edinburgh, 1966.
Feuerbach, Ludwig. *The Essence of Christianity.* Trans. Eliot. New York, 1957.
————. *The Fiery Brook: Selected Writings of Ludwig Feuerbach.* Trans. Hanfi. Garden City, 1972.
Fichte, J. G. *Science of Knowledge.* Trans. Heath and Lachs. New York, 1970.
Fromm, Erich. *Escape from Freedom.* New York, 1965.
Gardiner, Patrick, ed. *The Philosophy of History.* Oxford, 1974.
Gay, Peter. *The Enlightenment: an Interpretation.* 2 vols. New York, 1966-1969.
Goldmann, Lucien. *The Hidden God.* Trans. Thody. London, 1964.
————. *The Human Sciences and Philosophy.* Trans. White and Anchor. London, 1969.
————. *Marxisme et sciences humaines.* Paris, 1970.

————. *Recherches dialectiques.* Paris, 1959.

Gorz, André. *Le Socialisme difficile.* Paris, 1967.

————. *Strategy for Labor.* Trans. Nicolaus and Ortiz. Boston, 1967.

Habermas, Jürgen. *Knowledge and Human Interests.* Trans. Shapiro. Boston, 1971.

————. *Theory and Practice.* Trans. Viertel. Boston, 1973.

————. *Toward a Rational Society.* Trans. Shapiro. Boston, 1971.

Halévy, Elie. *The Growth of Philosophic Radicalism.* Trans. Morris. Boston, 1955.

————. *Histoire du socialisme européen.* Paris, 1974.

Hegel, G. W. F. *The Logic.* Trans. Wallace. London, 1892.

————. *On Art, Religion and Philosophy.* Ed. Gray. New York, 1969.

————. *Phenomenology of Mind.* Trans. Baillie. New York, 1967.

————. *Philosophy of History.* Trans. Sibree. New York, 1956.

————. *Philosophy of Mind.* Trans. Wallace and Miller. Oxford, 1971.

————. *Philosophy of Right.* Trans. Knox. London, 1952.

————. *Science of Logic.* Trans. Johnston and Struthers. London, 1929.

————. *Die Vernunft in der Geschichte.* Ed. Hoffmeister. Hamburg, 1955.

Hirschman, Albert O. *The Passions and the Interests.* Princeton, 1977.

Hobbes, Thomas. *Leviathan.* Indianapolis, 1958.

Horowitz, David, ed. *Marxism and Modern Economics.* New York, 1968.

Horowitz, Irving Louis. *Radicalism and the Revolt Against Reason.* Carbondale, Ill., 1968.

Hughes, H. Stuart. *Consciousness and Society.* New York, 1958.

Hyppolite, Jean. *Genèse et structure de la Phénoménologie de l'Esprit de Hegel.* Paris, 1946.

————. *Studies on Marx and Hegel.* Trans. O'Neill. New York, 1969.

Jacoby, Russell. "The Politics of Subjectivity," *New Left Review,* 79 (May-June, 1973), 37-49.

Jaspers, Karl. *Philosophy.* Trans. Ashton. 3 vols. Chicago, 1969-1971.

Kamenka, Eugene. *The Philosophy of Ludwig Feuerbach.* New York, 1970.

Kant, Immanuel. *Critique of Pure Reason.* Trans. Smith. New York, 1929.

————. *On History.* Ed. Beck. Indianapolis, 1963.

Kelly, George Armstrong. *Idealism, Politics and History: Sources of Hegelian Thought.* Cambridge, 1969.

Kierkegaard, Soren. *Concluding Unscientific Postscript.* Trans. Swenson and Lowrie. Princeton, 1941.

————. *Philosophical Fragments.* Trans. Swenson. Princeton, 1936.

Koestler, Arthur. *Darkness at Noon.* Trans. Hardy. New York, 1968.

Köhler, Wolfgang. *Gestalt Psychology*. New York, 1947.

Kojève, Alexandre. *Introduction to the Reading of Hegel*. Trans. Nichols. New York, 1969.

Kolakowski, Leszek. *The Alienation of Reason: A History of Positivist Thought*. Trans. Guterman. Garden City, 1969.

Krieger, Leonard. *The German Idea of Freedom*. Chicago, 1972.

——. *Kings and Philosophers, 1689-1789*. New York, 1970.

Laszlo, Ervin, ed. *Philosophy in the Soviet Union*. New York, 1967.

Lefebvre, Georges. *The French Revolution, From Its Origins to 1793*. Trans. Evanson. New York, 1962.

Lefebvre, Henri. *Critique de la vie quotidienne*. 2 vols. Paris, 1958-1961.

Lévi-Strauss, Claude. *The Savage Mind*. Chicago, 1966.

Lichtheim, George. *The Concept of Ideology*. New York, 1967.

——. *Marxism in Modern France*. New York, 1966.

Louch, A. R. *Explanation and Human Action*. Berkeley and Los Angeles, 1966.

Löwith, Karl. *From Hegel to Nietzsche*. Trans. Green, Garden City, 1967.

——. *Meaning in History*. Chicago, 1949.

Lukes, Steven. *Individualism*. New York, 1973.

Machiavelli, Niccolò. *The Prince and the Discourses*. New York, 1950.

MacIntyre, Alasdair. *Against the Self-Images of the Age*. New York, 1971.

MacPherson, C. B. *Possessive Individualism*. Oxford, 1962.

Makkreel, Rudolf A. *Dilthey. Philosopher of the Human Studies*. Princeton, 1975.

Malraux, André. *Man's Fate*. Trans. Chevalier. New York, 1961.

Mandel, Ernest. *Marxist Economic Theory*. Trans. Pearce. London, 1968.

Mandelstam, Nadezhda. *Hope Abandoned*. Trans. Hayward. New York, 1974.

——. *Hope Against Hope*. Trans. Hayward. New York, 1970.

Martin, Kingsley. *French Liberal Thought in the Eighteenth Century*. New York, 1962.

Mattick, Paul. *Marx and Keynes*. London, 1971.

Mead, George H. *Mind, Self and Society*. Chicago, 1934.

Meldon, A. I. *Free Action*. London, 1961.

Michels, Robert. *Political Parties*. Trans. Paul. New York, 1968.

Mitzman, Arthur. *The Iron Cage*. New York, 1969.

Mommsen, Wolfgang J. *The Age of Bureaucracy*. New York, 1977.

Myrdal, Gunnar. *The Political Element in the Development of Economic Theory*. Trans. Streeten. New York, 1969.

Pareto, Vilgredo. *Sociological Writings*. Ed. Finer. Trans. Mirfin. New York, 1968.

Parsons, Talcott. *The Structure of Social Action*. New York, 1968.

Peters, R. S. *The Concept of Motivation.* London, 1960.

Popper, Karl. *Conjectures and Refutations: The Growth of Scientific Knowledge.* New York, 1968.

Reich, Wilhelm. *Sex-Pol: Essays, 1929-1934.* Ed. Baxandall. New York, 1972.

Rieff, Philip. *Freud: The Mind of the Moralist.* Garden City, 1961.

Robinson, Joan. *Economic Philosophy.* Garden City, 1962.

Rosenberg, Harold. *The Tradition of the New.* New York, 1965.

Rousseau, Jean-Jacques. *The Social Contract and Discourses.* Trans. Cole. New York, 1950.

Ruggiero, Guido de. *The History of European Liberalism.* Trans. Collingwood. Boston, 1959.

Runciman, W. G. *A Critique of Max Weber's Philosophy of Social Science.* Cambridge, 1972.

Ryan, Alan, ed. *The Philosophy of Social Explanation.* Oxford, 1973.

Saint-Simon, Henri de. *Social Organization, The Science of Man and Other Writings.* Trans. Markham. New York, 1964.

Sausurre, Ferdinand de. *Course in General Linguistics.* Trans. Baskin. New York, 1966.

Schapp, Alain, and Pierre Vidal-Naquet, eds. *The French Student Uprising.* Trans. Jolas. Boston, 1971.

Schiller, Friedrich. *On the Aesthetic Education of Man.* Trans. Snell. New York, 1965.

Schutz, Alfred. *The Phenomenology of the Social World.* Trans. Walsh. Evanston, 1967.

————. *The Problem of Social Reality.* The Hague, 1967.

Simmel, Georg. *On Individuality and Social Forms.* Ed. Levine. Chicago, 1971.

————. *The Sociology of Georg Simmel.* Trans. and ed. Wolff. New York, 1950.

Smith, Adam. *Moral and Political Philosophy.* Ed. Schneider. New York, 1948.

————. *The Wealth of Nations.* New York, 1937.

Sorel, Georges. *From Georges Sorel.* Ed. Stanley. New York, 1976.

————. *The Illusions of Progress.* Trans. Stanley. Berkeley and Los Angeles, 1969.

————. *Reflections on Violence.* Trans. Roth and Hulme. New York, 1961.

Stirner, Max. *The Ego and His Own.* Trans. Byington. New York, 1973.

Sweezy, Paul. *The Theory of Capitalist Development.* New York, 1968.

Taylor, Charles. *The Explanation of Behavior.* New York, 1964.

Tocqueville, Alexis de. *Democracy in America.* Trans. Bradley. New York, 1945.

Toulmin, Stephen. *The Philosophy of Science*. New York, 1960.

Trilling, Lionel. *Sincerity and Authenticity*. Cambridge, Mass., 1971.

Valéry, Paul. *History and Politics*. Trans. Folliot and Mathews. Princeton, 1962.

———. *Monsieur Teste*. Trans. Mathews. Princeton, 1973.

Weber, Max. *Economy and Society*. Ed. Roth and Wittich. New York, 1968.

———. *From Max Weber*. Ed. Gerth and Mills. New York, 1958.

———. *The Methodology of the Social Sciences*. Trans. Shils and Finch. New York, 1949.

———. *The Protestant Ethic and the Spirit of Capitalism*. Trans. Parsons. New York, 1958.

White, Alan R., ed. *The Philosophy of Action*. Oxford, 1968.

Williams, Bernard. *Problems of the Self*. Cambridge, 1973.

Winch, Peter. *Ethics and Action*. London, 1972.

———. *The Idea of a Social Science and Its Relation to Philosophy*. London, 1963.

Winner, Langdon. *Autonomous Technology*. Cambridge, Mass., 1977.

Wittgenstein, Ludwig. *On Certainty*. Trans. Anscombe and von Wright. New York, 1972.

———. *Lectures and Conversations*. Ed. Barrett. Berkeley and Los Angeles, 1967.

———. *Philosophical Investigations*. Trans. Anscombe. New York, 1958.

———. *Remarks on the Foundations of Mathematics*. Trans. Anscombe. Cambridge, Mass., 1967.

Wolin, Sheldon. *Politics and Vision*. Boston, 1960.

Index